Walter Feinberg

Common Schools / Uncommon Identities
National Unity and
Cultural Difference

YALE UNIVERSITY PRESS NEW HAVEN AND LONDON

Published with assistance from the Louis Stern Memorial Fund.

Designed by Gregg Chase.
Set in Minion & TheSans types by Tseng Information Systems.

Library of Congress Cataloging-in-Publication Data
Feinberg, Walter, 1937–
Common schools / uncommon identities : national unity and cultural
difference / Walter Feinberg.
Includes bibliographical references and index.
p.   cm.
ISBN 0-300-07422-0 (hardcover : alk. paper)
1. Public schools — Social aspects — United States.   2. Nationalism and
education — United States.   3. Multicultural education — United States.
4. Citizenship — Study and teaching — United States.   5. Educational
equalization — United States.   I. Title.
LC191.4.F45   1998
371.02′0973 — dc21   98-14920

Printed in the United States of America.

A Catalogue record for this book is available from the British Library.

The paper in this book meets the guidelines for permanence and
durability of the Committee on Production Guidelines for Book
Longevity of the Council on Library Resources.

10   9   8   7   6   5   4   3   2   1

To Eleanor

CONTENTS

Acknowledgments

I wish to acknowledge the Spencer Foundation and the University of Illinois Research Board and its Beckman fund for providing support during the early stages of this project. I am especially grateful to the Benton Center at the University of Chicago for its support during the 1995–96 school year, when I was selected as the Benton Scholar. The conversations that I had with the faculty and students in the University of Chicago's Department of Education were very helpful at a critical point in my research, and I want especially to express my appreciation to Robert Dreeben, Carl Kaestle, Phil Jackson, and Fred Lighthall. A number of discussions with my colleagues Jeff McMahan and Belden Fields at the University of Illinois, Eric Bredo at the University of Virginia, and Yael Tamir at the University of Tel Aviv were very helpful. The conference on nationalism that McMahan coordinated with Robert McKim provided many useful conversations and debates about the role of nations in the modern world.

The assistance of Alan Phillips was invaluable. Kevin Mc-Donough, my research assistant, was most helpful in the early stages of the project, when we began to discuss the new and growing philosophical literature on minority rights. Maria Seferian served as my assistant during the later stages of the work, and besides reading and commenting on an earlier draft of the manuscript and maintaining a steady flow of new reading material, she alerted me to many of the legal issues involved in this area.

I am especially grateful to Alan Peshkin and David Blacker, both of whom read an early draft of the manuscript and provided detailed and invaluable comments.

The students and the faculty of the Department of Educational Policy Studies at the University of Illinois have created a unique, stimulating, and diverse environment where conversation within and across cultural difference is the norm. Discussions with my colleagues in the philosophy division, Kal Alston, Nick Burbules, Pradeep Dillon, Robert Ennis, and Ralph Page, have continued to alert me to new issues, material, and insights.

I owe a considerable debt to two of my teachers, Ken Benne and Marx Wartofsky, who introduced me more than thirty years ago to many of the concerns that I attempt to address in this book. Within the last few years both have passed away, but I hope that their generosity and intelligence continue to inform this work.

Discussions with my wife, Eleanor, about her work in the area of self psychology have begun to inform my ideas on selfhood. This, and her love and support, humor and charm, have helped me to see the importance of relationships with others in the development of the self.

1. Education: Cultural Difference and National Identity

My purpose in writing this book is to develop a justification for public education that is responsive to changing moral understandings about individual rights and community benefits. In doing this I hope to contribute to a renewal of public education as a progressive force in American society. My hope is that this justification will aid public school educators, school board members, policy makers, parents, and their communities to respond appropriately to claims from various subgroups, their own included, seeking to use schools to promote a particular group identity. I aim to develop a theory of education that is sensitive to the concerns of parents and community members who want the public schools to reinforce the values and identity of the home community. I also provide, however, a theory that maintains a commitment to what I call the "principled reasons" for public education. I show how these reasons are challenged by the present demands on education and how they can be maintained even while schools respond to different subgroups that wish to use public education to promote their various identities.

The book is concerned with issues of national and cultural identity in a multicultural society. I address the aims of education in a society that is committed to liberal democratic principles and to providing the conditions that members of different cultural groups need in order to flourish. A considerable amount of progress has been made by educators in showing the way in which cultural identity can be addressed in the classroom.[1] I deal with the philosophical concerns raised by multicultural education and with the fears engendered by a commitment on the part of the public schools to maintaining subcultural identity. The most important part of these is the concern that such an educational policy will weaken the thread of national identity, unity, and loyalty. In confronting this I join an international group of philosophers of education who have recently begun to address questions involving education and cultural and national identity.[2] Although I am hopeful that this work will contribute to the rich conversation that they have begun on the international level, the background for this book is the problems of education in the United States in recent years.

A few words need to be said about the way I use certain key terms. I use the somewhat archaic name *common school* in the title to indicate that one of the historical purposes of American education is to develop a shared national identity and a common loyalty. My use of the term should not be taken to mean that all schools are the same in their material or intellectual resources or in the way in which their curriculum and pedagogy intersect with the lives of the children. This is obviously not the case, and many studies show how schooling often differs along racial, gender, and social class lines. Nor should my use of the term be viewed as denying the problematic aspects of public education and the idea that schools are often used to reinforce and reproduce the class position of parents in their children. The point here is simply to focus attention on the schools' role in creating a national identity and a shared loyalty. The way in which we should think about that role is also an issue raised in this book, but it is not one that is answered by the choice of the term *common school.* It requires an argument that takes seriously many of the problems with this goal.

In using *common school* I have also avoided the term *government schools,* which has come into vogue recently, especially among those who want to advance the cause of private schools. *Government school* is an accurate way to identify the schools I am calling common as long as one keeps in mind that the term focuses attention on the way in which schools are supported and controlled but ignores their rationale and purpose. Moreover, in the present debate over educational vouchers, the term *government school* has become an instrument of those who would extend vouchers to support private schools, suggesting that the only critical difference between the public and the private is their source of support and thus shortchanging any discussion about the unique place of public education in American democracy.

I have used the term *uncommon identity* to mark the present moment in public education. In one sense there are no uncommon identities, and in another sense all identities are unique and therefore uncommon. My identity is as common to me as it may be uncommon to you, and clearly the opposite is the case as well.

My point in using this term is a historical and philosophical one. Historically schools were justified as critical in bringing different peoples together to participate in a common and shared identity, one in which every person was recognizable to every other person as a citizen of the same nation. Today the emphasis appears to have shifted, and what was once taken as an important role of the schools—advancing a single common identity—is sometimes viewed as advancing the interests of the dominant group over those who are different and powerless. Yet if the historical mission of the common school is now of uncertain value, the question remains, How should children from different cultural backgrounds be treated by the public schools, and what, if any, identity work is appropriate for public education? Hence the title of this book might best be read as a question: Given our new understanding of the value of cultural differences, is there any role for a common school, and if there is, then what is it?

The terms *culture, nation,* and *state* are used in more or less conventional ways. By *culture* I mean a network of meaning to which certain people have access and from which they draw to communicate with and recognize one another. These networks may be relatively thin, as, for example, when I speak to my colleagues about the Macintosh culture in our department and contrast it to the IBM culture across the campus. In this case, *culture* simply means the various things that we can take for granted when we interact with each other through our computers. Yet a culture can entail very thick and overlapping networks of taken-for-granted elements through which meaningful interactions develop and grow. A shared written and oral language, shared norms about marriage, child rearing, family membership and obligations, and land use, and shared understandings about the way we should interact with members of other groups and with nature are additional elements of the thickened web that we more normally call culture.

When I refer to a cultural group, I often mean what we usually speak of as an ethnic community, one that participates in a certain meaning formation and whose members identify and are identified with one another. My meaning here is close to that of *ethnicity* shared by Banks and Appleton: "Ethnicity . . . is understood to designate any group set off by race, religion, or national origin, or some combination of these categories which serve to create, through historical circumstances, a sense of peoplehood."³ I use the term *culture* or *cultural group* instead of *ethnic community* because the latter has become identified with *European* immigrants in this county, and I intend the term to cover a broader spectrum and to include, for example, African and Native Americans. Moreover, depending largely on the context, I may also refer to groups such as deaf people, women, or gays as belonging to a culture. This use is quite contentious, and except where an alternative would be awkward or where the meaning is clear, I try to avoid using the term to cover these groups. Nevertheless, given my understanding of culture as networks of meaning, there are times when it is reasonable to speak of a "gay culture" or a "women's culture," especially when members draw on taken-for-granted and somewhat exclusive meanings and when they identify themselves and are identified as belonging to these groups. In some cases the culture may be rather thin, more like the Macintosh culture in my department than like Chinese or Italian American culture, but for certain purposes one's Chinese or Italian heritage may be less important than the fact that one uses a Macintosh, and in other contexts it will be less important than whether one is a woman or a gay person.

The term *nation* shares considerable semantic space with the term *culture*. It too identifies networks of meaning that allow people to identify with one another. Yet the idea of nationhood carries with it more than this. *Nationhood* alludes to a real or ideal network of mutual aid, and in this sense it carries some of the connotation of "family" as well as of "culture." We may feel obliged to aid each other when we participate in the same network of meaning, but it is more than this that makes a nation. It is the perception that our participation in that network has created certain bonds of mutual support and continuing obligation that provides nationhood as a collective with a certain moral authority.

Nation-state indicates a significant overlap in the meaning of the terms *nation* and *state*, and there are times when I use one and then the other for the sake of variety. In certain contexts a distinction is needed, however. In these cases I use *nation* to indicate an imagined community of mutual obligation based on a perception of shared history and meaning. I use *state* to indicate the political instruments for meeting those obligations. In speaking of the state in this way, I depart somewhat from conventional usage, which defines the state as that which has a monopoly on violence. I do so for two reasons. First, it is rare for states to have such a monopoly, although they usually possess means for the greater violence. And second, the state does many things, and the legitimacy of what it does do — including threatening and exercising violence — is determined by the consensus that exists about the type of mutual aid that citizens as co-nationals should be expected to provide one another through the formal political organization of the state.

The terms *pluralism* and *multiculturalism* also retain a degree of fluidity and can often be substituted for one another in everyday discourse. They actually cover a range of concepts, however, which at times need to be distinguished. I have, where needed, attempted to do so by somewhat arbitrarily stipulating a definition for the two terms. Here I use *pluralism* to indicate the view that members of America's many different cultures should be allowed to pursue their own meanings and traditions in their homes, churches, mosques, or temples and in their communities, while the public school should actively strive to unify all children, regardless of their cultural affiliation, under a single national identity. Given this meaning, the public school is largely passive with regard to cultural identity. True, it does have the role of teaching children to respect cultural difference in general, but it does not have a role in advancing a child's cultural identity. Under pluralism cultural respect does not entail cultural recognition nor require the school to acknowledge the child's cultural membership in any active way. The school is, however, able to use the fact of cultural difference to teach about liberal tolerance and democratic ideals. In teaching these lessons, however, it is opportunistic with regard to the particular cultural groups on which it may focus to illustrate the more general points about tolerance and democracy. Multiculturalism is different. It involves the active recognition by the school of cultural membership and addresses the children not just as citizens of one nation but in terms of their identity as members of different cultural groups.

I am aware that other scholars use these terms in ways different from my use,[4] with some assigning meanings that are almost opposite the ones that I have assigned. These differences are inconsequential, as long as we are clear on what we are talking about. Moreover, since there is a range of meaning that both terms share there are times when either term could be used without distortion.

Nevertheless, there are times when meaning needs to be anchored along both the "private-public" axis and the "passive acceptance–active encouragement" axis. In using the term *pluralism* to anchor the private and the passive poles with regard to culture, I am following the tradition that tracks back to the debates of the earlier part of the century, when the alternatives to pluralism were assimilation and a view of national becoming that was then called the melting pot. The usefulness of stipulated definitions is simply that they help us to keep track of the terms of the debate, and they should not be mistaken for the debate itself.

By the term *principled reasons* I refer to the general ideals that historically have been used to advance public education as an individual and a common good. Principled reasons are justifications that appeal to people as human beings rather than as members of a particular social class, race, gender, or religious group. I call them *principled* reasons to distinguish them from more particular interests that have also influenced the course of public education but are designed to serve a specific class interest where the school is viewed by the dominant group as a weapon with which it can reproduce an arbitrary social class structure.

I call them principled *reasons* for public education to distinguish them from other, more particular ideals that appeal to specific cultural, historical, or religious groups whose experience separates them from others with equally legitimate ideals. Thus, for example, an Islamic school may appeal to a norm of devotion that marks the ideal Moslem, and this may differ from the norm of devotion for a Jew or a Catholic, who in turn will differ from each other. These norms are certainly principled, but none of them alone can serve as reasons for public schooling in a nontheistic, liberal democratic society.

The idea of principled reasons, then, is tied closely to liberal political philosophy, and this relation serves to distinguish public schools from both nonpublic parochial ones and private ones. The liberal political tradition's emphasis on individual choice requires public schools to enable children to develop the skills needed to choose their own conception of the good. This contrasts, for example, with nonpublic parochial schools that are founded on a particular conception of the good and whose mission is to reproduce this conception in their students. In addition, the liberal tradition's emphasis on equality requires that disparities in family background be compensated in ways that mitigate the disadvantage that poverty creates. In contrast, private schools, whether or not they advance a specific conception of the good, are allowed to provide an education that is based on the ability of parents to pay.

Principled reasons are the ideals to which people appeal to justify public education and to steer its development. Public education requires justification for two reasons. First, it uses tax revenues to accomplish its purpose and thus requires that one person's wealth be used to educate another person's children. Second, it requires parents to give up some of their parental authority for a period of time to enable the state to assume primary responsibility for educating their children. Both of these requirements have a coercive element. Some childless taxpayers will not want to pay for the education of children who are not their own unless they can control the curriculum. Some parents will feel that the state should not take advantage of their inability to finance their children's education by forcing them to study things that are inconsistent with the parents' values.

Public schools in liberal societies are justified as a public good because they perform two critical functions. First, in complex societies they advance public safety and development by socializing children into the general rules of the society, by establishing in them a commitment to the safety and well-being of their fellow members, and by providing them with the skills to advance both their individual and the social interest. Second, schools are critical instruments for reproducing the basic values of liberal society itself and of assuring its continuation across different generations. The three principled reasons that I address in this chapter — equal opportunity, freedom of association, and individual growth — are essential for advancing the ideals of liberal society and therefore serve the second of these goals.

Each of these reasons operates as an educational norm for the public schools — they are what schools should strive to accomplish and serve as standards by which they should be evaluated. Each operates in a different sphere, however. Equality of opportunity operates in the vocational sphere and addresses the important role of the school in developing socially and economically useful skills. Freedom of association operates in the political sphere and serves to reinforce the democratic principle that everyone has a basic right to form independent associations. Individual growth operates in the personal sphere and indicates that in a democracy we each have a right to form our own conception of the good and choose our own course of development.

As a vocational goal, equality of educational opportunity is intended to assure that children will be rewarded, both in school and afterwards in the workplace, according to their merit. When they follow this principle schools not only act according to an established principle of fairness, but they also provide a continuing stream of talent for the nation as a whole.

Equality of educational opportunity is intended to compensate for inequalities of opportunities that arise as an indirect result of other liberal commitments. For example, as a result of the commitment to individual choice, liberal society is also committed to allowing private wealth to be used to benefit one's own offspring. Other social systems might challenge this benefit on the ground that it continues even after death, when a person no longer has any wishes and is not around to worry whether past wishes will be honored. Extending the commitment beyond the life of the original creator of the wealth serves certain social purposes, however. By acknowledging that living people have interests that extend beyond their own individual lives and give their lives meaning, the extended commitment provides certain constraints on state authority. It serves as an incentive for long-term projects and contributes to a sense of extended responsibility.

Yet if unchecked there are serious indirect social costs to the exercise of this right, especially in societies that adhere to liberal democratic ideals. One of these is that the unearned advantages that inherited wealth allows distort and retard the development and rewarding of new talent. Less talented members are advanced over more talented ones because family background provides advantages that overwhelm relative deficits in talent. A commitment to equal opportunity seeks to mitigate this advantage by holding that children have a right to receive an education that is consistent with their capacities regardless of the circumstances of their parents.

The second principle, freedom of association, is a social

and a political reason, and it is critical to maintaining democratic societies. It holds that individuals have rights to form whatever friendships, alliances, and interests groups they wish, as long as in doing so they do not hinder the right of others to do the same. This principle requires schools to provide children with the capacity to understand the implications of the social choices they make. Under this conception of education children are not to be treated as if they were *destined* to relive the lives of their parents. The principle requires that children be introduced to ways of life that are different from that of their parents and that they be taught about the diversity of human cultures. But understanding the implications of different lifestyle choices also includes the *choice* to maintain the same political, cultural, and religious associations as one's parents.

The third principle, individual growth, is a personal one. A commitment to individual growth entails giving children a right to select their own conception of the good and to develop their talents and tastes in whatever way their inclinations and capacities allow, constrained only by the need of others to do the same. This principle requires the schools to challenge children in ways that they might not experience at home or in the community. It requires that they expand their understandings and broaden their horizons by engaging their present conception of the good with reasonable alternatives.

The principled reasons must be held as universals, applying to everyone regardless of social class, race, sex, or religion, and they must be viewed as reversible within liberal society in the sense that they must be acceptable to us even if we were to occupy a different position than the one we do. Thus, if individual children are to be granted equal opportunity, the right of free association, and personal growth, they must also learn that it is important for others to have these rights too. Universality and reversibility are essential for stabilizing these principles within the fabric of the liberal democratic state. If children are not taught that the rights they have for themselves are rights that should be extended to others, then the principles are not workable.

WHY SCHOOLS ARE OBLIGED TO TEACH VALUES TO OTHER PEOPLE'S CHILDREN

Whereas there are some who reject the principled reasons because they object to contributing their own wealth to the good of other people's children, there are others who reject them for their own children because they object to their exposure to an "unacceptable" conception of the social good. Some parents fear that this exposure could undermine their children's commitment to their own traditional values. These parents want to be able to recognize themselves in their children, and they want their children to cherish their values and way of life and not others. For example, parents often want to place strong limits on the principles of freedom of association and personal growth, believing that these will lead children to reject family and friends or to develop ideas and beliefs that will result in being ostracized by their community. Even the ideal of equality of opportunity, perhaps the least controversial of the three from the point of view of traditional communities, is problematic in cultural groups where a strongly gendered division of labor exists.

The fact that parents want to recognize themselves in their children means that when schools go "too far" toward remaking their children, parents may properly feel uneasy. This is one reason why the principled reasons are usually advanced in procedural terms by those who wish to defend public schools. It is thought to be acceptable to say of the schools that they "*provide* equal opportunity," not that they (should) *encourage* children to reject the sexual division of labor that their parents value; that they "*develop* the conditions for free association," not that this often results in youths' selecting friends or marriage partners from outside of their group; or, that they "*challenge students* to broaden their horizons," not that they introduce students to values that are in conflict with those of their parents. In other words, the argument goes, schools "teach children *how* to choose, not what to choose." This emphasis allows the possibility that many children will choose a life that is not alien to their parents'. Thus schools, in justifying their role, can also claim that they are doing nothing that would undermine traditional values when they advance the three principled reasons. In the schools' eyes, they are simply providing children with the means to make more informed choices.

Yet "procedural" goals are sometimes rightfully interpreted and criticized as more that just teaching children *how* to choose. They are often substantive in some very subtle but important ways. When the school makes an intended and predictable difference in what children hold to be right or true, then the school needs to defend that view of the right and the true as a substantive concern, not just as a procedural one.

In this book I show that advocates of multicultural education are providing children with more than just better instruments for choice or a wider understanding of different conceptions of the good. In an important sense, they are leading children to accept one conception of the good and to reject some others. Being granted license to do this requires a number of steps that are rarely articulated.

First, the school must show that it is appropriate, in a liberal society, to advance a certain conception of the good over competing ones. Given the commitment of liberal society to individual choice, this demonstration will require rather subtle distinctions if it is to be made successfully. Second, the favored conception of the good must be articulated and defended in the light of alternative conceptions, and, third, it must be justified as an educational good. These are the tasks that I seek to begin in the chapters that follow. First, however, I want to show why I believe that procedural concerns alone are not sufficient to justify the school's role as a multicultural educator.

THE PROBLEM WITH PROCEDURAL INTERPRETATION OF PRINCIPLED REASONS

The claim that schools are justified in exposing children to values and ways of life that are alien to their families cannot always be supported on the ground that the school is neutral about the choices children actually do make. In exposing children to different ways of life, schools teach children as much about *what* they should think as about *how* they should think. This does not mean that schools should abandon the alternatives that they present to children and teach only a parent-approved curriculum. Rather, it means that schools need to be able to justify the changes in children's ideas and values.

Consider the case of a New York superintendent of schools who failed to have his contract renewed after a fierce battle with one of the local school boards over the implementation of a new diversity curriculum that the board members claimed was overly sympathetic to gay lifestyles. "Sympathy" involved showing same-sex-parent households alongside a depiction of different-sex-parent households. The serious objection was not that the schools were in any way advocating homosexual unions; it was that they were normalizing behavior that the parents considered wrong. Certainly, parents would have a complaint if the schools were advocating homosexual behavior, but do they also have a valid complaint if the school is simply presenting homosexuality in a neutral way, as a choice that some people make, when the parents do not see this as a neutral choice? I believe that they do if we hold to the view that the schools are restricted to teaching children how to choose and are prohibited from teaching them what to choose. Once we understand the limits of this defense, we can understand that the school has an obligation to teach values and that the difficult problem is to justify the values that it must teach. To see this point requires that we shift our focus in the example above from the question of the future sexual orientation of the schoolchildren to the future norms of the community.

If the only issue were whether the curriculum would increase the likelihood that some children would become gay, then the argument that this is a procedural concern would be correct, and the parents' fear, while requiring a sensitive response, would clearly present no reason to interfere with the schools' teachings. Parents may fear many things, and the fact of the fear itself, even if somewhat justified in terms of cause and effect, does not establish a sufficient reason for rejecting a school practice. For example, parents might fear that science teaching will loosen their children's religious bonds, and for some children this might be true. Nevertheless, the fact of the fear is not a good reason for eliminating science classes. Or, at the dawn of integration in the South, many parents accurately feared that integration would lead some black and white people to intermarry. Yet this fear, though accurate, would not have been ethically right to act on and should not have determined the course of desegregation policy.

Suppose, however, as is likely the case, that the board objected to the inclusion of gay families not because they feared that anything the school did would lead the children to "change" their sexual orientation but because they held that the point of the lesson was to make their children more tolerant of behavior they considered "immoral" and "sinful." They did not fear that the children's sexual *behavior* would be influenced, but rather they knew that the school wanted to change children's *attitudes* about what is right and what is wrong in terms of sexual relationships. Given the likely success of the school, their children would become more accepting of behavior that, from their point of view, should not be accepted.

When looked at in this way the defense of the school on

procedural grounds alone is not sufficient. Rather, there is a hidden curriculum here. Children are being taught *that* they should be more tolerant of those who engage in behavior that their parents take to be sinful. Teaching children to be more tolerant in this case is not just a lesson in *how* to choose. The board is right; it is a lesson that *directs choice,* and it does so in a way that, if successful, could weaken community norms. The school is teaching children what to think, not just how to do so. The school is teaching the child to erase the boundaries that the community has constructed between normal and abnormal behavior (or, as some traditions would put it, between godly and sinful acts).

Of course, many traditional families would consider it a personal disaster if their own children became gay. Some, however, would also consider it a group disaster if the boundaries separating "normal" from "abnormal" behavior were erased from the minds of their community's children. To erase this boundary is to change the character of the community. From this point of view the issue is a substantive one and cannot be minimized as simply procedural. It has to do not just with choice but with the character and substance of beliefs about right and wrong and with the obligation that schools have, if any, to reproduce communal understandings and norms. And about this the board is correct. This issue involves questions about respect for traditional communities but also about whether the public school has a right, even an obligation, to face off against community norms in some situations. To argue the issue on procedural grounds alone is misleading.

In responding to these concerns, we cannot neglect the other side of this question: what parents of gay children, or gay parents, want for their children. For presumably the desire of traditional parents to have their values reflected in the construction of the curriculum is felt with equal intensity by others who have different sexual orientations and different values. Just as the traditional parents want to maintain the boundaries between "normal" and "abnormal," others want to break down these boundaries and develop children who are tolerant of others and willing to judge them on the basis of their trustworthiness, honesty, or academic ability rather than their sexual orientation. Without clear guidelines as to its responsibility to both children and their communities, schools are caught in an impossible dilemma whose result will only be determined by the relative political strength of the two communities. In order to address this issue we must examine the fundamental justification of public education in terms of its responsibility to both the ideals of cultural communities and the ideals of a liberal democratic nation.

What many parents, regardless of their cultural orientation, share is the desire for their individual children to have a school experience, public or otherwise, that will support their communal values. Yet, what supports the values of one group may go against those of another, and the values of both may conflict with one or more of the principled reasons that have formed the ethical foundation of the public school system. One curriculum guide that calls for a sympathetic treatment of gay lifestyles also suggests that Thanksgiving may need to be recognized as a day of mourning in some schools and for some groups. In some cities the demand by African Americans for separate schools for African American males is another instance of the same issue, as are the demands of certain religious denominations to have their ideas expressed in the curriculum. The idea of charter schools, where parents and teachers can bypass many state regulations and form publicly supported schools around their shared values, raises additional questions about the balance between different levels of pedagogical authority. Under some conceptions, the issues of how to treat controversial lifestyles need never arise, but only because topics might be routinely neglected or provided whatever slant the teachers and parents believe to be consistent with their values. Yet this ad hoc approach to one of the most important educational issues of the day is surely dissatisfying.

PLURALISM VERSUS MULTICULTURALISM

Although issues concerning the role of education in promoting national and cultural identity have arisen in the past, they have usually involved demands that the state *allow* groups to maintain a distinct minority identity, especially through the development of private or religious schools. The public school was not usually expected to *further* such identities; development of a distinct cultural identity was more often than not seen to be the job of the home, the church, or local after-school groups and organizations. Officially, the role of the public school was to establish a common, public identity that transcended the identities of particular communities. Pluralism as a social and an educational philosophy arose as a way to interpret and direct this transcendence.

Although pluralism and multiculturalism need to be distinguished as educational movements, they are often conflated because each is located between two other educational ideas. The first of these, assimilationism, holds that the role of public education is to erase past national and cultural identities and infuse children with a common American identity. David Tyack illustrates the assimilationist view as it was articulated by the New York superintendent of schools at the dawn of this century. The goal was not only to teach the immigrants " 'an appreciation of the institutions of this country' " but also to teach them an " 'absolute forgetfulness of all obligations or connections with other countries because of descent or birth.' " [5] This view is problematic to pluralists and multiculturalists alike, but for different reasons. To the pluralist, this view violates freedom of association. By denying people the opportunity to maintain a distinctive cultural identity, it is manipulating interests and shaping the purpose of association. Multiculturalists reject assimilationism too, but not necessarily because it denies freedom of association — although this may be a concern of some — but because it denies important benefits of community and affiliation.

Separatism stands opposite assimilationism. It holds that groups should form their own separate educational institutions and use them to maintain their own distinctive identity. Some forms of separatism, such as racial segregation, are clearly discriminatory because they are premised on a distinction between the absolute value of different groups. Other forms of separatism are benign in terms of assigning relative values to groups, however, and are advanced as effective ways to maintain a group's identity.[6] As Stokely Carmichael and C. V. Hamilton argued in a somewhat muted version of the separatist ideal: "Traditionally, each new group in this society has found the route to social and political viability through the organization of its own institutions with which to represent its needs with the larger society."[7]

Just as pluralism and multiculturalism are distinguished by their reasons for rejecting assimilationism, they are also distinguished by their reasons for rejecting separatism. To the pluralist, separatism violates freedom of association as much as assimilationism does, and thus must be rejected as antidemocratic. Separatism makes the mistake of presupposing a child's primary affiliation and then organizes education in such a way as to insure that the presupposed identity will become the child's actual identity.

Multiculturalists reject separatism for a different reason. They generally accept the importance that the separatist affords to cultural identity, but they question the price paid for achieving it. From the multiculturalist standpoint, separatism achieves one important goal of education — the development of cultural affiliation and pride — but it does so at the neglect of another goal — the understanding and recognition of different cultures.

Pluralism and multiculturalism locate themselves differently in the assimilationist-separatist polarity. Pluralism advances the idea that there are two separate spheres of identity formation, a cultural one and a public one.[8] For the pluralist, the public school is involved in preparing children for life in the public sphere, interpreted largely in political and economic terms. The goals of public education are to establish a common citizenry out of cultural differences and to shape certain attitudes and values that are consistent with political and economic life in modern industrial societies. For the pluralist, the development of a distinct cultural identity is the job of the home, the church, or local after-school groups and organizations. Indeed, it is because pluralists allow for a rich and diverse cultural life to be a significant part of American society that they also believe that the unifying role of the public school is so important.

Unlike assimilationism, pluralism neither seeks to eliminate cultural differences nor requires schools to discourage or be unresponsive to displays of cultural difference. Most pluralists allow that cultural respect is a part of a democratic society and are reasonably permissive about displays of cultural affiliation within the school. Yet on a day-to-day basis, the official school culture, operating under pluralist ideas, would aim for a "culture-neutral" environment, one that *allows* diverse cultural expressions but only *encourages* them as a means to a larger lesson about the value of a diverse but unified nation.

Pluralists will generally sanction minor symbolic expressions of local cultural commitments in the school such as allowing Jewish children to wear a yarmulke or Christian children to wear a cross around their necks, and most pluralists advocate the study of different cultures and ethnic groups. The difference between pluralist models and multicultural ones is that for pluralism the perspective for understanding and appreciating particular groups is that of a tolerant liberal nation. When pluralism shines the spotlight of significance on different forms of cultural expression it does so as a way to advance understanding among members of different groups but even more as a way to illustrate national inclusiveness. The ultimate goals are civic harmony and national identity, which sometimes, but only sometimes, may be achieved by a greater appreciation of the contributions that different groups have made to American society.

Pluralists hold that schools should teach children respect for *individuals* who are culturally different from themselves. They hold that this respect must be based on individual accomplishment, not on cultural background. Pluralists do not, however, hold that the school has a responsibility to develop cultural pride. Rather, schools must teach students to have pride in the nation as a whole and in the principles of opportunity and inclusiveness that it ideally embodies. Pluralists want schools to teach students from all groups that they belong to this larger national community. In pluralist eyes this allows for a form of equality in which everyone, regardless of their cultural background, can participate, and thus it serves to level cultural hierarchies.

To the multiculturalist, however, the pluralist's acceptance of a radical division between the public and the private, a division that relegates "local" cultures to the private sphere, does not really overturn the cultural hierarchy. Rather, these hierarchies are simply rendered less visible by pluralism. The culture of the schools reflects that of the dominant group, and to privatize so-called local cultures is, multiculturalists contend, to devalue them. Children quickly come to understand that the school curriculum and pedagogy label certain culturally grounded ways of thinking and doing more important than others. Hence multiculturalists seek not just to provide a token level of inclusion outside of the main work of the school. They contend that the school must express its commitment to diversity at every level of subject matter and pedagogy.

In contrast to the pluralist, the multicultural educator challenges the radical separation between the public and the cultural and wants to use public schools to establish respect for cultural variation and to promote pride in one's own cultural heritage. Multiculturalists question the pluralist assumption that there is a common identity that the public schools can claim for their own. They suspect that this idealized common identity is just a disguise for the dominance of one cultural group over others, and they believe that such dominance is inherently wrong. In questioning the possibility of a "decultured," or culturally neutral, public sphere the multicultural educator shares ground with the activists in the feminist, gay, deaf, African American, and Native American communities who seek a separate educational experience for their children. Yet the multicultural ideal rejects educational separatism and favors cultural fairness, an ideal in which no one cultural group dominates over others. The ideal of cultural fairness also serves as the multiculturalist's replacement for the pluralist's notions of a common public culture that is neutral with regard to "local subcultural" units that are supposedly expressed in the private sphere.

One example of the difference between the pluralist and the multiculturalist is the proposal, mentioned briefly above, before the New York Board of Education that Columbus Day and Thanksgiving be considered days of mourning for some groups because of the destruction that the Europeans brought to Native Americans. Multicultural educators often encourage interpretations that challenge traditional and officially accepted understandings of the American experience. The issue is somewhat open as to whether these interpretations are better than the standard ones, but there is a strong feeling that the lessons have been incomplete because these understandings have been systematically ignored, and the result has been a predictable and persistent degradation of groups that express them. This degradation results in continuing misunderstanding and stigmatization. Unless the school addresses this stigma, multiculturalists believe, its silence reinforces it. It is important to note, however, that in contrast to separatists, who would allow each group its own isolated interpretation without exposure to alternative ones, the multiculturalist allows for exposure to multiple ways to understand the same event.

Pluralists fear that these oppositional interpretations threaten national unity, and they object on this and other grounds. To pluralists such interpretations overemphasize the development of cultural pride, to the detriment of national unity. Usually this criticism is voiced in terms of a concern for political and social stability. It is feared that if interpretations are too diverse, national unity will be sacrificed.[9] Pluralists also fear that the emphasis on group pride will lead to a serious distortion of information, but this concern is really an offshoot of the concern for national unity since it is rarely voiced alongside an equal concern for the distortions that can be found in the standard textbooks.[10]

Pluralism and multiculturalism come from the same source — liberal political and educational theory — but they lead in different directions and represent distinct social visions. Pluralism seeks a society in which people from different cultural formations and orientations are allowed, if they wish to do so, to express their way of life within a separate cultural sphere and are treated as equal individuals in the public sphere. Pluralism wants equality of opportunity in the public sphere and freedom of association in the cultural sphere. Unlike assimilationism, pluralism does not seek to destroy memories or to obliterate cultural diversity. It does, however, allow for the dissolution of that identity should an insufficient number of individuals choose to pursue it. For the pluralist, society has no special obligation to maintain or support cultural structures. It must simply maintain the institutional conditions that make choice possible. It must assure, for example, that schools do not brainwash or indoctrinate children and that they develop an awareness of various alternative forms of life and the skill required to assess them. Thus, unlike assimilationism, pluralism is not hostile to cultural expression, but there is, as one commentator puts it, a certain quality of benign neglect.[11]

Multiculturalism values cultural difference and seeks to maintain it in ways that are not solely dependent on the momentary interests of individuals. Indeed, one concern of multiculturalist theory is that access to dominant, hegemonic, and unchallenged cultural forms may work to the disadvantage of local cultural affiliation by overly determining individual choice. Multiculturalism thus differs from pluralism in a number of ways.

First, it holds that the public is cultural. Its business is carried out in English, not French, German, or Spanish; its institutions are shaped by the traditions of some groups and not others; and educational and employment benefits are distributed unequally according to factors of ethnicity, race, and social class. Unlike pluralists, multiculturalists do not envisage even the possibility of a culturally neutral public sphere. Their ideal of cultural fairness is not therefore to maintain a wall of separation between the cultural and the public but to assure that no group dominates the public sphere in a way that excludes the bearers of other cultural forms. Hence, the public sphere is viewed as an arena for cultural negotiation where the goal is inclusion, culture and all. The public looks more like an open bazaar than a Tory courtroom.

Second, whereas pluralism *allows* cultural identity to flourish, multiculturalism *encourages* it to do so. Benign neglect is not sufficient for the multiculturalist. Nor is cultural diversity exhibited simply to teach lessons about the inclusive and benign character of the American nation — that is, as a means to a larger national goal. The nation's past and present practices of exclusion are as important to present to students as are its policies of inclusion. Hence multiculturalism seeks to give expression to the experiences of cultural groups not from the point of view of some benign abstraction called "the American nation" but from the grounded experience of men and women from different racial and ethnic groups and with different sexual orientations.

Third, whereas freedom of association and equal opportunity are the dominant principles informing pluralism, affiliation and cultural recognition are the principles that inform multiculturalism. For the multiculturalist, these cultural communities are the preconditions of individual growth.[12] In this view, individuals are part of collectivities that provide meaning to their lives, and multiculturalists seek ways to support these collectivities.

THE STAKES

Some, like Arthur Schlesinger Jr., arguing from a pluralist standpoint, fear that multiculturalism means the disuniting of American society.[13] They envisage a fracturing of its identity not unlike that which is happening today in the former Soviet Union. Others argue that a multicultural standpoint is the only way to provide the cultural recognition that individuals need to develop self-esteem and to lead happy, useful, and productive lives.[14] The difference arises because pluralism and multiculturalism build on different elements of liberalism and provide them with different interpretations.

To oversimplify, pluralists believe that the conditions for individual development are culture-neutral knowledge and the freedom to choose outside of the cultural framework into which one is born. Multiculturalists also believe in the liberal ideal of personal growth, but they hold that there is little knowledge that is culture-neutral and that the condition for such growth is affiliation and communal incorporation. They accept the idea that there may not always be a neat fit between different interpretations of the American experience, but they express less concern than the pluralists about the implications of this for national identity.

However large the differences may appear, it is important to remember that both positions are counterposed to the polarities of assimilationism and separatism and that both occupy the center of the educational spectrum. Granted, they arrive at that center from different starting points. Pluralism comes to the center while trying to accommodate the concerns of the assimilationist point of view; multiculturalism comes to it while trying to accommodate those of the separatist. Pluralism, like assimilationism, seeks a national consensus, but unlike assimilationism it is open-ended about the public character that should emerge from the deliberative process. Multiculturalism, like separatism, seeks cultural authenticity, but unlike separatism it allows that authenticity can be developed within an educational framework that includes different cultural groups. These different starting points mean that those who hold pluralist inclinations are likely to be more sensitive to issues of consensus, whereas those who hold multicultural inclinations will be more ready to allow dissent from the standard interpretation if it furthers cultural affiliation and authenticity.

In this book I show that there are ways to reconcile some of the differences between pluralism and multiculturalism and to make practical educational decisions about the merits of different claims for identity recognition and support. I do not hold that all differences can be reconciled, only that there are fewer irreconcilable ones than we might think. I show the conditions under which a liberal state that seeks a reasonable level of cultural neutrality (here I agree with the multiculturalists that no state could ever be completely neutral with regard to culture) may, under certain circumstances, allow publicly supported education to actively advance the collective identities of various subgroups. I show how the response to claims for recognition must differ for different groups depending on a number of considerations.

Because the challenge to the public school ideal has been so swift and has come from so many different quarters, there is a danger that all claims for special recognition will be treated or rejected on the same grounds. In this book I show why this would be a mistake and how it is possible to discriminate between different claims and to reconstruct an educational system that still embraces equal opportunity, freedom of association, and personal growth as principled reasons for public support. To answer the challenge to public education I examine the way in which we think about personal, cultural, and national identity. I show how a better understanding of these concepts and their interrelation can yield a more precise understanding of the points of conflict and possible points of reconciliation. A second set of relevant concepts includes education, democracy, and rights. I believe that there is an important distinction between political democracy and educational democracy that can help us to sort out different kinds of claims regarding the responsibility of schools in promoting certain identities. This distinction is frequently overlooked by educators who wish to use education to advance a certain form of enlightened, democratic understanding and who believe that one can determine the right thing to do politically on the basis of deciding what the right thing to do is educationally. It is also overlooked by political theorists who hold that the right thing to do educationally can be deduced by determining what the right thing to do is politically. I show how we can use this distinction to understand the limits that may be justifiably placed on schools by parents or minority groups in advancing otherwise desirable understandings and attitudes.

CONCLUSION

To summarize: In this book I develop an argument in favor of an inclusive national identity — one that takes seriously the claims of different cultural communities and other identity formations for public recognition. In this sense, I am treating two different things that are not usually brought together. First, I hold, alongside the pluralists, that, allowing for a rich diversity of cultural groups and individual orientations, there are important and justifiable reasons to take national identity seriously and not to view the nation as simply a shell for separate and unrelated groups. I argue for encouraging people to take on a common identity by participating in the nation's reformation. Ironically, one of the strongest reasons for doing this comes from the concern of some nonracist separatists for addressing injustices to groups. As David Miller argues:

> Radical multiculturalists portray a society that is fragmented in many cross-cultural ways, but they aspire to a politics that redresses the injustices done to hitherto-oppressed groups. Since, however, the injustices will be group-specific, how will it be possible to build a majority coalition to remedy each of them? Given finite resources, why should gays support favorable treatment for Muslims, or Jews for Blacks?[15]

Even if we accept the idea that there is an altruistic instinct which leads us to feel bad when others suffer, it is not clear, without an explicit effort to broaden identity around possible instruments of mutual aid and accountability, why we should direct this instinct to those who are "unlike us" when there are so many "like us" who need help.

Second, I hold, together with the multiculturalists, that there are cases in which groups are justified in seeking public support to maintain a subcultural identity, and I show how the merits of some different claims can be evaluated. In arguing this point I make a distinction between good political reasons and good educational reasons. In most of the literature on this subject, a literature that has been dominated by political theorists and political philosophers, the distinction between educational and political reasons has largely been collapsed, and educational considerations have been subsumed under the political. This is a mistake for many reasons, but among the most important are that it leads to blanket judgments about educational rights and it confuses educational rights with education.

To briefly state these points will serve to anticipate some of the more detailed arguments that follow: First, if one group has, for certain reasons, a right to *public support* to maintain its group identity, this does not mean that all groups should have such a right. I believe that the movement toward vouchers, the privatization of education, and school choice, if not grounded in some strong and encompassing norms about what the liberal democratic ideal allows and does not allow, commits precisely this error. Second, liberalism must separate rights and wisdom. If, for whatever reason, a parent is granted primary authority over the child's education, this does not mean that the parent will necessarily choose what is educationally best for the child. Parents may have rights without having wisdom, and those with wisdom may not always have rights. I may, to take one famous example, agree, which I do, that Amish parents should be allowed to decide their children's educational fate and have them leave school after the eighth grade. I need not, however, believe that this is necessarily the best educational choice. Third, if it is argued that the state has the authority to require children to experience certain kinds of education on the grounds that this advances a legitimate state interest, this argument is a political one, and it may still be questioned on educational grounds. The distinction between education and politics is important to maintain, as is the distinction between what should be educationally allowable and what is educationally desirable. Without these distinctions it will be largely impossible to sort out the issues that confront us in terms of identity and cultural recognition. Of course, the distinctions are only markers. They do not tell us what is educationally desirable or just how we should think about the proper balance between politics and education or between national and subcultural identity.

I am aware that there are some who might object to this project on the ground that the nation-state is on its way out and that globalization will soon render such a political organization obsolete.[16] We cannot dismiss this possibility, especially given the rise of regional organizations and the movement of capital around the globe. Nevertheless, the nation-state and its influence on individual rights and cultural development and well-being is still with us, and as long as it is there will be a need for publicly supported education to sort out the issues that are raised by a liberal multicultural nation.

In the chapters that follow I examine the moral obligations that the *public recognition* of cultural difference present for public education. In this book I advance a theory of public education that both shows why we need a common school and suggests guidelines for seeking to change it in ways that are required by liberal ideals in a society with many cultures.

2. Nature of National Identity and Citizenship Education

The American common school has always been concerned with the development of national identity and the transmission of "American" values — both individual and collective: "If a nation expects to be ignorant and free . . . in a state of civilization," declared Jefferson boldly, "it expects what never was and never will be." [1] Emerson saw the common school as critical to the unity of the nation. It was responsible for holding people together, providing a *national* identity as distinct from the chance coming together of people in a railroad station or the fellow feeling of friends at a picnic. Without the common school the very meaning of America — opportunity, freedom, power — is threatened. [2] Responding to criticisms that sound all too contemporary, he wrote of his vision of public schools and defended them as critical for forging a national identity around art and science:

31

I know that our schools are reproached as nurseries of vice, bloating our own conceit, sharpening our wits in trade, and even in some bad cases, making a more accomplished and dangerous rogue. I reply, "Let us stick to our school." . . . Cling to this despised common school. . . . this one point of plain duty we have — to educate every soul. Every native and every foreign child that is cast on our coast shall be taught, at public cost, the rudiments of knowledge, and at last the ripest results of art and science.[3]

In the minds of many proponents of the common school, liberty and democracy — understood as the distinguishing features of the American identity — depended on a well-educated citizenry. Jefferson wrote: "It is an axiom in my mind that our liberty can never be safe but in the hands of the people themselves, and that, too, of the people with a certain degree of instruction. This is the business of the state to effect, and on a general plan."[4] Jefferson's faith in the idea of education for "everyone"[5] was consistent with his understanding of the nature of knowledge and of liberty itself and, although it was an echo of Enlightenment ideals, it was one of the unique aspirations of the American nation at the time. It would "enable every man to judge for himself what will secure or endanger his freedom."[6] He thus proposed to the governor of Virginia that every county be divided into smaller units allowing every child to be "within reach of a central school."[7] Jefferson believed that reason and individual autonomy were the principle products of education and that, although these spoke to the character of individual citizens, they were the traits that together formed a "people" and created an American identity.

Even though compulsory education was many decades away, in these visions the common school was critical for the development of a people, an educated public who deliberated on behalf of the nation as a whole and in so doing advanced the cause of liberty. The school would develop the sentiments that attached children from different backgrounds to one another through a commitment to the nation. Moreover, in most of these accounts the nation served to link children to a common epistemological and moral order.

The vision was surely idealistic, and frequently many people were excluded from it. In the first place, school was not a part of the life of many Americans at that time, and when it became so, much of its work was often controlled by people who wished to advance the program of the dominant classes rather than to create an informed public. Nor did the arrival of the common school provide the same opportunities for blacks, women, Asians, and working-class people that it did for more privileged members of society. These failings of the common school—the persistence of race and gender inequality in American society, along with a growing gap between poor and rich—contribute today to a skepticism about both the common school ideal and the national identity that it is intended to support.

The skepticism is anchored in the belief that public education rests on and perpetuates an arbitrary foundation—the nation-state and its dominant groups. Moreover, this skepticism is not limited to the United States. People in other countries are coming to view the nation-state as an arbitrary social construction that imposes meaning and values onto the members of various subgroups, and some of these groups are reasserting rights to cultural and individual autonomy.

If this skepticism is well grounded and the common schools support an arbitrary national identity, then both the separatists who want to form schools around a given cultural identity and the market capitalists who want to form them around parental preferences have a strong case. And if they are persuasive then the idea that the common school must serve to develop a unified national identity is greatly weakened. A lot therefore hinges on what it means to say that the common school supports an arbitrary national identity.

ARBITRARY AS UNFAIR OR ARBITRARY AS RANDOM

There are two different meanings to the charge that education in liberal countries such as the United States is arbitrary. First, it means that the benefits of education are distributed in a morally arbitrary or unfair way and serve to reproduce the class, gender, and racial inequalities that exist in the larger society. Given this criticism, the principled reasons that I discuss in chapter 1 may serve to aid this arbitrary distribution by concealing, behind a great deal of ideological rhetoric, the real and unequal effects of public education.[8] Here, *arbitrary* should be taken to mean "unfair."

Yet this criticism actually reinforces the idea that the three principles are reasonable standards of fairness. The problem is not with the principles themselves or with their application within the nation-state. It is, rather, with the economic constraints that inhibit them from becoming effective and honest guides for educational reform. To be arbitrary under this criticism is to be unfair, but it is not to be random. Indeed, educational and economic benefits are distributed in a most predictable way—the haves get more and the have-nots get less. It is unfair, but it is predictable.

There is, however, another and a deeper meaning to the notion of the "arbitrary" nature of schooling: randomness in the way in which national identities are assigned and in the benefits and costs that follow from their assignment. Consider that the history of the common school is interwoven with the rise of the nation-state and that our standard, taken-for-granted interpretations of "universal" educational aims are implicitly contained within a national boundary.

This containment provides a certain instability to the educational ideals articulated in the previous chapter. The principled reasons that justify the idea of the common school are advanced as universals. They are said to apply to everyone, and yet one of the most important roles of the common school is to create, reproduce, and sustain a *particular* identity, not a *universal* one. This is the identity that we have as members of a nation, and this identity frames the way in which the "universal" principles are interpreted and applied. It is this identity that schools create through citizenship education. Yet it may be asked, What is so special about our national identity that we should seek to preserve it and treat others who have it as somehow special?

In order to see the problem raised by this question, consider how our understanding of the three principled reasons — equality of opportunity, freedom of association, and personal growth — are constrained, often unconsciously, by our membership in a nation. We appeal to them, say, when we want to show the injustice of the disparity in the money spent on the education of children in the wealthy suburbs and children in the impoverished inner city. Yet few of us register moral shock about the obvious fact that the vast majority of local, state, and federal educational dollars are spent on educating *American* children even though children in many other countries have much greater educational needs and could use the money for greater personal growth and development. There is probably more to be gained on some absolute scale by using $1,000 to teach, say, one hundred Bangladeshi students to read than in teaching advanced photography to, say, twelve American suburban high school students, but our debates over how to advance individual growth do not usually involve weighing the needs of children from Bangladesh against those from Skokie or the inner city of Chicago. Hence if the idea of advancing individual growth is intended as a universal, it is one that is circumscribed by national boundaries.

The same is true of the individual principles taken separately. Although some object to affirmative action on the ground that it violates the principle of equal opportunity by allowing less qualified people to advance over more qualified ones, few here give it a second thought if a less-qualified American is selected over a more-qualified Italian. What *is* expected for most positions is that one better-qualified *American* will not be passed over in favor of a less-qualified one and that a person from one cultural group within the nation will not favor a person from her own group over a better-qualified American from another group. Similarly, the staunchest defenders of freedom of association on the cultural and religious levels think nothing about all of the barriers — passports, visas, working permits — that are erected to limit association on the national level.[9]

Regardless of their cultural, religious, or racial differences, the men and women who graduate from our public schools are expected to view each other as belonging to the same nation and hence as sharing certain commitments to one another, many of which they do not share with members of other nations. When children learn that they are Americans, they learn certain rules about inclusion and exclusion. And so too do Mexican, Norwegian, and Japanese children when they learn "what they are." These rules are expressions of the ideal of nationalism.

If the logic is pressed, these two commitments, one to universal principles and the other to an exclusive national community, do not sit easily with one another. To learn to be a citizen of a nation is to learn how to apply the principles that justify the common school selectively, not universally. Yet if the principles can be narrowed from their universal framework to embrace only those within a national framework, why should they not be narrowed further to embrace only those within a certain racial, religious, or cultural framework?

This possible contraction of identity is one reason pluralists are concerned about the emphasis on cultural identity and recognition that they associate with multiculturalism. Pluralists are concerned that this emphasis contributes to the instability of the logic of liberal society by highlighting the arbitrary aspects of national identity. Thus pluralists worry that the multiculturalist cannot allow for any public that transcends particular cultural communities and will not support an education that attempts to create one. Of course multiculturalists, in return, are suspicious of the pluralists' attempt to apply "universal" principles in "neutral" ways and of their attempt to support an educational system that leaves cultural identity behind.

WHAT DOES IT MEAN TO HAVE A NATIONAL IDENTITY?

National identity does have a historically random character to it in the way it includes some and excludes others. As Ernest Gellner observes: "Nationalism is not the awakening of nations to self-consciousness: It invents nations where they do not exist."[10] As a system of ordered collectivities, the nation, as Benedict Anderson shows, comes into existence imagining itself as limited, that is, bounded by the other nations that surround it. Unlike, say, religions, which constituted an earlier organizing principle, nations do not, as Anderson observes, imagine themselves "coterminous with mankind."[11] Nations are inclusive but only in a limited way. And this limited way can present problems.

Serbs may imagine a Greater Serbia, but they will not imagine that all individuals now "occupying" the lands of "Greater Serbia" are, or ever will be, Serbs. The danger presented by the resurgence of European nationalism is not just that many nations imagine a "greater" space which is also part of their nation. Nor is it just that these "greater nations" are often coterminous. It is also that each nation imagines itself as holding exclusive authority within this space and has not been able to imagine ways to include the other as an equal while preserving what it takes as its own cultural heritage.

Each nation, as Anderson puts it, "imagines itself as a

community, because, regardless of the actual inequality and exploitation that may prevail, the nation is always conceived as a deep, horizontal comradeship."[12] Each unit comes to view itself "as *sovereign,*" and the relationship its members have to one another is imagined as ultimately one of equality even though visible differences in status clearly exist.[13] Although the common school is not the only instrument for enabling this imagination, at certain points and under certain conditions, it becomes critical.

HOW ARBITRARY IS MODERN NATIONAL IDENTITY?

The modern nation is characterized by an ideology of equal citizenship and sovereignty that is absent from the formative idea of hierarchy and obedience that marked many premodern societies. The idea that everyone has the capacity to reason and contribute to "the general will" forms some of the psychological and social conditions of modern nationalism, while the mass production of print is a critical material factor. It is difficult to think of these conditions as arbitrary, except for the fact that they arose at one time rather than at another.

Even if schools provided no direct instruction in patriotism—and it is well to remember that common schools and compulsory education usually did not follow the establishment of nations for many years—the reading of the same books and pamphlets in the same written language by people within a reasonably contiguous area would contribute to national unity. Anderson points out that the development of the printing press and the subsequent need to create a market of readers provided strong motivation to standardize many mutually incomprehensible forms of the oral vernacular into a sharable written script that could be marketed to a wider audience than the few elites who could read Latin.

What is arbitrary here is the manner of deciding which dialects to group together to form a national language—assuming a monolingual nation — and which of these dialects would assume supremacy in the written form. As Anderson writes:

> Speakers of the huge variety of Frenches, Englishes or Spanishes who might find it difficult or even impossible to understand one another in conversation, became capable of comprehending one another via print and paper. In the process they gradually became aware of the hundreds of thousands, even millions, of people in their particular language-field, and at the same time only those hundred thousand, or million, so belonged. . . . Print-capitalism created languages-of-power of a kind different from the older administrative vernaculars. Certain dialects inevitably were "closer" to each print language and dominated their final forms. Their disadvantaged cousins, still assailable to the emerging print language, lost caste, above all because they were unsuccessful . . . in insisting on their own print form.[14]

As different local versions of English, French, and German are standardized through print, previously distinct identities are clustered closer together, and people within those clusters begin to think of themselves, often of course after considerable conflict, as belonging to the "same" community, wrapped up in the same experiences, and sharing a larger set of interests. They also come to see themselves as distinct from other developing clusters whose dialects have been standardized under a different set of written norms.[15] At the same time, new ritualized practices develop that make visible this imagined community. Because print is a critical factor in tying the community together, some of the most powerful rituals are also practiced in silence and communal isolation.

> Hegel observed that newspapers serve modern man as a substitute for morning prayer. . . [reading one] is [a practice that is] performed in silent privacy, in the lair of the skull. Yet each communicant is well aware that the ceremony he performs is

being replicated simultaneously by thousands (or millions) of others of whose existence he is confident, yet of whose identity he has not the slightest notion. . . . At the same time, the newspaper reader, observing exact replicas of his own paper being consumed by his subway, barbershop or residential neighbors, is continually reassured that the imagined world is visibly rooted in everyday life. Fiction seeps quietly and continuously into reality, creating that remarkable confidence of community in anonymity which is the hallmark of modern nations.[16]

In this imagined (although no less real) community an identity is shaped that claims to override economic, social class, and gender inequalities, some of which are actually intensified as a result of the status tag that different dialects receive.

WHAT IT MEANS TO SAY THAT A NATION IS AN ARBITRARY CONSTRUCT

The arbitrary or random element reflected in the development of a national language was likely repeated in other realms as well. Whether a certain area became French or German was often a matter of dispute, with certain factors, say, religion, arguing for one assignment and others, say, language, arguing for a different one. Yet what is arbitrary is not nationhood itself. There is a perfectly reasonable story that can be told about why modern nations were formed and why they developed along the general lines that they did. This story includes not only the new possibilities for material advancement that arose as a result of new technology but also the need for more centralized administrative bodies to develop them. What is arbitrary is particular elements of a nation: why this dialect group was included while its next-door neighbor with a slightly different dialect was included in the neighboring nation. And even these marginal questions are only arbitrary if we place a strict and somewhat artificial standard of rationality on them. If language was not a deciding factor in certain situations, then geography or religion may have stepped in to decide the question. With the exception of marginal cases, hindsight will allow us to understand reasonably well the various factors that lead to this placement rather than to that one.

Yet the margins are very important for understanding the formative role of the common school. One of the school's roles is to connect the margins to the center. It provides the training needed to reconstruct the strange marks and pronunciation into meaningful words and sentences. It also is the primary instrument for reshaping marginal identities into a national configuration.

Thus a major task of the early common school was to help to bring this imagined community to life by developing the literacy that was required to expand the child's relevant affiliation beyond that of his local village or town. This is done not only by teaching the new script and introducing children to a wider array of stories but, as Dewey observed, by extending the connections children perceive between their own actions and that special but invisible community affected by them.[17]

CONSEQUENCES: INTENDED AND UNINTENDED

The nation-state is arbitrary at the margins, and it is also arbitrary, perhaps even immoral, from the perspective of feudal or religious virtues that it replaced. Yet it is wrong to generalize from arbitrariness at the margins to the view that everything about the modern state is an imposition, and it is wrong to also assume that the nation and the state, even when essentially wrapped up with one another, are arbitrary in the same way. Kwame Anthony Appiah makes this point very nicely when he argues against the view that the state is arbitrary. He writes:

> If anything is morally arbitrary, it is not the state but the nation. Since human beings live in political orders narrower than the

> species, and since it is within those political orders that ques-
> tions of public right and wrong are largely argued out and
> decided, the fact of being a fellow-citizen — someone who is a
> member of the same order — is not morally arbitrary at all.[18]

In contrast to his view of the state as a reasonable expression of human organization, Appiah argues that the nation is
arbitrary. This does not mean, however, as postmodern suspicion
would encourage us to believe, that nations are simply impositional and controlling.

> The nation, on the other hand, is arbitrary, but not in a way that
> permits us to discard it in our moral reflections. It is arbitrary
> in the root sense of that term, because it is . . . "dependent upon
> our will or pleasure." . . . The reason nations matter is that they
> matter to *people*. Nations matter morally . . . as things desired
> by autonomous agents, whose autonomous desires we ought
> to acknowledge and take account of even if we cannot always
> accede to them.[19]

The claim that the nation-state is inherently arbitrary, if
taken to mean that all of its values and practices have only power
and position to legitimize them rather than other alternatives, is
simply wrong when viewed in a historical context. Many of the
practices of the modern state make sense within a modern historical context. True, given another context, say, that of a local culture
or that of a global world order, they may appear arbitrary and dys-
functional. They are evaluated not for all contexts, however, but for
a certain set of them. When viewed within this set their legitimacy
is a matter not just of power and position, but also of the liberating
possibilities they allow.

For example, technology not only provided, through
print, the new linguistic uniformity that made possible the imagined national community; it also provided real material possi-

bilities, possibilities that required greater centralized power and wealth to exploit than feudalism could allow. This in turn pressured archaic moral constraints, such as those on usury, constraints now seen as sacrificing capital accumulation, exploration, and material development to an anachronistic, face-to-face, imposed harmony. The unification of peoples from many different regions, speaking many different dialects, representing different forms of life with their often conflicting habits and customs, called for an extended administrative apparatus, a unified code of justice, and an elaborate system of courts, fines, and prisons.[20]

The change in the attitude toward usury mentioned above is one example of the way in which modern citizenship is tied to a shifting conception of virtue. The passage in the Bible forbidding usury ties it to the coherence and solidarity of a visible community. "Thou shalt not lend upon usury to thy brother; usury of money, usury of victuals, usury of anything that is lent upon usury. Unto a stranger thou may lend upon usury."[21] Yet the nation now creates a dual role — brother *and* stranger — allowing the rules that govern lending to one's own to change as economic development strains to take off, the volume of trade rapidly increases, and the real practices of people force a change in the notion of virtue.[22] And the application of the Bible's injunction becomes more complex as citizens are brothers abroad when serving the nation's cause, but when they return home, they are strangers. This change from Christian charity to practical business sense is consistent with other developments, such as the consolidation of national "communities" into state administrative bodies. Given the changes in material conditions and the possibilities that were created by newer technology, it would have been more arbitrary to maintain the strict rejection of usury than to accept it while finding other ways to preserve and extend the needed solidarity.

To provide this needed cohesiveness to a community spread out in space and extending both forward and backward in time was one reason that, as time passed, the common school and compulsory education increased in importance. Sharing part of the crop with the lord of the manor in exchange for protection is different from paying taxes to a distant government for unseen activities and invisible benefit. And helping a neighbor in need by harvesting his crop is a long way from putting money in a bank at a given interest rate so that the bank can lend it to your neighbor at a higher rate. The maintenance of adequate vocational skills, appropriate meanings, good and virtuous habits, and a single collective identity is no longer a by-product of living in a certain community. It is the assigned function of a state institution—the common school.

These developments have the effect, as Dewey observed, of separating the child from many of the social and productive forces of the society. Although it is not hard to see the results of the accumulation of capital in such things as new factories, towns, and ships, it is very hard to see it in the abstract, without an elaborate theory to explain connections between supply and demand, capital and labor, savings and investment, and so on. Moreover, whereas one does not need special institutions or elaborate training to learn to speak one's native language or dialect, this is not the case when it comes to learning how to decode letters and assign to them sounds that, when combined, result in meaningful words and sentences.

The common school was and continues to be the instrument for providing the technical, conceptual, and cultural skills that enable individuals to think of themselves as belonging to that fictive, invisible community called the nation. Or, to put it another way, the fact (as opposed to the ideal) of multiculturalism—so important throughout much of the Western world today—is not a new one for public education. The need to shape multiple cultures is one very significant reason public education came into being. Especially since the rise of modern urbanization and technology ushered in the age of immigration, one key job of the common school has been to provide children from multiple cultures with a common identity as members of a single nation.[23] An important justification and motivation for this identity in the United States is the inculcation and the stabilization of the three principled reasons that I elaborated in the first chapter. The public school is held out, accurately or not, as an avenue for equal opportunity, personal development, and new associations *within* the context of a national identity. The principles affirm the connections that are supposed to exist in some way among people within the same nation and are intended to express the horizontal character of its institutions and the underlying equality of its citizens.

NATIONAL IDENTITY IN MULTICULTURAL SOCIETIES

Traditional nation-states that base their membership on stories of ancestry and blood have boundaries that are usually less porous than those of constitutional democracies that base membership on the acceptance of certain institutions and practices. And because there is no single and easy test of identity, constitutional democracies that embrace people from many different cultural groups need practices that reproduce their national identities. For more than a hundred years the common school has been the most important instrument for doing this.

Nationalism involves the view that states must develop a shared sense of national membership and that their citizens must be partial to their fellow nationals in many of the ways suggested at the beginning of this chapter. Culturally pluralistic nations—that is, those consisting of people with different cultural backgrounds and experiences living and governing together under a principle of equal citizenship—do not come by this lesson naturally or as a result of family affiliations. Lessons in national partiality often must be explicitly taught, and they contain a number of additional tenets. These include the understandings that (1) citizenship in the national community is shared by members of different cultural groups; (2) members of this national community are expected to be morally partial to it [24] and, under certain conditions, to their co-members regardless of cultural affiliation; and (3) culturally different citizens are to be partial to one another (in certain kinds of situations) even if this involves distancing themselves from culturally similar citizens of a different nation-state.

In pluralistic nations where people often hold special cultural allegiances, the development of this kind of partiality has often been a special project of the common school. To learn this partiality is a complex accomplishment. There are no obvious concrete events that are "a national unit," only flags, songs, stories, recounting of historical events, representatives, or institutions, and so on, and there is no obvious type of person who can be shown as an example of an American or a Canadian citizen. Indeed, one of the things that citizenship means in a consciously multicultural society is that there can be no such single example.

Instead there is a complex conceptual map about nationhood that children need to grasp as they come to understand themselves as members of one particular nation. For example, in learning to view themselves as nationals of a certain kind, children also learn a complex set of personal obligations and nonobligations that apply very differently to citizens of their own country than they do to citizens of other countries.

In taking on an identity as a member of this nation, and in developing the intuitive understanding that co-nationals in every nation have special obligations to one another, children grasp the concept of nationhood and begin to understand the philosophy of nationalism, which enables their nation to coexist within a field of other nations. In order to understand that this identity can and must belong to them, they must also understand that it is situated in a field of other like identities that are not available for them to grab.

When they understand this, they do more than simply

embrace one national identity; they also grasp the concept of nationalism. They see that nations exist in time as well as in space and that this temporal existence extends backward to memories of a past, memories — historically constructed, to be sure — that have to do with promises made and obligations to be met. They understand that one must be a member of one of these units and rarely of more than one; that membership is not usually voluntary; that one is born a member and then (usually) accepts that membership and the obligations it entails later. They also see that there is a connection between being a member of a nation and being subject to the nation's laws. Children are unlikely to be able to articulate all of this, just as people who know how to write a grammatically correct sentence may not be able to articulate the rules they are following. Yet as they take on a national identity children also acquire tacit rules imbedded in the idea of nationalism.

To put it simply, modern nations are expressions of the philosophy of nationalism, and to take on a certain national identity is to grasp that relationship in its general form.[25] The relationship here is analogous to the way people assume a system of numbers when they complete a multiplication problem. One need not know everything about mathematics to do the problem, but one must have a sense of the ordered relations that allow multiplication to be performed.[26] Following Gellner and Anderson, without an underlying conception about nationhood there would be no nations, and without an understanding of this conception, children could not take on an identity as co-nationals.

What children pick up when they take on a national identity is the idea that nationhood involves collective inclusion and exclusion in a past, present, and future stream of activities, sufferings, and anticipations. They learn that as they become a member of that nation they enter this stream and, ideally, that as they become citizens they take responsibility for interpreting and directing it. Through the nation individuals are brought together as *a people* and as such, and they stand in distinction from others who are brought together as a *different people.*

This understanding is expressed every day in the small details of private lives—the reporting of news from this center of interest rather than that, the reading of literature from this author rather than that, the retelling of this history rather than that history. When children learn to read in school, they are not just learning a technical skill; they are learning to experience a very large set of events from a particular point of view, from a center of subjectivity shared by their co-nationals. Learning to view events from this center but not that one allows a nation's identity to be expressed through its individual citizens.

Recognition of the ideas of identity and difference constructed through nationalism is a by-product of something else— learning to think of oneself as American or British or Mexican—and is not by itself sufficient to enable children to "have identities" as co-nationals. Thus, in addition to the assumptions about nationalism that people in all nations share, each individual nation expresses through its members certain ideas, norms, self-understandings, and practices that distinguish *it* from other nations. These are found in such things as political and juridical practices, in literature, and in normal everyday expectations and behaviors. In Japan, for example, the judicial system serves as much as a way to cement community ties as an instrument to convict the guilty and free the innocent. In the United States the secret ballot is an expression of individualism and the ideal of individual authenticity.

This authenticity is also expressed in the nation's arts. "Doing it my way" is more than just a song. In America it is a national expectation. The practices must be crystallized and reproduced in subsequent generations through institutional memory. And they must be both understood and taken on as one's own. To do so, however, does not require that one agree with them. It only requires that one see oneself as responsible for them.

THE PROBLEM OF MULTICULTURALISM AS THE PROBLEM OF LEARNING TO BE MODERN

If the common school is a development of nationalism, then nationalism, as we know it, is a development of modernity and of the requirement of large-scale coordinated action to exploit the possibilities made available by advances in scientific knowledge and technology. These changes include the way in which we think about morality, taste, authority, identity, and thinking itself. They require cooperation among groups previously separated and sometimes antagonistic to one another, and thus they also require a commitment to a common authority that can override local interests, local decisions, and local ways of knowing.

The connection between modernization and science involves more than just the exploitation of technology. It involves a new source of understanding, one that serves to extend thought and judgment beyond a person's immediate environment. In practical matters this involves changing the way people think, and in moral matters it involves changing the way they judge.

In addition to teaching children to be members of a modern nation, the common school has to teach some of them how to be modern. Many of the issues raised by multicultural education arise out of conflicts between the modern nation — viewed as the instrument of scientific and technological progress by its advocates — and traditional cultural formations, viewed as victims of the state's inexorable march toward modernity. Yet public education, as flawed as it may be, cannot simply be dismissed by postmodern sound bites such as "totalizing" or "hegemonic" without addressing some of the specific goals that its advocates hoped to accomplish. If the projects of education are to be refined one needs to understand the vision (along with its limits) that inspired public schooling in many different nations during the latter part of the last century and much of this one.

Luria and Improving Thinking

Consider thinking first: When A. R. Luria, the Russian psychologist, studied illiterate peasants in the Soviet Union in the 1920s and 1930s he found that many of the logical processes that form the foundation for modern thought, such as categorizing objects or determining similarity and difference, were guided by the peasant's idiosyncratic experiences. Hence, for example, if the subject was asked to decide which of the following doesn't belong—a potato, a tractor, a train, or a truck—he might name the train and then, if asked to provide a reason, he might say that it was the only one not related to the harvest. For Luria the answer indicated that the peasant had not acquired *higher*-order thinking skills.[27]

From a nation-building point of view the peasant's thinking process is problematic because it changes depending on the immediate experience the subject has in mind and because this experience often is not shared with people outside of his immediate environment. This limits the ability of others to follow the thought process and to coordinate action.[28]

Because of their inability to link the premises and conclusion of a syllogistic argument, Luria felt, the peasants were limited in their ability to comprehend events outside of their own immediate environment. For example, in response to the question "In the far north, where there is snow, all bears are white. Novaya Zemlya is in the far north. What color are the bears there?" many of Luria's subjects refused to draw any inferences, commenting, for example, that "they could only judge what they had seen": "We don't know what we haven't seen."[29] These answers are telling. To learn to *re*think in the way Luria wants presupposes an ability to experience a world from the point of view of someone who knows little about you and will likely never be a part of your immediate community.

This explains Luria's observation that schools make a considerable difference in changing the way these people think:

> This tendency to rely on operations used in practical life was the controlling factor among uneducated and illiterate subjects. Subjects whose activities were still dominated by practical labor, but who had taken some school courses or had attended training programs for a short time, were inclined to mix practical and theoretical modes of generalization. The somewhat more educated groups employed categorical classification as their method of grouping objects.[30]

Changes of this kind were obviously connected to education at that time. They are important not just because they provide opportunities to think in different and broader ways but because they contribute to reconstructing and widening the community that is identified as one's own. They allow one to think beyond the horizons of local meanings and enable those from different communities to communicate with one another. In the process both the nature of the community and the object of thought undergo change. The object of thought, now disengaged from specific traditions and associations, is available to manipulate beyond the perimeters of present experience and provides possibilities for new responses to a changing environment.

As we will see in the next chapter, from the point of view of traditional culture, the change is not always benign. As ways of thinking change, so too do ways of relating, and long-standing ways of life become threatened by larger alterations. Yet this judgment is largely after the fact. At the time (both from outside and from within a cultural grouping) it is difficult to see all of the other changes that a change in logical thought will bring about. This is no less so when it comes to the changes that reformers wished to bring about in moral and ethical judgment.

Durkheim and Moral Reconstruction

At the end of the nineteenth century scholars and reformers came to believe that many traditional and religious values were retarding the progress that advances in science and technology were making possible. Some argued that the public school should become the instrument of a new kind of morality—one linked to science and technology through the collective endeavors of the state. This attempt had reflexive implications. As the school was to become the instrument for such a change, it was also one of the critical institutions that the change was to justify and legitimize.

This move also carried with it implicit comparisons between the morality of tradition and the morality of progress and created the most persistent conflicts for public education, as well as one of the most perplexing ethical problems: How does a democratic society justify *imposing* education on groups of citizens who want to maintain their own values and to reproduce them in their children? That there are times when these groups desire to reproduce values that are not especially democratic is a factor that complicates the issue severely. Yet this is one of the critical issues for multicultural education and for the remaining chapters in this book. What does a liberal, democratic education require of the different cultural groups that are a part of it, and what, if any, obligation do the public schools have to these groups as collective entities?

Emile Durkheim believed that moral education must be freed from its religious moorings in faith and anchored to the modern state and to reason. He wrote: "There is nothing in reality that one is justified in considering as fundamental beyond the scope of human reason."[31] Many scholars, including Durkheim in France, Dewey in the United States, and Green in England[32] believed that the public school (or in Dewey's case the scientific method) was the instrument of reason and that it, more than the church, was the legitimate bearer of moral education. Public schooling, because it provided children with the training needed to reason well, was itself a moral project. As Durkheim wrote in explaining the importance of providing the public school with the moral authority previously granted to the church:

> From the fact that nations, to explain [morality] to themselves, have made it a radiation and a reflection of divinity, it does not follow that it cannot be attached to another reality, to a purely empirical reality, through which it is explained, and of which the idea of God is indeed perhaps only the symbolic expression. If, then, in rationalizing education, we do not retain this character [of dignity] and make it clear to the child in a rational manner, we will only transmit to him a morality fallen from its natural dignity. At the same time we will risk drying up the source from which the schoolmaster, . . . feeling that he was speaking in the name of a superior reality[,] elevated himself, invested himself with an extra energy. If we do not succeed in preserving this sense of self and mission for him — while providing, meanwhile, a different foundation for it — we risk having nothing more than a moral education without prestige and without life.[33]

Durkheim believed that the nation is the primary source of morality because it avoids the narrowness of the family and the incoherence of a universal but amorphous collective depicted by the noun "humanity."[34] And the school is "the only moral agent through which the child is able systematically to learn to know and love his country."[35]

Durkheim failed to provide a fully convincing rationale for the monopoly of public education over moral training because he was unable to reconcile two principle elements in his argument. On one hand, the object of moral action had to be a social one.

It was not to be driven by individual desires and inclinations. For this reason, even charity, since it was merely a reflection of the wishes of the individual benefactor, could only serve as an example of a kind of protomoral behavior.[36] Only where the individual will was hitched to the larger purpose of the nation was moral action truly expressed. Yet, on the other hand, when responding "scientifically" to the question as to why individuals should choose to so link themselves to such a project, Durkheim was able to respond only in terms of individual benefits — such as to avoid an increased likelihood of suicide or to be happy[37] — benefits that were not, of course, unavailable in many traditional cultural groups.

The inadequacy of Durkheim's justification is important to note for, unnoticed, it allows a monopoly of public education over moral training. Once noted, this monopoly becomes more complicated. Not only did Durkheim fail to consider the possibility that the nation may organize itself to serve immoral purposes, one of the sad lessons of this century, but he allowed little space within which other collective formations might arise to challenge national goals formulated by government agents. Nevertheless, to fail to establish that public education should have a monopoly over moral education is a far cry from denying, as some separatists do, that it should have a significant role to play or that the home or the church or the cultural unit should be given a monopoly on the moral education of an individual child.

Dewey and the Social Justification of Morality

John Dewey was considerably less admiring and more skeptical of the state than Durkheim, but he was a strong advocate of public education. Convinced that modernization and the methods of scientific thinking provided a new framework for moral action, he believed, with Durkheim, that the school was the agent of the new ethics. Equating evolution and ethics, he argued for an expansion of human agencies of control. Early in his career he argued that ethical behavior is consistent with evolutionary activity and growth because in the long run the survival of the fittest means the survival of the ethically best. Dewey argued for this position by noting that the success in overcoming the difficulties we encounter with part of nature always entails the intelligent use of other parts of nature. He then proposed that success in overcoming such difficulties depends on our skills in cooperating with one another and concluded that the struggle for survival would be won by those who were most intelligent and cooperative. These two qualities were also the two that were central in the critical role that he gives to education. Yet, as with Durkheim's, Dewey's justification was not fully convincing.

Dewey stated boldly: "We have reason to conclude that the 'fittest with respect to the whole of conditions' is the best; . . . The unfit is practically the antisocial." [38] He illustrated his point by arguing that a society that cares for its old, sick, and feeble develops in the process habits of foresight that contribute to the development of the skills of warfare. Moreover, he wrote, "such conduct would pay in the struggle for existence as well as be morally commendable." [39] Obviously, if Dewey is correct in this point then a new and nonarbitrary foundation is available for using the common schools as an instrument for ethical and moral development.

Yet ultimately this conception of ethical behavior fails on a number of grounds. The problem with his claim is not just that modern anthropologists have shown us cultures whose survival may depend on an abandonment of the old when they are unable to advance with the group. It is also that Dewey's understanding of what is to count as ethical behavior is actually derived independently from his ideas about evolution. This suggests that there is a valid reason to maintain the distinction between evolution and ethics. In other words, in order to judge whether behavior that is sound from an evolutionary standpoint is also ethical, we need to have some independent idea about what to count as ethical.

It is one thing to claim that what is ethically best is also what is most appropriate for survival. This is an empirical claim that evidence can, in theory, show to be true or false. It is quite something else to decide just what is to count as ethical behavior. Dewey seems to be saying that something is ethical if it contributes to the survival of the group broadly conceived.

Yet surely this is not an adequate explanation of what we are to count as ethical. True, it does make sense to say that if an act is undertaken knowing that it will seriously hurt the chances for the survival of a group—assuming the group is itself ethical— then the act is unethical. To assume that a group is ethical, however, requires an independent standard of behavior, and therefore, we cannot just reverse the principle and say that because an act contributes to the survival of the group it is ethical. Ethics involves the intent as much as it does the consequences of an act. The person who cares for the sick out of concern for their well-being, for example, is acting ethically. The person who cares for the sick because it is the only job available is not usually singled out for ethical commendation, although certainly there is nothing necessarily wrong in acting out of this motive. To do nothing wrong is not necessarily to act out of ethical concern. The failure to understand this distinction led Dewey throughout his career too easily to connect science and an evaluation of consequences with ethics as such. And this led to a sympathetic yet sometimes shallow understanding of education's obligations to traditional communities.[40]

A RECONSIDERATION OF THE ARBITRARY CHARACTER OF THE COMMON SCHOOL

The inability of these projects to fully establish a moral basis for the common school is telling for two reasons (which I will address more fully in the chapters that follow). First, the common school is an instrument of individual and cultural change. It alters the way people think, changes basic moral understandings, and alters commitments and loyalties. Some of these early changes were driven by the seemingly inexorable movement of technology and the development of the modern state that grew in tandem with it. Yet this movement for compulsory public education was not unconscious. Schools developed as a result of a self-conscious decision to advance a certain kind of identity and, by implication, to short-circuit local ways of life. Even though I have argued that the arbitrary qualities of nations and hence their schools are much more circumscribed and specific than the postmodern climate of criticism allows, from the point of view of another self-conscious but more local way of life, the development of compulsory public education may well appear to be an imposition[41] and as the purveyor of what Bourdieu calls symbolic violence.[42]

The arguments on behalf of the common school were unable to make the finer distinctions that are needed to determine the obligation schools have toward specific cultural groups, whose history and traditions might differ as much from each other as they do from the practices of modernity.

These flawed justifications encourage theorists and groups who wish to maintain their traditional identity to turn the tables and view the school only as an instrument of domination, oppression, and hegemony and view traditional culture always as the source of liberation and authenticity. In other words, the assumption on the part of its defenders that the common school could be justified in terms that inevitably placed science above tradition left little room for argument about a particular tradition or a particular conception of science and set the stage for many of the seemingly irreconcilable clashes that we are experiencing today.

SUMMARY

The failings of the common school should be viewed alongside its benefits and its possibilities. The school played an important role in the move from a rural, agrarian society to an urban, industrial one, it provided opportunities for some to advance economically and socially, and it was and continues to be a critical battleground in the struggles to end racism and sexism. The task now is to provide a vision of public schools and national identity that allows for both the development of unifying national sentiments and the recognition of cultural differences.

Even though I have pointed out some of the weak spots in the traditional justification of public education, I believe that the argument that I have presented in this chapter reinforces the idea of citizenship education against the contention that national identity is simply an arbitrary matter and that the common school can only serve to reinforce the ideology of the dominant group. I have suggested that although there are indeed certain arbitrary elements to any given national identity, there are also many needs served by the development of such an identity.

Granted, the arguments developed by Durkheim, Luria, and Dewey for the importance of modern schools do not provide a fully adequate justification for advancing a child's national identity, but they are not to be dismissed either. Modern education at its best can add considerable power to our modes of thinking, and the modern nation-state, for all of the problems, all of the horrors associated with it, has allowed for an unprecedented degree of coordinated action and mutual aid.

In order to formulate a more acceptable justification of the public school we need to understand the elements that were left out of these defenses and begin to replace them. I believe that the justification of the common school can be strengthened by extending its public-forming role to include the idea of enabling culturally different formations within the same nation to flourish. Yet before this argument can be completed I need to explore the concerns that advocates of individual cultures have expressed about the public schools.

3. Cultural Difference

*All pedagogical action is, objectively, symbolic
violence insofar as it is the imposition of a
cultural arbitrary by an arbitrary power.*

PIERRE BOURDIEU AND JEAN-CLAUDE PASSERON,
Reproduction in Education, Culture, and Society

INTRODUCTION

There are two significant challenges to the identity formation role
of the common school in a liberal nation. The first is to Luria's
claim that a common school can provide a neutral form of knowing. This challenge is voiced frequently by many feminists and
spokespeople for other liberation movements, but it also issues
from people who are concerned about the encroachment of modernity on traditional cultures. I speak of this challenge as the "strong
culturalist" position, and in this chapter I draw on our understanding of the concept of culture to explain its relevance to the common
schools ideal and to show its concern for capturing the way marginal groups may experience nonrecognition by the schools.

Some people use the term *relativism* to describe part of
what I want to indicate by the label "strong culturalism." Relativism, however, is largely an epistemological doctrine that addresses the nature of knowledge and holds that there are thick

boundaries between groups or individuals such that what is true knowledge for one need not be true knowledge for the other, and that there is no neutral system of true knowledge that can serve to adjudicate the differences between the two. The idea of strong culturalism captures this understanding, but it goes further and describes what is at stake when a particular system of knowledge is forced on a community. In this sense strong culturalism is a moral as well as an epistemological doctrine. It holds that there are collective experiences that can only be authentically understood from the inside and that attempts to describe them using general categories not only are likely to fail but can result in distortion of the group's experience to others and, more important, to itself.

This distortion, when reproduced through the educational system, is seen as a form of symbolic violence leaving a group's collective experience unrecognizable by its own members. Whether the experience involves a tradition-imbedded culture such as the one in which Luria worked or women seeking to validate their collective experience, the emphasis of the strong culturalist is always on the uniqueness of the experience and on the distortions that arise in trying to express it in general terms by "neutral" third parties.

The second position, which I call the communitarian idea, challenges beliefs like those of Durkheim that a common school, especially in the liberal state, can provide an adequate moral education.[1] Whereas the strong culturalist is concerned about imposition of meanings from the outside, the communitarian is concerned about the inability of modern society to develop moral norms and understandings. If the challenge from the strong culturalist spans the space between traditional cultures and liberation movements, the communitarian challenge spans the space between traditional culture and a nation-state conceived, not in liberal terms, but as a community of moral understanding and education. The communitarian involves an assertion of the importance of traditional cultural authority that theorists such as Luria and Durkheim believed needed to be superseded by modern institutions and scientific rationality.

These two challenges stress different concerns about public education. The first holds that it is a hegemonic exercise of authority and questions its legitimacy on its own terms — as providing new liberating possibilities for individuals. Instead it holds that, rather than liberating people, schools distort the collective experience of many groups of people and then conceal the fact that they have done so. The second challenge holds that the neutrality claimed by the liberal state and the public school is inadequate for the development of moral citizens, and it asks for a reexamination of the value of traditional culture as a moral educator.

The first challenge, which I consider in this chapter, holds that collective identities, broadly conceived as including gender, race, and class, as well as culture, are unique and often incompatible with one another. Thus the very idea of a common school where identities are molded together is seen as an imposition on a more primal identity. The second challenge, which I will examine in chapter 4, holds that the liberal, multicultural state can never be an adequate source of moral education because it is inadequately related to the source of moral authority — a tradition-imbedded community. Both are arguments about identity. One suggests that public schools in liberal societies are inadequate in representing collective experiences; the other that they are inadequate in enabling children to identify with a strong moral ideal and that as a consequence their moral identity will remain underdeveloped.

The two critiques are similar in certain ways. Besides rejecting liberal ideas as the basis for education, each focuses attention away from formal political units such as the liberal state. In one instance the focus is on a group with shared experiences and meanings. In the other the focus is on a community with shared moral norms.

The difference may appear slight. After all, shared norms entail shared meanings. Nevertheless, there are a number of important distinctions. For example, the first tends to assume that there is an irreconcilable antagonism between most cultural units and the state as a whole, and it views the school as imposing meanings that are often unfamiliar to a group and incongruent with its experience. School meanings are imposed meanings that serve the dominant group and maintain oppressive relationships. The narrative is governed by a tone of suspicion or of resignation about advancing cultural meanings in a fair and impartial way through the public school. One reason for this tone is the underlying assumption that meanings and norms can only be group-specific and cannot transcend differences between groups, but this idea in itself is not sufficient to generate the tone that I am trying to capture. The strong culturalist emphasizes the incommensurability of meaning across collective experience and the fact that all practices and institutions are culturally imbedded. Given this basic incommensurability, it calls attention to attempts by the liberal state, under the guise of neutrality and through the public school, to impose a hierarchy of meaning.

Communitarians focus on the problem of moral education in the liberal state. They are skeptical about the ability of public schools in a *liberal state* to teach any meaningful moral doctrines. This skepticism does not rest on the belief that moral norms are incommensurable (although incommensurability is an issue) and is thus not the same as the suspicion that governs the tone of the strong culturalists. It arises because of liberalism's apparent unwillingness to develop a commitment to any particular conception of the good, and, as a consequence, to allow unformed children to determine their own conception of the good.

In the sections that follow I am especially interested in understanding the way in which certain kinds of provocative and often insightful ideas can, in some writers, come to take on a tone that is highly suspicious of any claim that public education can enable children from cultural communities to flourish. Since this is a claim that is largely insinuated (see the epigraph) it is hard to find any one person who has developed the idea fully. Yet it seems now to have become such a staple of certain elements of the educational left that it is not hard to find representative statements.[2]

I believe that the tone builds on a variety of different kinds of literature, and once we understand the different kinds of claims that are involved in this body, the reason for the tone will be clear. Then it will be possible to understand how advocates of public education can address the concerns to which the tone gives rise. One word of warning: since I am addressing the way in which research findings get their tone it should not be assumed that all of those whose work is cited here to support this tone actually agree with it.

THE ROLE OF CULTURE IN EDUCATION

The strong culturalist draws on certain general understandings about the role of culture. These understandings include the idea that culture involves structures of meaning and feeling that develop communally. These structures both make possible and constrain the formulation of individual and collective goals. They also include the idea that learning never occurs outside of culture but always within and because of it. Culture provides the social and material support through which individuals develop meaningful lives. It provides shared frameworks and instruments of understanding, but not necessarily a unified outlook. To "share" the "same" culture does not necessarily mean that people see eye to eye on every issue. Chinese in Taiwan and Chinese on the mainland share a written language, a moral and religious system, and for many centuries, a history, as do Koreans in the North and Koreans in the South. And a similar situation existed in the former East and West Germanys. Despite a shared culture, however, many important political differences exist between and within these groups.

Culture provides the conditions for learning and makes learning possible, but at the same time that it facilitates some kinds of understandings, it makes others more difficult. For example, in providing the language through which skills, attitudes, insights, and norms are communicated from expert to novice, from one generation to the next, it provides an important tool but one that is not infinitely flexible. To learn one natural language as a child makes it quite difficult for most people to pick up another "natural" language—or at least to pick it up as natural.

Culture expands and limits us in other ways. It provides the categories that render some understandings of the world "intuitively" available and allows others to be known only self-consciously and deliberately. In a word, we learn through culture in the sense that culture provides both the instruments that facilitate learning and the constructs and practices that constitute the objectives of learning. When we enter culture—that is, when we are born—we begin to pick up certain horizons of understanding about ourselves and others and about our relationship to our so-called natural environment. Culture sets before us a kinship system—a network of relations and obligations that we choose within but not beyond, at least not ordinarily or easily. It also provides us with a language that, among other things, reflects this kinship system and not others. Our language allows us to communicate many things but probably not all things. It provides a common standpoint from which voices from "our" past, present, and future participate in a common enterprise.

Culture is implicated in self-development because the "I" is implicated in the "we." The "I" is always formed in the context of the "we," and it is the "we" that provides the ideas of identity and attachment that constitute the "I." Culture as a system of meaning provides the material through which self-recognition occurs. It is through these materials—language, beliefs, systems of kinship, and moral systems—that we are bound together, and it is also through these that our separateness is developed and recognized. "What we are," as Jonathan Glover writes,

> is influenced by how we think of ourselves. But we do not think of ourselves according to a private conceptual scheme of our own. We use the concepts of language we have learnt, and that language is the product of a particular society. . . . It is surely plausible that societies show conceptual variations and that our thinking, at least in part, is shaped by the categories of our own society. This would only be worrying if the use of a pre-existing language excluded thinking anything original or distinctive, which it clearly does not.[3]

FEATURES OF RECOGNITION

Culture stands as the system of meaning that enables individuals to make sense of their own and others' experience. Yet making sense—or experiencing nonsense—is not an easily willed process. We can no more will that something *not* make sense than we can will that it can make sense. Listen to two people talking in English, but try to hear the conversation as if it were but the babble of an unfamiliar foreign language. Or, try to see a no-longer-incomprehensible painting as again incomprehensible. The problem with meaning is not just that it is hard to come by. It is also that once we have it, it is hard to let go of. The strong culturalist draws on many of these insights and holds that children learn through culture in the sense that there are deeply ingrained but culturally specific patterns of apprehending the world that start at birth and develop through adulthood. Bourdieu calls these patterns of apprehension a *habitus* in order to indicate both a deep-seated location and a pervasive and habitual way of apprehending and responding to events. To deny the importance of these patterns is to reject the supporting and constitutive role that all cultures play in learning.

The strong culturalist holds that there is something special about the relationship between child, culture, and knowledge, that the child learns through culture, and that the object of knowledge is constituted by culture. Given this view, it is thought to be a supreme violation of the educational mandate to ignore the fact that learning and knowledge are culturally constituted. The question to be asked, then, is, Just what does it mean to say that a child learns through culture and that learning and knowledge are culturally constituted?

THE STRONG CULTURALIST VIEW AND THE PROCESS OF EDUCATION

The end of colonialism in its political form and the rise of the post-modern multicultural state raises three important challenges to the public school's role in advancing a common identity. First, given the diversity of experiences and beliefs among people from different groups, is there any way to use schools to connect children's sentiment to national understandings, memories, and norms that is not impositional and does not violate the collective experience of the child's primary group? Second, is there any presentation of memories, interpretations, and aspirations that can acceptably represent the experience of the many different groups within the state, or must the memories, interpretations, and norms that are advanced as constituting a national identity really be those of the dominant economic, racial, gender, or social class groups? Third, is it justifiable to take systematic steps to use schools to develop a favored representation of the national experience?

The view of the strong culturalist that the systematic development of a national identity through the schools is a form of imposition and symbolic violence arises in part as an antidote to a frequent although not invariable history of insensitivity and violence against different cultural practices. This view properly challenges, for example, the taken-for-granted assumption of past and some present educators of Native American children that the greatest benefit they can provide these children is to separate them from the practices and values of their parents' culture and to replace these with the values of the dominant society. One of the consequences of this belief was the forceful removal of children from their native culture and their parents in order to place them in boarding schools where they would learn to be "Americans."

The assumption itself is an outgrowth of certain misappropriations of the Enlightenment tradition and has been influenced by additional misappropriations of liberal thought. It is, for example, one of the possible implications of the idea represented in a benevolent way by Luria that there is a single form of rationality and that tradition often stands in the way of rational thinking. It is also the outgrowth of views such as that held by John Stuart Mill — that it would be disruptive to have more than one cultural group represented within a single state.[4]

This view fails to consider the element of cruelty that is involved if a child's taken-for-granted understandings and cherished beliefs are redescribed by public school practices as marginal, primitive, or inadequate to the benefits of modern life. Indeed, one of the historical problems with liberal theory is that it has often neglected cultural concerns in favor of political ones. Yet the failure to consider the relationship of the self to culture leads to an inadequate view of the self, one in which we wrongly believe that we are independent in some acultured sense, that all of our achievements and failings are our own doing and all of what we count to be an achievement or a failing is universally given.

The strong cultural critique is often expressed against the assumption that schools constitute some kind of culturally neutral site of learning and that the evaluation of children in school is an objective, culture-free assessment of their ability. Against this, the strong culturalist correctly holds that schools are not culturally neutral and that they express their own culturally situated point of view.[5]

An important presupposition of the strong culturalist is that there are many forms of cultural competence and that people develop theories that are compatible with life in a specific culture. Shirley Brice Heath illustrates some of the alternative theories of education that are found within cultural communities and the competence involved in implementing them. As one of her respondents explains:

> He gotta learn to *know* 'bout dis world, can't nobody tell 'im.
> . . .White folks uh hear dey kids say sump'n, dey say it back to 'em, dey asks 'em 'gain 'n 'gain 'bout things, like they 'posed to be born knowin'. You think I kin tell Teegie all he gotta know to get along? He just gotta be keen, keep his eyes open, don't he be sorry. Gotta watch hisself by watchin' other folks. Ain't no use tellin' 'im: "learn dis, learn dat. What's dis? What's dat?" He just gotta learn, gotta know: he sees one thing one place one time, he know how it go, see sump'n like it again, maybe it be de same, maybe it won't. He hafta try it out. If he don't be in trouble; he get lef' out. Gotta keep yo' eyes open, gotta feel to know.[6]

Heath does not express her own views about the value of this learning, but the passage illustrates an important aspect of the strong culturalist's view — that competence must not be defined by standards that are external to a practice and imported from the outside. Rather, the strong culturalist will mark as significant standards that arise from within the practice and ideas of the community and will extract from these the learning that is important. Again, Heath's work provides a nice example of such internal standards:

> Preschoolers, especially boys, are always being presented with situations and being asked "*Now* what you gonna do?" The children must think before they respond, and as Annie May realized, must feel the motivation and intentions of other indi-

viduals. They are powerless to counter physically; they must outwit, outtalk, or outact their aggressor. Across sets of situations and actors, children learn the domains of applications of a particular word, phrase, or set of actions, and the meanings conveyed across these are often neither literal nor predictable.[7]

She illustrates the point by describing an incident with a preschooler who, when teased by the men in the community, came up with an ingenious solution. An adult would take the child's candy, saying, "What you gonna do, I try to take dis? Let me keep it for you. Come on, I just be keepin it." He would then eat the candy, giving some to the other children, and then return it to a now-crying boy. After unsuccessfully trying to enlist the aid of the other adults, who would themselves eat some of the candy, the boy's solution was to stick the candy in a small hole between the boards of the porch where his tormentors could not reach. To win the game, as Heath sums up, the boy "had to size up the possible responses of other adults, to figure out a tactic which made the most of his strengths and caught [the adult's] weaknesses. Their relative size had been the key to the solution."[8] For the strong culturalist, finding the key demonstrates cultural competence and validates the indigenous learning theory articulated above by Heath's native respondent.

METHOD AND PRESUPPOSITIONS

The concern to display cultural competence is an important element in the strong culturalist view. A moralist looking in from the outside might question the appropriateness of a pedagogy that largely leaves a child to his or her own devices or could be alarmed by adults who tease children until they cry. These are, however, at least from the strong cultural viewpoint, incidental. Much more significant is the understanding that there is an internal theory that explains the interaction between adult and child, that there are im-

plicit standards that are internal to the culture by which these interactions can be judged, and that the interactions that are consistent
with the indigenous learning theory result in important learning.

From the point of view of the strong culturalist, culture
not only makes a difference in how we learn, it also makes a difference in what we learn and in what we count as an object of
knowledge. This strengthens the incommensurability thesis that I
mentioned earlier. Heath provides a useful example involving the
difference in the way stories are told in two Appalachian communities. One, Roadville, is white and working-class. The other,
Trackton, is black and working-class.

> In Roadville, a story must be invited or announced by someone
> other than the story-teller. Only certain community mem-
> bers are designated good story-tellers. A story is recognized
> by the group as an assertion of community membership and
> agreement on behavioral norms. The marked behavior of the
> story-teller and audience alike is seen as exemplifying the weak-
> nesses of all and the need for persistence in overcoming such
> weaknesses. Trackton story-tellers, from a young age, must be
> aggressive in inserting their stories into an on-going stream
> of discourse. Story telling is highly competitive. Everyone in a
> conversation may want to tell a story, so only the most aggres-
> sive wins out. The stress is on the strengths of the individual
> who is the story's main character, and the story is not likely
> to unify listeners in any sort of agreement, but to provoke
> challenges and counter challenges to the character's ways of
> overcoming an adversary. The "best" stories often call forth
> highly diverse additional stories, all designed not to unify the
> group, but to set out the individual merits of each member of
> the group.[9]

In Trackton, though a story often begins with a grain of
truth, it is quickly embellished so that this grain is quickly lost

sight of. In Roadville, "any fictionalized account of a real event is viewed as a lie."[10] The people in Trackton, Heath tells us, would not be able to view a Roadville account of "real life" as a story, and the resident of Roadville would see a tale from Trackton as a pure and simple lie.[11] In other words, children from both communities are learning, through different cultural forms, what to count as a story, the learning is in fact different in each of the communities, and the norms by which one could say that a story was really told are incommensurable across the two communities.

THE MEANING OF "LEARNING-THROUGH-CULTURE"

Heath does not tell us what she thinks of these different cultural modes, but for the strong culturalists they serve to show that learning occurs through culture and that culture determines both how we learn and what is counted as genuine learning. To say that learning occurs through culture may mean at least four different but related things. The strong culturalist means all of them. First, it means that we cannot apprehend the world except through the conceptual and emotional frames that are both the products and the elements of culture. The most obvious of these frames is language, which both makes possible and constrains the way we can know the world. To ask a Japanese person, for example, whether it is more important for children to learn to respect or to be critical of authority may provide a misleading response since it is difficult to translate "be critical of authority" in an appropriately Western, neutral way. This difficulty is itself a sign of different ordering principles for American and Japanese society.

Second, "learning through culture" means that culture determines the elements of development that are to count as learning; learning occurs in a context that gives significance to some ways of developing and not to others. Imagine a person in a far-away land who has developed the ability to shoot a ball into a hoop consistently at fifteen feet or more but whose culture has no game like basketball. The activity is idiosyncratic and largely meaningless.[12]

Third, it means that the world as apprehended is dependent on instruments such as language, norms, relational possibilities, shared meanings, and symbols that constitute a culture and in which individual members participate. Fourth, it means that different instruments from different cultures create different apprehended worlds. To hold all four of these meanings is to hold the strong view of the relationship between culture and learning.

None of this is to say, of course, that culture alone determines the way the world is seen or that it does so in such a way that some parts of the world are not available to people from more than one culture. Cultures are responses to certain constraints; they develop in part to service collective needs. There are obviously certain needs and activities that all human beings require — food, shelter — and any culture that did not meet these would quickly disappear through no fault of anyone outside. Hence, on the very broadest level there will be common features between cultures. It is the variety of ways in which these needs are met that provides the vast array of differences that are found among different peoples. Nevertheless, culture provides the framework that is necessary to understanding the world, and without some such framework the world is incomprehensible and meaningless. Moreover, within some frameworks the world looks vastly different than it does from other frameworks. For the strong culturalist this means that interference with cultural forms is a serious matter.

THE GIFTS OF CULTURE

Except perhaps for the newest infant, experience does not come to us culture-free and uninterpreted. The problem of epistemology is the problem of culture. If culture did not mediate experience, there would be no difficulty understanding the nature of knowledge. The problem arises because for every group (with the possible exception of our own, whatever "our own" may be), culture mediates knowledge. The question of what to count as knowledge arises because cultures weave taken-for-granted horizons of discourse, and through these horizons people shape their experience in ways that give it particular meanings but not others. Certain elements of experience become "intuitively" visible to members of some groups but not to members of other groups. From the point of view of one culture, the experience of members of another seems mediated and indirect. It needs to be translated and explained, rather than just lived: "*Their* language has this peculiar way of thinking about authority relations," or, "If you want to understand why *they* are so dependent on each other, you need to know their unusual history." This mediation is a problem the strong culturalist points out only because we continue to think that there must be universal ways to experience the world—when we think, for example, that my green must also be your green, that my loving must also be your loving, or that my classic novel must also be your classic novel.

Consider what it takes to *appreciate* a story (to have the "right" feelings) in "the right way." Laura Bohannan is a cultural anthropologist who, armed with a copy of *Hamlet* to occupy rainy days, started off from England to spend time living with and studying a people in the African bush. After many rainy days, on which tribal members would tell one another stories, she was encouraged to tell them the story of Hamlet. She began:

> "Long ago. . . three men were keeping watch outside the homestead of the great chief, when suddenly they saw the former chief approach them."
> "Why was he no longer their chief?"
> "He was dead," I explained. "That is why they were troubled and afraid when they saw him."

"Impossible," began one of the elders, handing his pipe on to his neighbor, who interrupted. "Of course it wasn't the dead chief. It was an omen sent by a witch. Go on."

Slightly shaken, I continued. "One of these three was a man who knew things" — the closest translation for scholar, but unfortunately it also meant witch. The second elder looked triumphantly at the first.

"So he spoke to the dead chief saying, 'Tell us what we must do so you may rest in your grave,' but the dead chief did not answer. He vanished, and they could see him no more. Then the man who knew things — his name was Horatio — said this event was the affair of the dead chief's son, Hamlet."

There was a general shaking of heads around the circle. "Had the dead chief no living brothers? Or was the son chief?"

"No," I replied. "That is, he had one living brother who became the chief when the elder brother died."

The old men muttered: such omens were matters for chiefs and elders, not for youngsters; no good could come of being behind a chief's back; clearly Horatio was not a man who knew things.

"Yes, he was," I insisted. . . "In our country the son is next to the father. The dead chief's younger brother had become the great chief. He had also married his elder brother's widow only about a month after the funeral."

"He did well," the old man beamed and announced to the others, "I told you that if we knew more about Europeans, we would find they really were very like us. In our country also," he added to me, "the younger brother marries the elder brother's widow and becomes the father of his children."[13]

The experience illustrates the way in which our conceptual and emotional frames condition the way in which we grasp the world. *Hamlet* only works as *our Hamlet* when we can assume a structure of kinship relationships and obligations that are then violated by the antagonists. When these assumptions are not in place and moral horizons are not shared, the play loses its dramatic power. Why *would* Horatio bring the news to Hamlet and not to Hamlet's uncle?

Hamlet works for *us* in the way that it does because our culture provides us with a taken-for-granted but shared set of understandings and norms about kinship relations. These understandings allow us to appropriate the play in a certain way and to expect that others like us will appropriate the play in the same way. When young children fail to appreciate a certain play or story it is sometimes because they have not yet grasped the cultural understandings and norms that must be assumed in order for the play to work. This is also the reason why the appreciation of jokes and literature is often an important sign of an individual's successful assimilation into another culture.

Culture tells us what elements of personal change should be counted as development and learning. There is evidence that at least some of the cultural patterns into which we fall are stamped very early and remain relatively fixed in adults. Recent research on language, for example, shows that infants are able to distinguish the phonemic distinctions in different languages but that this skill is lost by the time the child is a year old and has begun to learn its native tongue.[14] This suggests that learning occurs in a context that gives significance to some ways of developing and not to others, and that as it does occur certain possibilities become more difficult to recapture.

THE ANTIHUMANIST THESIS

But the strong cultural thesis is bolder than the idea that culture picks out some responses as meaningful in the course of development and renders others inconsequential. It is that the world as apprehended is dependent on culture and that different cultures create differently apprehended worlds.

There are actually two claims that can be contained in this proposition: one about the way the subject relates to the world, or apprehends it, the other about the object — about the world that is apprehended. The strong cultural thesis should be able to deal with both sides of this claim. That is, (1) culture makes a difference in how we apprehend the world, and (2) culture makes a difference in the world that is apprehended. To see the importance of these claims consider a counterclaim that "we are all the same under the skin," which means that despite superficial cultural differences, we all experience and react to the world in similar ways. Our behavior may be dependent on our culture, but our feelings are not. Given this view, the way in which we react, say, to a pleasant song or to a suffering child are the same regardless of our cultural differences.

Now consider the possibility that this humanistic doctrine is wrong in an important way and that culture not only conditions the way we behave but also makes possible the feelings we have. I believe that this is a critical component of the strong culturalist's view. The argument is that we are not all the same under the skin and that there are radical differences between the feeling states experienced by members of different cultures, differences shaped by the cultures.

The strong culturalist claim is not just the obvious one that two people may feel differently about the same event — say, the victors and the losers in a battle. It is that the kinds of feelings available to certain cultural groups may differ widely from the kinds of experience and feelings available to members of another cultural group. Although we may all be born with the capacity to experience the same range of feelings, our culture actually shapes us into the kind of people that experience one segment of that range rather than another, and, then, our own individuality refines that segment even further. Even when we may be having a similar feeling, our cultures often tone that feeling in different ways. Consider, for example, the way guilt is experienced in a deeply religious, pre-

Freudian society—unself-consciously—and the way it is experienced in a post-Freudian society—self-consciously, perhaps even *guiltily*. In one it calls for confession and forgiveness—absolution. In the other it calls for self-reflection and self-understanding—therapy. In one it is imbedded in a theological map; in the other it is imbedded in a psychological map.

Not only is the "same" feeling toned differently by different cultures; it may be valued differently as well. Takeo Doi, a Japanese psychiatrist, describes with some misgivings Americans' commitment to independence and contrasts it, with some unfavorable overtones, to the Japanese idea of *amae,* or "the desire"—as Doi's translator explains, "to be passively loved, the unwillingness to be separated from the warm mother-child circle." [15] In contrast to the American's drive for independence, *amae,* which Doi sees as a characteristic drive of the Japanese, could be called a quest for dependency.

The idea that somehow there could be a strong and universal urge for dependence seems to run counter to our "Western" moral intuition that there is a strong and universal drive toward independence. Moreover, Japanese and American cultures are organized in such a way that both accept the *truth* of their own *particular* universal, and the organization reinforces *that* particular as universal. For example, American college-age students often cannot wait to leave home to be "on their own," hence realizing their nature as independent beings. Japanese companies, however, perhaps in response to the discomfort over separation from family, provide elaborate family-style dormitories for their young, unmarried, college-educated workers.

Liberals often hold the humanistic doctrine that all human beings have essentially the same feelings, only, in different cultures, these feelings may be triggered by different events. I may feel repulsion when I see a Japanese person eating raw fish, whereas the Japanese person may feel the "same" repulsion when she sees me cutting into a large chunk of rare meat. Similarly, a Japanese and an American worker both may feel pride, but the Japanese may do so when he feels he is a member of an important company, whereas the American may feel it when he surveys his own individual workmanship. Nevertheless, the liberal argument continues, the pride — that inner feeling that makes the heart beat faster, the chest expand, and the chin rise — is the same in the Japanese and in the American.

Strong culturalists take a different view. Although they may not deny that some feelings are shared, there are others that are specific to a cultural group. As Richard Shweder asks rhetorically: "Human infants come into the world possessing a complex emotional keyboard; yet as they become Eskimo, Balinese, or Oriya only some keys get played. Do the others get stuck because they are hardly played at all?"[16]

Shweder's question begins to get at the problem of the relationship between culture and emotions, but the issue is perhaps even more complex and difficult than his question implies. Shweder seems to share with the liberal the view that feeling states are located "under our skin." He simply questions whether, given our cultural differences, these feeling states will be the same.

Yet the strong culturalist would question the liberal assumption that feelings are just names for inner states and would argue instead that feelings are tied inextricably to systems of belief. The liberal may grant that beliefs and feelings are linked in that certain beliefs can provoke or cause certain feelings: I believe that you stole my watch and thus I become angry. I find out otherwise and feel guilty for doubting you. In both cases, the liberal will grant, the belief causes the feeling. The strong culturalist wants more, however. She believes that the relationship between belief and feeling is more than just causal. It is constitutive as well.

Culture not only directs the way objects are felt — as good or bad, attractive or unattractive — it also drives the character of apprehension. Culture creates feelings, and in doing so it builds a world. Yet more than this, it weaves together beliefs, feelings and institutions so that each is required by and requires the other.

Consider, for example, how much my anger about the "stolen" watch is tied to a complex system of belief about the viability of individualized private property. Consider too how much my guilt is tied to a belief that individuals are responsible for their own "private" thoughts and feelings. And note as well how both are tied to institutions that spotlight the individual location of action — the criminal justice system — and feelings — the church and the therapist's office — which then develop intervention strategies to reinforce the idea that beliefs and feelings belong exclusively to individuals.

FEELINGS, BELIEFS, AND INSTITUTIONS

The relation between feelings, beliefs, and institutions may be seen by comparing the feeling of pride as it is experienced in different societies, one governed by a code of honor and the other by a sense of dignity. Charles Taylor has insightfully argued that these two different sentiments are tied to the tenets of different belief systems concerning the nature of the self and the proper relationship between the self and society.[17] In the case of honor the key factor involves a conception in which the self is incomplete unless it exists as part of a hierarchical structure in which members are at each other's service. Honor is bestowed on one person but participated in by all. Whether one is the head of a great household or a simple butler, honor is derived from membership and service.

To participate in a household is to occupy an important place in an institution that has a public face and public obligations. To do one's own job well at whatever level it may be is therefore to facilitate the dispatching of those obligations and thus merits inclusion in the honors that are bestowed on the head of the household. To take pride in these honors is allowed, even expected. Yet pride has its limits and is expected to be taken with expressed individual humility and without boastful displays. One can feel pride about one's role, and about having performed it well, but not about oneself.

In contrast to the notion of honor, which serves as part of the ideal of service and thus sanctions hierarchy, the notion of dignity is a part of the ideal of equality, in which each person deserves respect in her own right rather than as recognition for serving the purposes of a well-ordered hierarchy. To be treated with dignity is to have one's voice heard not simply as a member of a well-oiled household or corporation, but on its own terms and within the larger political enterprise. Here, when I feel pride, it is because of something that I did myself, something that enabled me to stand out from others. Thus both honor and dignity entail some feeling of pride, but "pride" is experienced so differently in the two cultures that it is not clear how appropriate it is to call it by the same name.

Once we understand that the feelings we refer to as "pride" may be imbedded in different beliefs about the proper relationship between self and society, and once we see how these contrasting beliefs are constitutive of different institutions, then we can better understand how the feeling itself may be experienced differently in different cultural contexts. In the system that values honor, praise is accepted with modesty and one continues to serve with humility. In the system that values dignity, pride requires a person to demand that her very being, let alone her accomplishments, be recognized.[18] The humanist fails to understand that given the very different contexts in which the two forms of "pride" are imbedded, the different expectations that they entail, the different cognitive horizons that give rise to them, and the contrasting institutions that support them, it is neither the *same* pride nor is it *just* under the skin.

There is more, however, to culture's creations than beliefs, feelings, and institutions. Culture creates objects of understanding that those on the inside call "reality" and those on the outside call "belief." It sustains these objects as reality by highlighting evidence that confirms the experience of them. For example, our own world consists of atoms, electrons, molecules, and so on, all of which evade direct sensation. It also consists of planets in motion, of gravitational forces, and other unseen matters. This world is not without evidence, of course, but the evidence for it is indirect and inferential. Scientists tell us that this is what it is like, and for some of us they provide explanations of everyday phenomena, such as the shifting positions of the sun and planets, which help us to understand why we think in these terms. Shweder provides a nice example of how other worlds can be supported by similar inferential steps by noting some of the everyday phenomena that would support a belief in reincarnation:

> Fact: Identical twins reared together not infrequently display marked difference in personality; for example, one but not the other may become schizophrenic. Fact: The personality of siblings who grow up in the same family are no more similar to each other than are those of random pairs of people drawn from different families. Fact: Children often have fears or phobias that cannot be accounted for by any known trauma and are not shared by any other members of their family. Fact: Children sometimes have skills or talents, such as mathematical or musical abilities, unlike those of relatives, abilities that could not have been learned through imitation or instruction. Each of these facts seems resistant to either genetic or environmental explanations. . . . But . . . [for] the believer, the concept of reincarnation is not without explanatory appeal.[19]

Once we have been acculturated, usually we need not think about the horizon of expectations that enables us to share meanings or feelings with others who have been similarly acculturated. Nor need we think very much about the fact that such meanings are indeed shared. We do not have to unpack the codes that enable us to evaluate and communicate in the way that we do. For the most part culture remains invisible except, of course, when things go wrong. At that point we may begin to seek out the tacit elements of understanding, elements imbedded in current practices and historical meanings that, during normal times, enable communication to flow.

THE QUESTION OF TRANSLATION AND EVALUATION ACROSS CULTURAL DIFFERENCES

This way of viewing culture raises the question of whether it is possible to translate an experience from one culture to another and whether it is also possible to really evaluate a practice in a way that is independent of the standpoint of a given culture. The issue arises because once it is accepted that culture conditions the way the world is viewed, then we always look at another culture through the lens of our own. Hence what appears to be a translation is likely a projection of one culture's ways of seeing on another. Since we would be using our own standards—standards that are already constructed through our own culture—to evaluate the culture of others, our picture will always be distorted. This concern is perhaps one of the most important reasons for the strong culturalist's reservations about the role of the common school. If we cannot truly know or evaluate another culture, then how can educators, concerned to promote autonomy, justify a common school for children from many different cultures?

LIBERATIONIST VERSIONS

In liberationist versions of the strong culturalist thesis this question is complicated further because the liberationist believes that the distortion is systematic and serves to conceal, under the claims of democracy, persisting unequal power relations. Hence the middle and upper class distort the experience of the lower and working class, whites distort the experience of blacks, and men distort the experience of women.

One problem with some liberationist accounts, however, is that they straddle two separate and contradictory standpoints. One is that of the strong culturalist and its view that one group is bound to misunderstand and distort the experience of another. The other is a scientific one that posits that we really can locate persistent structures, such as capitalism, which cause and maintain distortions. The problem is that from the first standpoint it is hard to see how any claims can be made about a structure beyond culture and from the second standpoint it is unclear how any claim can be made without threatening to distort the view as experienced from within some culture. This is not to say that liberal society is off the hook, but only that where liberationists are unclear about the source of their criticism, they may need to discard one of the hooks. Yet liberal democracy has a similar problem in terms of its stance on cultural freedom.

THE PARADOX OF THE COMMON SCHOOL UNDER LIBERAL EDUCATIONAL THEORY

The idea that culture provides the material for norms to be created and for evaluations to take place presents liberal educational thought with a vexing problem. Insofar as liberal theory requires appreciation and tolerance of difference, it would seem to require the widest possible leeway for different cultures. To override one culture's norms for the sake of more "liberal" or "democratic" ones seems paradoxically undemocratic. "We will force people to be democratic" may be as cynical as the statement attributed to an official during the Vietnam War: "We will destroy the village to free it." Even without the strong culturalist thesis, the idea of a school that overrides cultural differences in order to develop a single, national identity presents a serious problem of ends and means.

The project for liberal, democratic education is to find a way to acknowledge the importance of culture and the ways it is implicated in learning while affirming broad-based educational goals that reflect a national identity. In other words, liberal nations must recognize cultural differences but liberal democracy is more than the recognition of cultures. In subsequent chapters, I explain how I think this balance might be accomplished — that is, how we can work toward a liberal and democratic society while providing places for cultural practices, not all of which may be liberal or democratic. To begin this task requires a more critical evaluation of the strong culturalist position.

PROBLEMS WITH THE STRONG CULTURALIST VIEW

There are three problems with the strong culturalist view. The first has to do with the way in which some, such as Bourdieu and Passeron, characterize the movement through one set of cultural understandings to another as symbolic violence. If this characterization is accepted literally, it either sanctions violence as an unavoidable feature of all education or it paralyzes educational action. The second has to do with an inappropriate leap from a basically reasonable idea that different cultural groups have different ways of constructing meaning to the self-contradictory claim that cultures are impenetrable and that translation between them is inherently impossible. The third is the way in which this conception of culture can be abused to further cultural neglect. I treat the problem of neglect first.

The Problem of Cultural Neglect

There are certainly times when the appropriation of educational institutions to effect a systematic shift from one set of interpretations and aspirations to another constitutes symbolic violence and when re-description from a cultural to a national story is indeed a form of cruelty. A great deal depends upon how and why re-description is undertaken, however, and how the cultural and the national identities intermingle.

Violence and *cruelty* are too broad to capture every shift in identity formation, even those where pain is present. True, pain may be caused by random acts of violence, but pain has other causes and other results.[20] Certain forms of educational change have been disrespectful and oppressive and are rightly characterized as violence. Yet to see all shifts in identity in this way requires that much more be said about the circumstances as well as the means and the purpose of the change.[21] There is no reason, for example, why a greater understanding of the particular meaning system of a child's cultural group may not be used to reduce the difficulty with which the child is introduced to the meaning system of the larger society, or why both cannot coexist reasonably well.[22]

A great deal of cross-cultural transmission is initiated by members of the receiving culture who see some major benefit in adopting the new way of understanding. Consider an extreme example, such as why members of a past culture that used visual and concrete cues to communicate direction—walk to the river, paddle to the fork—might have wanted to understand directional coordinates such as north, south, east, and west. And consider how learning these would likely have changed much of the character of the culture.

The fact that this reconceptualization would have had a profound effect on any culture that chose to adopt it is weak ground to suggest that it should neither be adopted nor taught. Clearly this is an extreme example, but any educational system that failed to provide children, regardless of their cultural background, with the conceptual tools that are required to make a reasonable life in the modern world of science and technology is guilty of cultural neglect. When evaluating the work of people such as Luria, it is most important that the consideration to reduce cultural violence be balanced against the equally important concern to avoid cultural neglect. Theorists such as Bourdieu overemphasize symbolic violence and underemphasize cultural neglect.

Can Members of Other Cultures Know What We Mean?

The strong culturalist writes as if there were some impenetrable wall between cultures and that, even were it desirable, we could not really understand why members of other cultural groups do what they do. Given the problem of translation, then, whenever the common school is introduced to children of a different culture, it is always a matter of uninformed consent and hence of imposition.

I believe that this is too strong an indictment of the common school, in part because I reject the idea that the notion of "a wall of impenetrable meaning between cultural groups" is meaningful or clear. Consider some possible meanings that "the wall" might have. It may refer to our feelings and to an inability to understand the emotions of people from other cultures. It may refer to an inability to grasp the conceptual framework of another culture. It may involve the belief that it is impossible to understand the way in which people from other cultures think. Or it may refer to our moral understanding and to the idea that it is impossible to understand how people from other cultures form judgments. All of these are problematic.

The claim of incommensurability, when applied to feelings and understanding, is wrong on two counts. First, it is wrong because there is no reason to believe that certain experiences will be better understood by a person from the same culture than they will be by a person from a different culture. For example, although parenthood differs quite drastically from one culture to the next, it is likely that parents across many different cultural groups have a better understanding of aspects of each other's experience as parents than do nonparents within their own cultural group. This is one reason why liberation groups that seek to unite certain classes of people — women, gays, blacks — across cultures make sense. Certain experiences are better understood by people who have participated in them regardless of their culture. Yet this cannot be accurately said for all experiences; some are better grasped by calling on the robust context that culture provides.

Second, the claim is self-contradictory in that there must be at least one person—the person who pronounces it—who knows two cultures well enough to know that they are incommensurable. Yet to know this is to know also that in principle they are commensurable in the sense that each is understandable to someone who also understands the other. Hence, two systems cannot be incommensurable in a conceptual sense to anyone who claims that they are, on the basis of knowing each. That is, unless the person making the claim is wrong.

This also suggests that they may not be incommensurable with regard to feeling and that even those who have not shared a certain experience (for example, motherhood) can be brought to an awareness of how it might be to feel in such and such a way.

True, there may be feelings that I do not experience in quite the same way as people subjectively experience them through another culture. For example, some writers claim that Japanese people have a sense of obligation which is different from that of Westerners because it is perpetual and has no way of being satisfied. It may be that one would have to be born Japanese to experience obligation in this way. That does not mean, however, that one cannot understand how it *might be* to feel an obligation of this kind, and commentators make valiant efforts to convey the sense of such a feeling. They do so through analogs to what one owes one's parents for life itself and try to show how such an obligation is not repayable. The feeling may not be reproduced in the sense that we now come to feel Japanese, but this does not mean that we cannot understand how it *might be* to feel a Japanese sense of obligation.

The language of feeling is actually very complex, but there are a number of different ways to explain one's feelings to those who have not experienced them. We can explain anxiety to someone who has never felt anxious as long as we can draw on her experience of fear. And we can probably explain fear to someone who has never felt afraid as long as we can lean on her observation of animal behavior. A culture may very well produce interesting and unique emotional keys, as Shweder suggests, but this does not mean that someone from another culture with a different set of keys cannot learn to understand the emotional content.

There is also no reason to think that culture establishes a conceptual incommensurability. To see this, return for a moment to the example from "Shakespeare in the Bush" and notice that it is inadequate to support the strong cultural thesis for two reasons. In the first place, the story does not support the idea of an incommensurability between cultures. After all, it is told by an American living in the twentieth century about a play (which presumably she understands) written by an Englishman in the sixteenth century, regarding the apprehension of the play by members of a bush culture that (she also) understands as a result of two complex sets of tacit moral norms (of which the bush people understand one but not the other) that evoke a competing set of moral evaluations (which she is able to describe to us).

It likely would require a lot of work to get the bush people to understand *Hamlet* in the way that a European or an American might, but there is nothing secretive about what would constitute such an understanding or about the way in which tacit moral norms would have to become the focus of the explanation in order to achieve it. The author has provided us with ample material to comprehend the reason for the misunderstanding, and presumably the same could be done for the people in the bush.

True, at its foundation this is still a translation that deals with understanding and interpretation, rather than one in which the moral norms are themselves made commensurate. After all, if one is *obliged* to marry the wife of one's deceased brother, one cannot also hold such a marriage to be *taboo*. Yet one can understand what a taboo is, why societies have them, why different societies may have different taboos, and why, given different circumstances, such differences might be appropriate. To see all of this is to allow that neither conceptual nor moral judgments are incommensurable and is to encourage considerable discussion about them both.

ACCOMMODATION OF STRONG CULTURALIST AND LIBERAL EDUCATIONAL IDEALS

There are at least two possible ways in which liberalism could accommodate the strong culturalist positions. The first is from the point of view of choice, and the second is from the point of view of harm. From the point of view of choice the argument is that support of different cultures is a precondition of liberalism because cultures provide us with material for different conceptions of the good. In other words, a conception of society that protects the right to choose which conception of the good one is to follow is of little significance if there are not robust conceptions of the good from which a choice can be made.[23]

One objection to this view is that respect is something which individuals give to one another. It is not given by cultures to cultures or by cultures to individuals. Although it is true that cultural recognition is important for dignity, it is not true that dignity can only come through the recognition of one's birth culture.

This objection is correct as far as it goes, but it runs the danger of being too cavalier about the way in which culture is involved in individual choice and neglects important reasons why members of liberal society should be concerned about the existence of cultures other than their own. There is more to this issue than individual choice. Culture is a certain kind of good, one created when people exercise it. It is a value something like that of "conviviality" at a party, which, as J. Waldron nicely observes, is a "benefit they will have enjoyed together, not merely in the sense that to be enjoyed by one guest it cannot practicably be denied to others . . . , but in the sense that its enjoyment is essentially a property of the group rather than of each of the individual guests considered by himself." [24]

In an important sense, then, culture, like conviviality, is a value that depends on being shared, and it may well be that in fact different cultures are experienced quite differently from one another. The idea that one culture can be substituted for another without loss is an incorrect idea. Cultures are not like protein, of which one can get one's daily requirements in many different ways. They are more like beans and rice, steak and potatoes, which are enjoyed for their particular qualities by those who eat them.

Given these observations, the liberal position requires amendments that acknowledge that conditions that endanger the existence of a viable culture also reduce the choices that people have available to them in a special way. Consider that the very existence of a culture depends on its being practiced by a reasonable number of people and that the greater the number of people who opt out of this practice, the weaker the culture is likely to become.

For example, the existence of a language as an organic mode of communicative interaction is increasingly impoverished as fewer people know the language or choose to speak it. This impoverishment is experienced often by immigrants who find that certain forms of feeling become strained and often lost as they lose the opportunity to speak to others in their native tongue. [25] Where a sizable but not overwhelmingly large community exists, every person who chooses to leave the community and to practice different cultural forms is an additional incentive for others to do the same, until at some point the cultural community is no longer a viable unit no matter how much it once served as a good in its own right. Like a game in which we all participate, the value comes about just because it is a collective enterprise, and without the collective there is no value. Hence if a culture is not sustained, choice itself is diminished, and individual lives may be harmed.

Thus from inside the cultural community there is good reason to develop incentives for encouraging people to continue speaking the language, reciting the history, practicing the rituals, and following the moral norms. There is also considerable reason to limit the number of attractive options outside of the cultural unit. In other words, from inside the culture there is a continuing drive to affirm cultural forms and to develop enforcement procedures to see that they are followed. This should not be surprising. People have a stake in the frameworks and meanings that they hold to be their own, and they work to hold on to them. Certainly liberals must allow such support to continue.

The question that the liberal must ask is whether there is any reason for those outside a given culture to support these efforts through the public school. Although I do not agree with the argument that endangerment by itself is sufficient to constitute an obligation to a given culture, liberals cannot be indifferent to conditions that foster cultural uniformity and thus diminish the available conceptions of the good.

Finally, the liberal needs to note that the strong culturalists sometimes advance their case by insinuating a false dichotomy between cultural identity as authentic and spontaneous and national identity as constructed and impositional. A nation exists in part because a group of people have invested much in shaping and reshaping a certain identity, and this identity and its continuation should not be a matter of indifference. Nations are often connected to states precisely because of the need to protect this identity as well as to further it and reflect upon it, discuss it and reshape it.

CONCLUSION

This chapter shows that the strong culturalist view is incorrect. Schools *need not* do violence when they teach children to move beyond the memories, interpretations, and aspirations of their cultural group. There is no reason to think of *all* educationally initiated change from cultural meanings to national meanings as acts of violence or imposition. Indeed, to do so in a grand, metaphysical way actually runs the risk of excusing real schools that do exercise real violence, physical and symbolic, against real children. And it also may encourage a form of cultural neglect that excuses schools for not providing the cultural tools and conceptual instruments needed to live in the larger society.

4. The Possibility of Moral Education in a Liberal Society

In this chapter I want to consider a second challenge to the common school, one arising from communitarian theory. This challenge can be read as a rejection of Durkheim and Dewey's belief that the common school can serve as a substitute for the moral instruction provided by traditional communities. Communitarians are especially critical of the capacity of the common school in a liberal state to teach moral norms and conduct. They believe that the liberal theory of education places too much emphasis on the student's right to choose among different conceptions of the good and fails to emphasize the community's obligation to instruct students in the specific values and virtues that are identified with their community. In this chapter I show how this criticism can be answered within the framework of the liberal state and the common school.

In subsequent chapters I address citizenship education in a liberal, multicultural society.

Most communitarians hold to the following set of beliefs:

1. Morality is only learned within the context of a tradition.

2. Different traditions have incommensurable moral systems.

3. There is no necessary moral framework that exists across traditions and communities.

4. Traditions maintain themselves by controlling membership and education.

5. Individuals have a special responsibility to the traditions that have nurtured them.

6. The core morality is not always taught rationally, but ceremony and rhetoric often play important roles.

7. Liberals wrongly reject these communal and nonrational features of morality.[1]

Communitarians believe that the idea of moral education within the context of political liberalism is incoherent. Liberal theory requires individuals to *choose* their own conception of the good, whereas moral education, according to the communitarian viewpoint, requires children to establish a *commitment* to a certain way of life and especially to the community that nurtures them and that provides the environment for their moral and spiritual growth. Communitarians object to the liberal state because they believe that it cannot lend sufficient support to a shared moral identity. They believe that more shared moral authority is needed and that anything that would help to bring this about would be welcome.

According to the communitarian, the problem is thus not with the idea of the common school and the importance of developing a shared identity. The problem is that in a liberal society, where the emphasis is on individual choice and individual reason, such an identity will never be sufficiently robust to establish a moral community worth maintaining.

In contrast to what they take as the prevailing liberal view, communitarian theorists argue that human beings are not isolated individuals. They are fundamentally communal animals, and their affiliations with others need to be nurtured. Because humans are essentially communal beings, any policy that works against the community also ultimately works against the personal self. The self is constituted through the practices of its particular group, deriving from it not only meanings and capacities, as the strong culturalist believes, but most important, moral character. A moral self is a self related to a particular community, positioned and concerned to reproduce its traditions.

Communitarians are concerned about the relationship between the community and its members, and they highlight the responsibility that individuals have to their communities and their nation. They believe that people who are brought up in liberal societies are too concerned with their own individual rights and not concerned enough with the needs of the community. Communitarians want rights talk to be replaced by a discourse of obligation and responsibility, and they want the direction of the flow of benefits from the nation to the individual to be reversed. Communities should have moral claims on their members. "Rights talk," as one commentator puts it, "encourages our all-too-human tendency to place the self at the center of our moral universe." [2]

An example of the kind of moral authority that the communitarian wants could be found in the early years of the Israeli kibbutz. In those years, a bright child might have been expected to put aside her or his ambitions to be, say, a physicist because the community needed gardeners or chefs. In this situation there is a three-way set of obligations and responsibilities: from the individual member to the community to the nation. The member paid back the obligation to the community by serving a communal need rather than a private ambition, and the nation allowed the community to shape its members' desires. In turn, both the individual and the kibbutz were strongly committed to the survival and well-being of the state of Israel.

The idea that the schools should just promote individual achievement and teach children to develop their own conception of the good life, an idea that the communitarian associates with liberalism, is seen as insensitive to the important role that communities play in the development of moral character. Communitarians believe that schools overemphasize autonomy and independence and reinforce the destructive imbalance between rights and obligations. They are concerned that in our schools, as well as in our adult lives, we emphasize individual rights over collective responsibility and thus continue to erode the social foundation of moral behavior.

Liberalism, according to this view, is mistaken because it views moral education as a matter of open choices. An example of the communitarian's concern is the value clarification curriculum. Children are given opportunities to discuss fundamental values such as honesty, truth-telling, respect for others so that they might clarify their importance for themselves, but the teachers are discouraged from steering them to a single correct answer. For the communitarian this wrongly encourages children to believe that values are just a matter of individual opinion and that lying and stealing have no greater inherent value than truth-telling and respect for property.

Even the liberal approaches to moral education that allow that some value choices are more defensible than others are problematic if they also allow the child to determine the value of different choices on the basis of her individual reason alone.[3] A stage theory of moral education, according to which children move through different levels of moral understanding in step with their developmental clock, is insufficient because it neglects the important role that the community must play in this development. More-over, this role is not simply bound to developing universal principles of rationality as developmental theorists define the end state of moral development. Rather, communitarians believe that moral education has elements of the particular and the nonrational as well.

Feminist approaches to moral education that stress caring and maintaining relationship might seem to fare somewhat better for the communitarian, but this is not necessarily so.[4] Where care or the concern to maintain a given relationship is governed by the sentiments of the individual and not guided by communally sanctioned norms, the same problem exists. If the theory of care is indifferent to whether the care be directed toward one's wife or toward one's mistress, then it repeats the liberal's mistake of assuming that the individual is the foundation of moral development. Only in this case, it is not the individual's reason but the individual's sentiment that is the problematic feature of the theory.

Similarly, if the theory is indifferent to the terms of the relationship there is a problem for the communitarian. It makes a difference for the communitarian whether the relationship has the sanction and support of the community in the way that, say, traditional marriage does, or whether it is dependent on continuous negotiation in which the sentiments of each partner must be re-aligned in constant adjustment to the other's. The liberal fallacy is to believe that the common school should teach children to allow sentiments to shape the relationship rather than to have the community's understanding of the value of certain relationships over others shape the sentiments.

For the communitarian these approaches are mistaken because they view the moral aspect of a child's schooling to be to a matter of individual reason or sentiment and because they fail to recognize and honor the communal attachments that make our lives as human beings possible.

THE COMMUNITARIAN ARGUMENT

Beginning with Alasdair MacIntyre's important book *After Virtue*, a growing appeal to the ideals of communitarianism has developed in both the scholarly literature and the popular press.[5] This appeal cuts across traditional ideological boundaries of left and right and is directed against contemporary works within the liberal tradition. MacIntyre directs much of his criticism against two of America's most important contemporary liberal theorists — John Rawls[6] and Robert Nozick.[7]

Although Rawls and Nozick are at opposite ends of liberalism — Rawls arguing that material difference should be minimized, Nozick that redistribution is theft — they both develop their case from the point of view of individual rights and liberties. Both assume that the individual person is the unit that ultimately makes claims on public resources and for whom claims may be granted. And both assume that the basic problem for political democracy is to determine what should count as an individual's legitimate share of property and opportunities.

In countering this view, MacIntyre argues that liberalism is grounded in an incorrect conception of the individual and that it understates the role of tradition and community in the development of individuality and moral authority. MacIntyre traces much of the present-day social crisis (crime, drug use) to the loss of clear moral guidelines. He blames the Enlightenment idea of individual rationality as the source of moral misunderstanding and misbehavior. MacIntyre objects that virtue is not the product of free-floating rationality rooted in individuals. It is the product of a tradition imbedded within a community and woven into the stories that the community tells about itself and its heroes.

It is the traditions of communities and nations that determine what will count as legitimate rights and obligations. According to MacIntyre, we do not have abstract rights and obligations that are independent of the role that we play in a communal structure. Rather, each of us has the obligations we do because of the roles that we occupy within a communal tradition, and we are judged by how well we conform to the idea of excellence that is associated with the performance of our role.

In well-functioning communities, according to communitarians, claims are made from the point of view of one's role and are legitimized in terms of the requirements attached to the proper exercising of the functions associated with that role. Thus the community serves as the foundation for all individual claims and, as a result, judges the merits of such claims within the context of its history and traditions.

Communitarians hold that children need a moral community in order to grow up as morally sensitive human beings, one in which members are willing to act and sacrifice on the basis of some collective conception of the good. For the communitarian this means that appeals to reason can only go so far and that at the foundation of all worthwhile ideas of the good is the commitment to a living community. The educational implications for children are profound. Rather than provide an open setting where children are encouraged to determine their own conception of the good, the communitarian believes, it is important for schools and other educational institutions to develop nonrational rituals and teaching methods that appeal to the sentiments in order to shape the child's desires according to the community's ideas about the good life.

LIBERALISM AS ONE TRADITION AMONG OTHERS
Communitarians believe that goodness and virtue arise only from a life within a community. They hold that the liberal ideal of a free-floating good is both unrealistic and undesirable. "The good" is a communal construct, and education needs to reaffirm the importance of community and tradition in the formation and constitution of morality. They believe that the liberal's rights-based theory both neglects the importance of community in the construction

of an individual's identity and preferences and fails to acknowledge itself as just one among many traditions. This neglect helps to explain why liberalism, in the communitarian's eyes, underemphasizes the relationship between tradition, community, identity, and moral judgment. Hence the opposition between traditional communities and liberal, rights-based ones is really, according to communitarians such as MacIntyre, a conflict that arises when liberalism forgets that it too is a tradition like all others. The implication of this argument is that liberalism should not presume to occupy an independent platform from which other traditions can be judged. Rather, it stands alongside them.

MacIntyre sometimes writes as if the reason liberalism cannot claim superiority is that standards of judgment are developed from and imbedded within a specific tradition, and thus there is no standpoint outside of any and all traditions from which a judgment could be made. Since an evaluation that I make of your tradition must come from within my tradition, I am bound to misrepresent and to distort it if I appeal to universal principles in support of my judgment.[8] Liberalism errs, according to this reading, because it misunderstands itself and immodestly assumes that it is more than just another tradition. Yet there is another reading as well, one that emphasizes more than liberalism's character as a tradition alongside other equally valid traditions. In this alternative reading, to which I will return shortly, the emphasis is on liberalism as an inferior tradition in comparison to its competitors.

Both readings are developed in MacIntyre's *Whose Justice? Which Rationality?*[9] Here he explores the internal workings and rationality of a number of different traditions, showing how each deals with conflict and gives rise to different conceptions of justice. He argues that beliefs about truth and falsity and ideals about justice are interrelated and self-referential and often make little sense outside of the tradition in which they were constructed. MacIntyre develops his argument indirectly through an examination of the ebb and flow of a number of different Western traditions and the various ways in which they managed internal philosophical conflicts and institutional crises. His own view is more often expressed through a commentary on the thoughts of Aristotle and other philosophers, especially Thomas Aquinas and David Hume, all of whom recognized that "to reason apart from any such a society is to have no standard by which to correct the passions. . . . It is qua member of some form of social order and not merely qua individual that someone exercises determinate practical rationality." [10]

As I mentioned earlier, MacIntyre does not completely reject the liberal, rights-based view. Rather, he views it as one tradition among many. Liberalism arose out of a set of historically specific circumstances as an attempt to enable individuals to free themselves from the arbitrary rulings and morality of particular traditions by

> appealing to genuinely universal, tradition-independent norms.
> . . . Liberalism, which began as an appeal to alleged principles
> of shared rationality against what was felt to be the tyranny of
> tradition, has itself been transformed into a tradition whose
> continuities are partly defined by the interminability of the
> debate over such principles. [11]

To see liberal ideals as simply the products of a particular tradition rather than as universals that transcend particular traditions requires that we reject the idea that the individual has a natural status and stands as the unit of all social organizations. Rather, we must come to understand that the individual is a relatively recent social and cultural artifact, invented by liberalism and forming a new and competing foundation for the exercise of practical reason.

> In Aristotelian practical reasoning it is the individual qua citi-
> zen who reasons; in Thomistic practical reasoning it is the

> individual qua inquirer into his or her good and the good of
> his or her community; in Humean practical reasoning it is the
> individual qua propertied or unpropertied participant in a
> society of a particular kind of mutuality and reciprocity; but in
> the practical reasoning of liberal modernity it is the individual
> qua individual who reasons.[12]

MacIntyre believes that in the liberal tradition, in contrast to older ones, the connection between reason and obligation
has been loosened, and he laments the fact that it is now accepted
as normal for a person to reason to one conclusion about the good
and yet to decide for any number of reasons not to act on behalf
of that conclusion.[13] Consider, as an example of MacIntyre's point,
that many people find the arguments of animal rights advocates
persuasive on the rational level but still continue to eat meat and
wear leather without any strong sense of guilt. MacIntyre believes
that because it does not enjoin the support and sanctions of a community, liberal morality leads to hypocrisy.

PROBLEMS WITH MACINTYRE'S ARGUMENT
AGAINST LIBERALISM

MacIntyre's communitarian argument rests on a historically uncritical and idealized conception of past traditions. He writes as
if hypocrisy were a problem only for liberalism. Moreover, in describing his favored traditions, such as those of classical Greece and
of the church in the Middle Ages, he draws only on their most coherent and innovative philosophers, but with liberalism he allows
all of our everyday knowledge to color his treatment. Thus, he
mentions the prevalence of lawyers in today's liberal societies but
seems ignorant of the mind-deadening theological disputes and
the hypocrisy that came to characterize the ecclesiastic tradition. In
pitting an idealized community against the everyday messiness of

contemporary liberal society there should be little doubt about the victor. But this is only because the contest is rigged to begin with.

In addition, even if his argument—that there is greater consistency between belief and action within traditional communities—is correct, there are still great inconsistencies across traditional communities—one tradition's witch is another tradition's martyr. This inconsistency may have been acceptable when intercourse between communities was limited, but this is not the case in today's world. This in part explains the gap between belief and action that MacIntyre laments. People have to live together with others who hold very different value systems, and in doing so some come to hold their belief more tentatively. In modern society citizens are exposed to a variety of conflicting beliefs and convictions often not reinforced only by one single-minded community. Hence what MacIntyre views as a gap between belief and action is really the result of conditions that allow for more open-ended and changeable beliefs. MacIntyre treats this as if it were some kind of flaw, but it is a problem only if the change takes place without adequate evidence, reflection, and deliberation or without a consideration of the various interests and points of view involved.

Moreover, few traditionalists are likely to take seriously MacIntyre's understanding of their own systems of values and beliefs. They want to privilege the norms of their own traditions and are unwilling to place them on a par with those of every other tradition, as the communitarian actually does.[14] Hence if liberalism suffers from hubris, as MacIntyre believes it does, it does not suffer alone.

Thus the first reading of MacIntyre leads to inconsistency, but the second leads to incoherence. In the first reading MacIntyre writes as if all standards of judgment and evaluation are imbedded within specific traditions, but in the second he writes as if there are standards that can be used to evaluate competing traditions to determine their relative worth. Given this reading, when these standards are applied to liberalism, it falls short in comparison to other traditions.

A close reading of MacIntyre reveals that he is actually of two minds about liberalism and, indeed, about traditions in general. By arguing that liberalism is a tradition he intends to show that "any hope of discovering tradition-independent standards of judgment such as universal principles of equality and justice turns out to be illusory."[15] In this sense, instead of being the bearer of universal standards of the right and the just, liberalism is simply another tradition, and as such its standards are limited and self-contained. They are not worn easily by other traditions. "Like other traditions, liberalism has internal to it its own standards of rational justification. Like other traditions, liberalism has its set of authoritative texts and its disputes over their interpretation. Like other traditions, liberalism expresses itself socially through a particular kind of hierarchy."[16]

Hence, by classifying liberalism as just another tradition and by affirming the view that standards are simply internal to the specific traditions that express them, MacIntyre has brought liberalism down a peg or two. Liberalism fosters liberal traditions just as Catholicism fosters Catholic traditions.

MacIntyre does considerably more than place liberalism on the same plane as other traditions, however. He also provides in the second reading a harsh evaluation of its practices, finding its debates barren and nonrational. Without any substantive theory of the good, according to MacIntyre, liberalism strives merely to count preferences and to resolve conflicts without any significant philosophical guidance. "The lawyers, not the philosophers, are the clergy of liberalism."[17]

Yet, if MacIntyre is ultimately to hold on to the position that traditions cannot be evaluated from the perspective of other traditions without risking significant distortion, then one must wonder about the source of his negative response to liberalism.

Whereas MacIntyre grants to most traditions the internal resources to address their own conceptual problems, he seems to deny these resources to liberalism. If this denial is accurate, then it would appear that he wants to make liberalism a tradition just like any other while at the same time denying that it has the same resources as others. Given these two readings, liberalism is both the same as every other tradition and inferior to them all.

MacIntyre's ambivalence toward liberalism reveals a more general problem with the communitarian's overall conception of tradition. If MacIntyre is correct that liberalism does not have a way to evaluate its own tradition from the inside and must therefore be content simply to add up preferences, then his point must be taken as strongly critical. Liberalism is not just *another* tradition, as suggested by the first reading; it is an *inadequate* tradition because it does not have the means to generate internal criticism.

Yet if the logic of this criticism is extended to other traditions as well, it would seem that legitimate criticisms of traditions are not just generated internally. Rather, they can, it seems, be legitimately criticized from some external standpoint, through some general conception of how traditions are supposed to work and what distinguishes richer from poorer traditions. If traditions can be evaluated using a defensible external standard, then the communitarian must give up the first reading—that standards are only internal to traditions. Yet once this is done, then it becomes harder to distinguish the communitarian and the liberal positions.

Given these two readings, the second should be favored as a better description of the way tradition works, and the view that standards are simply internal to a tradition should be rejected as inadequate. The implication of this rejection is that an education that seeks norms beyond that of a single tradition—an education

consistent with liberalism — is both defensible and desirable. Indeed, one of the benefits of liberalism is that it seeks to establish
a national identity in which the conversation across traditions is
seen as a condition for both individual and collective growth.

MORAL EDUCATION

Whatever else moral *action* may be, it is, as the liberal suggests,
action that is, at some level, self-chosen. If I accidentally push a
child, thereby propelling her out of the way of a speeding car, I have
not performed a moral act no matter how beneficial the consequences. If, however, I see the car coming and choose, at some risk
to myself, to push the child out of harm's way, then the act is moral.

The communitarian is also correct, however. Moral behavior is usually not so heroic or spontaneous. And even if moral
action does involve dramatic moments of choice, the *object* of
much moral action — my family, our community, our country —
is not self-chosen. Even given the modern notion that all identities are negotiated products, the communitarian is right that the
point from which certain negotiation begin is unnegotiated. Our
involuntary affiliation with *this* family, *this* community, *this* nation
makes our relationship special and unlike that which we have to
another family, community, or nation. And this is true even if we
choose to reject the standard accounts, interpretations, and aspirations of our family, community, or nation. This is because I cannot
reject the memories of units in which I have no membership. I can
only *reject* what is in some sense already mine. I can only *disagree*
with the others. The communitarian is right. Our so-called involuntary relationships make a moral difference.

Nevertheless, the fact that our involuntary relationships
make a moral difference does not establish the communitarians'
point about moral education across traditions. To say that we have
a special relationship, even a special obligation, to some groups
that we do not have to others is not the same as saying that our

sense of right and wrong or our rational skills are somehow forever imbedded in and constrained by the norms and understandings of that group. Nor is it to say that we can never stand in a position to draw on critical insights from outside our group in order to appraise its practices and standards.

The communitarians fail to consider that the moral learning developed in one community and expressed through initially nonrational means is often rationally defensible on grounds that appeal to people in other communities. They also fail to consider that it makes an important difference whether moral education is conducted in a way that encourages or discourages reflection on existing practices.

Given the way in which modernity constantly strains existing moral norms, any moral education that is grounded in a commitment to an ongoing community must involve the development of a critical, reflective moral understanding. Consider, for example, the way a moral precept such as "thou shalt not kill" requires new commentaries and interpretations as medical science finds ever more ingenious ways to keep our lungs pumping and our hearts beating.[18] Unless the communitarian understands the "community" as an ever-static entity that has no reason to interact with the larger natural and social world, the job of moral interpretation is inevitable, and such interpretation always involves the ability to reflect on, critique, and change existing moral norms. And if it is such a static entity, why would anyone choose to continue to adopt its moral precepts unless they were indoctrinated to do so? And, if this were the exclusive means for a moral education in my community, it is questionable whether other communities should choose to honor or support it under normal conditions.

One of the arguments that communitarians sometimes make in support of their notion of moral education is that it is actually more tolerant than moral education within a liberal framework. It is claimed that people who are raised with a strong commitment to one community are likely to be sympathetic to the demands of various and different communities. It is argued that when children are taught to honor their own community then they can appreciate the value that other communities serve. Although they may not be able to understand every aspect of the other community, and although elements of its moral code and theirs may differ fundamentally, they can see why members of that community value it in the way that they do. Hence, the claim is that they will be less likely as adults to impose their norms on others.

Given this argument, communitarians hold that their view has the advantage of encouraging mutual respect across different communities. MacIntyre believes, for example, that the idea of incommensurabilities across traditions lends support to the principle of tolerance for different traditions. This is probably because once we realize that moral norms are tradition-bound, we may have less reason to impose our norms on others. In point of fact there is a serious question about where respect for other traditions comes from. It might come from the fact that traditions are the source of morality,[19] but this assumes a tradition that knows this fact and that knows it for other traditions.

This argument that the idea of incommensurability breeds tolerance is problematic because it rests on a confusion between the point of view of the communitarian philosopher and the point of view of the community dweller. It is true that those who hold that membership in a community is a supreme good probably value all communities. These people are not necessarily members of any single community, however. They are philosophers and theorists, communitarians, if you will, who stand outside of particular communities when they write about the benefits of membership in communities in general.

The situation is quite different, however, when one moves from the standpoint of a communitarian advocate to the standpoint of a community member. Given the position of the member of a specific community with a specific set of traditions and beliefs, the argument for greater tolerance is correct only if that member holds her values in a certain way, believing, for example, that they need not be applicable to every member of every community. As I will argue in a later chapter, this is a crucial element of citizenship education in a liberal society.

Given the communitarian's suspicion of claims to a universal morality, it is not clear why members of any one tradition should respect another tradition—unless, of course, one of the norms within their own tradition is to respect other traditions. It is an empirical question whether communities have such a principle of respect, and the most likely answer to the question is that some do and others do not and that most will respect some traditions but not others. If, however, the principle of respect for traditions does not come from within a tradition, then it would seem as if the communitarian is appealing to some kind of universal principle and then using this principle to argue about what communities should do. This, however, does not seem like a very communitarian way to argue.

Nevertheless, to hold one's values in this way is consistent with the liberal idea of tolerance. I can both hold onto a strong moral idea and express tolerance for those who disagree with me. As a liberal I may not believe what you believe, but I respect your right to believe it. If, however, I hold onto the traditions and beliefs of my community as the only true ones, and believe that I have an obligation to spread their truth to others, then there is no reason why membership in a community should give me reason to tolerate the practices of members of other communities with different beliefs.

Communitarians correctly recognize that moral behavior and therefore moral education are only occasionally about individual rights or national obligations. More often they have to do with the fabric of everyday interaction, which is reflected in mutual service and civility. Morality and moral decision making are only occasionally about the heroic aspects of existence and usually are about the everyday activities required to sustain a community and its traditions. To frame morality in terms of either-or decisions, as Lawrence Kohlberg's influential liberal proposal for moral education does,[20] is to neglect the subtle interactions that enable community life to persist from day to day, allowing the needs of people to be met on a consistent basis. This either-or version of moral education overemphasizes the students' ability to correctly identify universal moral principles but neglects moral commitment and moral action. Here moral decision making has the quality of a game in which people use one principle to trump another and in which moral education is conducted in terms of puzzles about heroic, but still marginal and unusual, cases.[21]

One of the important communitarian insights is that morality, although sometimes heroic, is usually more mundane—although no less important. Nevertheless, despite this important insight the communitarian doctrine about moral education is as confusing and incoherent as its ideas on tradition and community.

Here the confusion arises because communitarians reject, at least explicitly, the possibility of moral norms and ideals that transcend individual communities or individual nations and thus come close to sanctioning any and every community- or nationally grounded norm—although, as we have also seen, the absurdity of doing so leads to a second reading in which some traditions, namely liberalism, falter, while others, such as Aristotelianism or Thomism, acquire intellectual vigor.

MACINTYRE AND PLATO

We can gain an appreciation of the relation between liberalism and moral education by unpacking the reasons for some of the confusions in the communitarian doctrine. Specifically, I want to compare and contrast MacIntyre's account of the virtues with a close but quite distinct historical analog: Plato's portrayal of the heroic Socrates in the *Crito*. Although few would argue that Plato was a liberal, the difference between the two accounts provides an important insight into the liberal understanding of the relation between moral and state action.

MacIntyre holds that because of the essential role played by the nation in moral development, people owe it a special debt and allegiance.[22] Note that this argument is different from Durkheim's, in which the nation is to develop loyal citizens because it is a superior moral entity. Unlike Durkheim's, MacIntyre's point is not a comparative one. To him Durkheim's claim is like saying "I should love my family better than John's family because it is more moral," with the implication that if John's family should prove more moral than mine, I should stop loving my family and love John's instead. Rather—and here I think MacIntyre is correct—we love our family, our community, our nation because they are ours, and for better or for worse, they have provided the conditions for our development.

One of the most compelling communitarian episodes in Western literature occurs in Plato's *Crito*. Here Socrates refuses to cooperate in a plan that would allow him to escape Athens after he had been condemned to death by a hasty and biased court. Socrates argues with his friend against the idea of escape on the ground that to escape would be to reject his own moral identity. He tells his friend that by having lived his life as an Athenian citizen he has implicitly accepted Athens's practices and laws. To choose to avoid its sentence would be to reject his life's commitment.

MacIntyre's account looks much like Plato's. He too believes that the state or the nation is the foundation of our individual moral life and that because of this we owe it a special debt. Nevertheless, there is an important difference between Socrates' and MacIntyre's communitarianism. Socrates was, after all, applying a rule to *his own* behavior. He did not oblige any other Athenian, wrongly condemned to death, to follow the same rule, and the power of Plato's dialogue develops precisely from the fact that this was a self-imposed rule.

Had Socrates been talking to someone else about what *he* should do, the dialogue would have read like an unconvincing morality play. And, of course, the reason that Socrates had been condemned to die was precisely that he was teaching about a higher set of virtues, one that was not necessarily grounded in Athenian tradition.

Just how we interpret this "higher" set is a complex question, but the idea of moral progress requires the possibility of new moral understandings that enable us to deal with new and problematic situations. Sometimes these situations become apparent precisely because the norms of our traditions are not adequate to the existing situation. Whether we view new moral norms as human *inventions*—instruments that we create in respond to new problems—or as *principles* that we discover to enable us to live more perfect lives, moral progress requires that our norms reach beyond our traditions. Thus moral progress is possible for Socrates precisely because we humans can act both within and beyond our traditions. We can understand more than our traditions provide while honoring the importance of traditions in our own lives.

What Socrates did in the *Crito* is exactly what MacIntyre criticizes liberals for encouraging. He allows for moral understanding to exist within an individual who has moved beyond his tradition by behaving according to an implicit distinction between the "good" and the "allowable." This is precisely the distinction that MacIntyre fails to understand when he criticizes liberalism for encouraging hypocrisy. Yet once we understand the importance of the distinction between the good and the allowable, we can also understand the proper role of moral education within a liberal society.

In choosing to accept the verdict for himself, Socrates was choosing a good of sorts—the good that is involved in leading a consistent, principled life—even though he was not establishing the acceptance of unfair death sentences as a general principle that everyone should follow. This view of morality foreshadows liberalism. When liberal moral education insists that, within limits, children should learn how to choose among different conceptions of the good, it is not claiming that stronger arguments may not exist for choosing one version of the good over another. The point is that, however strong the argument in favor of one or another choice, there are many forms of life that are allowed regardless of what our own rational deliberations tell us.

Moral education in a liberal society may well encourage students to act on the basis of the best argument, but it must also enable them to choose allowable ways of life even if they are not supported by the best argument. Moral educators may err in both directions. They may neglect to encourage students to explore the relative costs and benefits of one way of life over another, or they may fail to teach students that many forms of life are acceptable within a liberal society.

MUST MORAL EDUCATION AND MORAL PROGRESS BE COMMUNITY-SPECIFIC?

Another modern communitarian, Michael Walzer, is more convincing than MacIntyre on the question of the source of moral principles. Like MacIntyre, Walzer accepts the importance of community in the formation of moral authority. Walzer's belief in the fundamental role of the community in the development of a moral order does not, however, lessen the importance for him of the generative role of the social prophet, and Walzer would have an easier time accommodating the moral lesson of the *Crito*.

Unlike MacIntyre, Walzer's critic may seek truth outside the present community, say, in an original covenant with God. Once such truth is found, the critic then serves to interpret the community to itself by reminding it of the covenant that binds it together. Nevertheless, for Walzer, this covenant is viewed as community-specific, and the truths it reveals are truths for that community. Thus Walzer's account maintains the basic communitarian framework and is skeptical of norms and principles that go beyond the specific community.

Walzer illustrates his point by contrasting the biblical figures of Amos and Jonah. He presents Amos as the quintessential prophet and social critic. Amos challenges the conventions and the ritual practices of his own society in the name of its own shared values and norms. Whereas Amos reminds his own community of its moral roots, Jonah, acting as God's messenger, according to Walzer's account can merely warn a foreign nation, Nineveh, about failing to live up to God's minimum international standards, standards which that community does not necessarily share. Amos is the embodiment of the communitarian's internal critic, and Jonah is the bearer of liberalism's minimum moral principles. Yet this contrast is unfair both to Jonah and to liberalism. If the standards themselves are simply internal to a community, then who is Jonah, a Jew from another land, to deliver any message, unless the content of the message can be heard in Nineveh as well as in Jerusalem, unless Jerusalem's standards are Nineveh's as well?

It may be that internal critics, because they are able to draw on the stories, metaphors, and understandings of a society, are generally more believable and more effective than external ones. It may also be that the internal critic is able to see reasons for practices that an external critic would not understand except in inappropriate ways. Yet none of this should be taken to mean, as Walzer's contrast suggests, that the standards for internal and external criticism are inherently different. And in fact Walzer fails to see something important about the message Jonah delivers to the people of Nineveh: their reaction. They decided not simply to stop their wicked ways but to repent for their past transgressions. And the king "arose from his throne and . . . sat in ashes and . . . pro-claimed 'Let neither man nor beast, herd nor flock, taste any thing: let them not feed, nor drink water; but let them both be covered with sackcloth, both man and beast, and let them cry mightily unto God: Yea let them turn every one from his evil ways.' " [23]

In contrast to the claim that morality is community-spe-cific, this repentance suggests that there is also a universal aspect to moral authority and that the stories of Amos and Jonah suggest the plausibility of moral teachings that are not confined by communal boundaries.

PROBLEMS WITH COMMUNITARIAN MORALITY

The mistake of communitarians at this point results from their fail-ure to separate two different claims: the first, that morality is com-munally grounded; the second, that it is communally confined. This confusion leads Walzer to mistakenly suggest that when treat-ing moral relations across communities, social criticism can only operate at a minimal level. Communitarians, much like strong cul-turalists, take incommensurability too seriously. What is required is a conception of tradition, morality, and community that is more open and more porous than the one with which they provide us.

Nevertheless, Walzer is an advance over MacIntyre, and his understanding of the role of the social critic can be used to begin to build a bridge between rights-based and communitarian theories. To acknowledge the importance of the social critic, as Walzer does, is to do two additional things. It is, first, to acknowl-edge the added value of communal structures in which social criticism has a recognized and exalted role, and, second, to ac-knowledge the importance of cultural understandings and politi-cal structures that encourage the critic's voice to be heard. These are key aspects of liberal society, and the doctrine of individual rights is its foundation. Given the relationship that Walzer posits between the community and its critics, it is possible to develop some principles which both are imbedded within a communitarian standpoint and transcend the framework of any single community.

Nevertheless, the problems with the communitarian view are many. For example, the claim that the community is the source of individual morality is obviously correct in some sense, but that does not say much about the character of the community or the nature of the morality. The morality of revenge persists in some communities, but it is a morality that generates continuing fear and retaliation. It is helpfully replaced by a morality that submits grievances to parties who will be rejected as illegitimate if they are widely perceived to be acting partially. Whether we should accept a certain moral system should not be determined solely by the fact that it is endorsed by a certain community. Acceptance or rejection should have something to do with the character of the moral system itself: whether it helps us resolve old issues, address new problems, lead better lives.

If the incommensurability thesis is accepted in its strong form, communitarians will have difficulty explaining how to distinguish adequate and inadequate traditions. MacIntyre attempts to address some of these problems by developing a stage theory of traditions whereby traditions develop from immature and unselfconscious practices to mature and self-conscious ways of apprehending their own problems and assessing the resources of other traditions in resolving them.[24] The solution rightly presupposes a tradition that has become conscious of its boundaries and limits and has now to confront some of the issues that such limits create. To recognize the limits of one's own tradition is to recognize the viability of traditions that exist outside of one's own and to begin to engage the truths of one with those of the other. Yet it is exactly this recognition that leads to certain important elements of liberalism and to the belief that many tradition-imbedded truths can be subject to evaluation and renewal. Indeed, one of the key errors of some versions of communitarianism is to fail to understand the great benefits that can occur within a traditional way of life from the positioning of members in more than one tradition.[25]

COMMUNITARIAN THEORY AND TWO KINDS OF MORAL COMMUNITIES

One of the major contributions of communitarian theory is to remind us that there are two kinds of moral communities and that each requires a somewhat different moral relationship between its members. There are, first, those that we enter more or less voluntarily, and the voluntary character of such communities is often taken for granted in liberal discussions about general issues involving identity and moral activity. Here the rules of freedom of association, good-faith negotiation, and uncoerced agreement constitute the basic standards of moral action. And there are, second, those to which we belong as a result of accidents of birth or history. Here, nurture, commitment, and loyalty constitute the basic standards of moral action. This description fits membership in families, traditional communities, and nations.

Because few of us choose the nation to which we belong, and few would renounce one national identity without subscribing to another one, national identity is not generally a matter of freedom of association. Being an American is somewhat like being a Jones. We do not usually choose it, and sometimes we may prefer the ideals, values, or practices of another country. Nevertheless, if I am a Jones, I am a Jones, and if I am an American, I am an American. I do not like my country's policies toward poor people, I object to its military aggression and its support of dictators abroad, but it is still *my* country and my objections do not erase my identification with it. (Although there are, of course, many voluntary immigrants who do actually choose to be Americans, once this choice is fulfilled, their relationship to the ideals, values, rights, and obligations are much the same as that of those who were born here.)

One of the things that being a member of the Jones family and being an American have in common is that they create specific obligations that are sometimes unforeseen and that one may prefer not to have. The Jones's boy is obliged (in a way that the Greens' boy is not) to aid *his* (Jones's) parents, and this is true even though he never chose those particular parents. He is also obliged in a way that the Green boy is not to share Thanksgiving with *his* sister and her husband even though he would never choose her husband as a friend and even though he and his sister recently had such a strong and painful disagreement that, had they not been related, they would have severed all ties. Moreover, if our parent or our child or our sibling needs help, we have special obligations to provide it, obligations that do not fall on strangers to the family in the same way. One may decide for good reasons that other obligations override these, but it is wrong to be indifferent to them. It is the same with co-nationals, only in this case membership in the same nation creates special obligations among strangers. As Yeats wrote of the thoughts of an Irish pilot: "Those that I fight I do not hate, those that I guard I do not love." [26]

The obligations we have as members of a national community transcend our liking and disliking for one another and require us to recognize our common membership at certain moments and for certain ends. And although there are demonstrable benefits that accrue to both the individual and the society at large, the argument for the salience of national identity is not best demonstrated by science, as Durkheim thought. [27] Rather, it is implicit in the nature of our membership. We may not like the obligations that membership entails, but they come with the territory. To have such obligations is just part of what it means to be a Jones or to be a U.S. citizen. If I were a Smith or a Canadian citizen I would have other obligations, perhaps even ones that I would prefer to those I have now. These obligations cannot be swapped. A Jones cannot say to a Smith, "If you take on my Jones obligations, I will take on your Smith obligations." Nor can a Canadian say to a Mexican, "I will assume your national obligations if you will assume mine." These relationships do not work that way. They are in some important ways involuntary relationships — we do not have much of a choice about whether to be a part of them or not. We may, of course, disown our family or renounce our country, but we cannot do so in some neutral way as if, say, I were to reject your family or decide "well, France be damned." If I leave France it is just a physical act. If I leave the United States *for good* it is a moral statement.

This kind of partiality is different from, say, the racism that is involved when people declare "white power" as a way to uphold their partiality to people with similarly shaded skin. Here race is an erroneous signal for something else, such as intelligence, purity, or kinship, which under certain circumstances might require special relations but which has nothing to do with skin shading. This is why the slogan "black power" is different from "white power." The former involves a rejection of subordination and appeals to principles of fairness and equality in order to end it. The latter is an assertion of domination and an appeal to continue an arbitrary exercise of power that is justified by the false claim that skin color, an irrelevant trait in its own right, is a sign of something more profound.[28]

The source of national identity is often connected, as we saw in chapter 2, to the belief that a people share a common origin in terms of historical experience, culture, or language. It is also connected to a web of mutual aid that extends back in time and creates future obligations and expectations. The assumption that others outside of this web are imbedded in different webs in part justifies the partiality that we provide to co-nationals. This is similar to the way that assumptions about multiple webs of family obligations justify one's partiality toward one's own children.[29] It is a particular obligation, but it is justified in terms of universal principles about the right that we all have to be partial and the obligations that we develop toward those who are partial to us. Similar justifications work in terms of our partiality to co-nationals, but this is also why, in the larger scheme of things, vastly unequal nations are morally problematic, and it is one reason why nations have an increasing obligation to submit aspects of their sovereignty to regional and global authorities.

National identity and the obligations that flow from it are not determined by science. Rather, national identity is nonrational in the sense that it involves obligations that are not subject to rational deliberation or cost-benefit analysis. A person is born into a certain historical tradition and carries the weight of that tradition. I cannot, for example, just choose *not* to be an American because I disapprove of the historical treatment of slaves. My birth as an American places me in a special moral relation to the history of slavery. Moreover, people who are able to change their nationality do not do so simply as free-floating individuals. When people become Americans, they take on the American citizen's benefits and burdens, including obligations that have accrued as a result of historical injustices. Hence, when a new immigrant becomes an American (by choice in this case) she does not just do so as a rights-bearing person who now has opportunities that were not available before. She takes on new obligations, ones that she may not have had before.

It is in this sense that the nation is nonrational and not subject to scientific appraisal. It provides the conditions of rational or irrational choices and is not merely its object. This is why the communitarian is right about moral education in at least one re-spect—common schools must teach children the standpoint from which rational choice for them is deliberated. An early task of moral education is to teach children to identify with the political, social, and cultural factors that make being a self possible and that connect one self to other selves. Roger Scruton makes the point well in an approving description of Hegel's views on the legitimacy of the state:

> In Hegel's view, man owes his identity as a rational chooser to a process of development that implicates him inescapably in obligations which he did not choose. These obligations of piety are both pre-contractual and pre-political. . . . The legitimacy of the state depends in part upon its ability to recuperate these non-political obligations, which form the original of its own non-contractual order.[30]

Yet to see this obligation — to be partial to relational webs we do not choose — is to understand a larger principle that connects our tradition to others and serves to both support them and limit their encroachment on each other.

COMPLICATIONS OF THE MULTICULTURAL STATE

This traditional view of national identity is complicated by the multicultural state because different cultural groups have different origins. They do not share all of the same historical experience, and their original languages and histories differ from one another. It is also complicated by the fact of immigration and adopted citizenship, in which choice is a factor in identity formation, at least at the stage of immigration. To the extent that a multicultural state is formed through voluntary immigration, the choice to be a citizen carries with it an involuntary obligation to all other citizens. This act constitutes the origin of the new national identity for members of different cultural groups and provides the framework for thinking of the multicultural state in terms of a national identity.

Under these circumstances, cultural membership alone cannot stand as the exclusive object of the educational formation of the self. Once a people is reconstituted through a multicultural state, they form a different people. Italian Americans are not Italians, and Irish Americans are not Irish. They are Americans who maintain certain affiliations on a cultural basis. Because these cultural affiliations are voluntary, people may choose to forget or to remember them without political penalty.[31]

Public schools often have good educational and political reasons to acknowledge a child's cultural meanings. For example, many children learn better where they feel they are respected and their background honored. Where voluntary immigration is the occasion for new citizenship, however, the obligation is to the child, not to the culture. For example, teaching a child in her native language may be a bridge to learning other subjects such as math or science. Where this is the case schools have an obligation *to the child* to incorporate bilingual instruction. The obligation, however, involves the instructional aid required to enable the student to become a functioning citizen of this country. The obligation is not primarily to the child's original community. This is why, with a few exceptions, if a child already speaks English but doesn't know the language of her parents, the school usually has no special obligation to the parents' culture to teach their language to the child. These exceptions are the topic of the next chapter.

5. Aims of Multicultural Education

Multicultural education has three goals: to inform students about cultural diversity; to encourage respect for the practices of other cultural groups, especially disempowered minorities and women; and to encourage members of these groups to have pride in their own cultural heritage. Where multicultural education is practiced there is considerably more diversity than usually represented in textbooks and the curriculum, and more attention is paid to "minorities" and especially to people of color, women, and sometimes gays. The idea is to allow students from different backgrounds to appreciate the variety in American society and to embrace their own cultural heritage.

Multiculturalism differs from pluralism because it uses the school to raise consciousness about group membership and identity. In contrast, pluralists believe that schools should not be involved in the business of promoting cultural identity. Rather, they hold that this identity should be developed and nurtured within the child's home or local community. They do not, of course, believe that all issues relating to people of color or women or gays should be ignored in areas such as social studies, history, and literature. Promoting group identity, or pride, is not an acceptable rationale for inclusion for pluralists, however, and they are suspicious of these goals for fear that they retard national coherence. Whereas pluralists object to material that they believe threatens national cohesion, multiculturalists object to material that they feel fails to give adequate recognition to cultural groups.

Pluralists fear that multiculturalism conflicts with the values of equal opportunity, freedom of association, and personal growth because they perceive that it counts group membership more than it counts individual merit. Multiculturalists believe that the pluralists' emphasis on individual merit protects the status quo because it advantages privilege by creating additional cultural barriers for minority children.

In this chapter I address this conflict and provide an interpretation of the goals of multicultural education and of pluralism that I believe will reduce their incompatibility. I argue that the most defensible interpretation of multiculturalism arises, as with pluralism, from the values of liberalism and a commitment to liberal ideals. In contrast to many pluralists who see all minority issues as part of a single ideal of tolerance, however, I argue that the multiculturalists are right to defend a more refined, historically specific conception. I begin this argument by showing the openness of the stated goals of multicultural education to various interpretation and then show why some interpretations are more desirable than others.

CONFLICTING GOALS OF
MULTICULTURAL EDUCATION

Consider the potential conflicts among the different goals of multicultural education. Let's begin with the goal of providing children with information about cultural groups and encouraging children to respect cultural difference. Respect for cultural difference is not a guaranteed result of greater information about a given group. Consider, for example, the problem that a teacher might have in realizing both of these goals in certain situations.

In one instance, the *New York Times* reported that among certain African communities living in Ghana ritual slavery is practiced. Young girls are given as unpaid servants to priests in order to atone for the sins of their relatives. The *Times* goes on to relate that the girls are then used to provide sexual favors to the priests and that when a woman is no longer appealing, a priest sends her back with the expectation that she will be replaced by a younger, more appealing girl.[1] There is little in the information that is provided in the *Times* about this practice that would increase respect for the priests, for the tradition itself, or for the relatives who, believing that sin and atonement are communal rather than individual, follow it.[2] After reading the article we may have more information than we did before, but we likely have no greater respect for the practice than does the Ghanian Baptist preacher who, the *Times* reports, has been campaigning against it for sixteen years. True, a good teacher, like a good anthropologist, could use this information to lead students to understand the worldview that advances such a practice. Whether this broader understanding will or should lead to more or less respect for its participants is an open question.

A teacher bent on realizing all the goals of multicultural education could decide to convey only that information that will lead to a more favorable attitude toward a particular group. This is indoctrination, however, and it is problematic, whether we are teaching about a child's own culture and expect to increase the child's pride, or whether we are teaching about another culture and expect to increase the child's level of respect.

Consider for a moment the practical question of how to increase a child's respect for a certain culture. Suppose we tried to accomplish it by removing from the curriculum any information that portrays the culture in an unfavorable light. This strategy assumes that the relationship between information and attitude is clear-cut. It assumes that if teachers provide unfavorable information then children will develop an unfavorable attitude and that if teachers provide favorable information then children will develop a favorable attitude. Yet this relationship is not at all clear-cut. Consider for example the potential for a negative impression of England derived from reading, say, *Richard III.* Students generally do not form a negative attitude toward England just because of the depictions of its leaders in plays and stories. Rather, they usually read behind the plot and understand that the "greatness" of England is reflected by the greatness of the author of the play.

Let us assume, however, that we really do know how to shape children's attitudes toward their own and other groups. Why should we believe that this is an appropriate educational mission? On what basis will educators decide which group children are to feel positive about and which, if any, group they are to feel negative about? Neither whole-hearted endorsement nor whole-hearted condemnation seems to be compatible with helping the children learn to decide these things for themselves. If the exercise is educationally defensible it will require that students are provided with enough varied information and perspectives to allow them to form their own opinions, and generally, the more nuanced these opinions the better.

There is a similar concern about the school's role in fostering cultural pride. Take the issue of whether African American children should be taught that their culture extends back to ancient Egypt and that many of the accomplishments of civilization have been erroneously attributed to other cultures. The question as it stands is only interesting because our society devalues dark skin and because some people believe that the harmful effects of this on dark-skinned children will be relieved if they know about the past contributions of dark-skinned peoples. In a nonracist society the color of Egyptian skin would have no special interest, since culture is derived from more than complexion.

In the present debate about what children should be taught about the complexion and contribution of the ancient Egyptians, interesting educational questions go unaddressed. Few children are asked to consider whether ancient Egypt should be valued because of its contribution to the civilization of the region or devalued because it was a slave society. Those who believe that children should be taught that African American culture can be traced back to Egypt and those who believe that it cannot should both be concerned to teach children about the problems involved in evaluating slave societies that have also made significant historical contributions.

Given a society such as our own, which devalues dark skin, there are at least two reasons for developing cultural pride, and they call for different treatment. The first justifies instillment of cultural pride as a way to develop individual self-esteem, and it views high self-esteem as a condition for academic achievement. In this case the goal of self-esteem sets the conditions in which schools need to be concerned about developing cultural pride: instances in which there is a strong causal relationship between low achievement, low self-esteem, and low cultural pride. One may argue about whether cultural pride is related to self-esteem in any given case and whether self-esteem is related to academic performance, but given this relationship, the aim is to improve performance in academic work by helping students feel better about themselves. Where an individual student's academic advancement involves enhancing feelings about her cultural group, then it makes good educational sense to do so. Given this rationale, teaching students to feel good about their cultural group is only a means to academic achievement and is perfectly compatible with a noncontroversial aspect of public education—improving academic performance.

Some people might object to using group pride as a means to this noncontroversial goal, and I will look at this issue shortly. If we accept the means, however, the goal places limits on when and where it is appropriately applied. If a student from a given culture is performing adequately and feels pretty good about herself, then, given this justification, the focus on cultural pride is gratuitous and distracting. The same is true where students are not performing adequately or where they do not feel good about themselves but where their attitude toward their own culture is not a factor in their performance or self-esteem. For example, Ogbu notes a number of situations in which low academic performance is linked to high group identity and self-esteem. Here the problem is that the students identify their youth culture as antagonistic to academic achievement.[3] It is not that they lack pride in their youth culture, at least as they see it. It is that they have a limited understanding of what constitutes their culture.

The second possible reason for seeking to develop cultural pride is to enhance the likelihood that a child will draw her identity from her cultural group and in doing so will in fact strengthen the group and increase the likelihood that others will draw their identity in the same way. The implication of this argument is that the development of cultural pride is a legitimate goal even if a student is not doing poorly in school. This is a considerably more problematic argument, and, as we will see, its justification requires a special set of circumstances. For now it is sufficient, however, to note that the two reasons for developing cultural pride point to very different obligations for the public school.

The goal of respect brings similar questions: What are we

teaching students when we teach them to respect another culture? Are we teaching them to respect people's right to express their traditions in the way they choose? Are we teaching them to respect the accomplishments of the members of that culture, and if so, then what do we do about "accomplishments" that we do not like? If respect for the accomplishments of people from different cultural groups is the goal, must we tag all accomplishments by individuals in terms of their cultural background—Chomsky, the Jew, Jordan, the black, Kennedy, the Irishman, and so on? If so, then what about those whose origins are lost or mixed—Sammy Davis Jr., the black Jew?—or those whose origins are no longer known—Eleanor Roosevelt, the white [blank] woman? Perhaps respecting other cultures simply requires that we respect the right of people who identify with the culture to continue to do so? Yet this is just the alternative that the pluralist allows. From the multiculturalist we expect something different.

Although both group recognition and individual self-esteem are important, enhanced understanding, reflection, and growth are the primary considerations for educators. Just as the adjective *multicultural* modifies the noun *education* so that we expect a multicultural classroom to be different from others in certain ways, so too should the noun *education* modify the adjective *multicultural*. We should expect a multicultural experience that is also educational to be different than representations of different cultures for exclusively political, economic, or psychological purposes. If multicultural education does not advance reflective understanding and growth, then it has limited educational value.

To put the matter differently, consider the way in which multicultural programs are defended in terms of national economic growth and political stability. Those who defend the programs in this way believe that schools should adopt multicultural programs in order to develop a workforce that will reflect, at all levels, the diversity in the society. Given the demographic changes in the population and the declining proportion of white men in the workforce, the idea is certainly reasonable, and one would expect it to get a hearing in schools. If not, then we may face the prospect of a future workforce stratified along lines of color as well as social class and gender— a formula for social unrest. Thus enlightened business leaders believe that the future success of their company will depend on their ability to identify talented people from all cultural groups and to place them in positions of authority. And, they also believe that the success of their company depends on effective teamwork from people of many different cultural backgrounds. Yet this rationale both goes too far and does not go far enough.

It goes too far because there is little evidence that teamwork and political harmony require cultural understanding. Teamwork requires sufficient respect for cultural difference to allow the task at hand to be accomplished by people who look and act differently from one another. Political harmony requires a pervasive sense that one's place in life is better than the alternatives, or not worth the risks or the effort involved in seeking change. Neither of these requires a great deal of sensitivity to cultural differences. True, there are certain instances in which cultural differences can be misunderstood and generate unnecessary conflict, but it seems overly idealistic to believe that workers must understand each others' cultural history and practices in order to function on the job.[4]

The argument does not go far enough because it assumes an incomplete notion of educational equity and fails to provide a reason why cultural factors that retard achievement should be given special consideration, whereas other factors, say, poverty, should be treated as incidental. In addition, the argument addresses the benefits of multicultural education from the point of view of business and fails to consider the educational needs of the child.

Regardless of the benefits that may or may not be derived

by business from multicultural education, many people justifiably wonder why schools should be used to raise children's consciousness of their cultural differences. These critics pose important questions about the nature of the self and about the character of cultural and national identity. Perhaps the most difficult of these involves the point at which multicultural education comes closest to the separatist position and argues that public schools should be instruments for developing cultural pride.

THE ISSUE OF CULTURAL PRIDE REEXAMINED

There are two sides to multicultural education. The first involves the way in which members of one culture will become informed and feel about others. The second involves the way in which they will become informed and feel about themselves. The issue of group pride, an offshoot of this second, is one of the most controversial aspects of multicultural education. Critics fear that curricular material will be *selected* not for its educational merit but because it is likely to have a positive influence on the way in which students think about their own culture. The concern here is less with the actual results of using certain material than with the educational principles involved when material is used not because of its intellectual merits but because it will change the thoughts and attitudes of students in certain predetermined ways. There is no reason to find fault with a unit that happens *incidentally* to raise the value that students place on their own group. The objection is to cases in which the intention to produce certain attitudes about a cultural group predetermines the selection and in which material is accepted or rejected not because it is truthful or distorted but because it will likely lead to a more favorable attitude toward "one's own" culture.

This concern is raised by pluralists against those who seek a more representative literary canon, although it is often raised with the faulty presupposition that few truly worthy works can be found outside of the Western tradition. Similar concerns are expressed in the areas of history and social studies by those who believe that the requirement of cultural respect will lead to a partial and incomplete presentation of the practices of some ethnic communities in order to emphasize the positive contributions and deemphasize the negative ones.[5]

Pluralists also object on the ground that this kind of representation is designed to advance the solidarity of particular subcultures. They believe that this is often harmful for individual students who are identified with those subcultures but who find a single cultural identity confining and limiting.[6] The concern is that an exclusive emphasis on cultural pride will lead students to think of themselves in one-dimensional terms and will inhibit their desire to explore other dimensions, including other *cultural* dimensions, of the self. If cultural pride leads to cutting off contact with members of other groups who have expanding interests, then it will inhibit growth and development.

Pluralists also believe that some forms of cultural pride are harmful to the nation as a whole, especially if they overemphasize points of difference with other groups and underemphasize points of similarity. They fear that instead of thematizing all relevant groups as related to one another through nationality, the emphasis on cultural pride may devolve into an emphasis on cultural exclusivity and national disunity.[7] They object to the idea that the school should serve to legitimize some groups and delegitimize others by assuring that the perspectives of certain groups are given priority within the officially framed curriculum and pedagogy. And they especially object to the idea that cultural pride should be developed by encouraging "particularistic" interpretations of historical events or social formations, for example, presenting Columbus Day or Thanksgiving as a day of mourning for Native Americans. They are concerned about the political implications of multiculturalism and the danger of advancing the sense that there are *only* cultural groups and that there is no common American culture.[8] They believe that if this approach takes root it will distort both the character of American culture and the "root cultures" which are supposed to be its base. As Ravitch puts it:

> In the particularistic analysis the nation has five cultures: African American, Asian American, European American, Latino/Hispanic, and Native American. The huge cultural, historical, religious, and linguistic differences within these categories are ignored, as is the considerable intermarriage among these groups, as are the linkages (like gender, class, sexual orientation and religion) that cut across these five groups. No serious scholar would claim that all European and white Americans are part of the same culture, or that all Asians are part of the same culture, or that all people of Latin-American descent are of the same culture, or that all people of African descent are of the same culture.[9]

Ravitch goes on to rightly criticize the notion that the development of ethnic pride will necessarily result in higher achievement in traditional academic subjects such as math and science.[10]

Ravitch is right to object to the idea that one's origins exhaust one's potential identities, but this should not be taken to mean that cultural differences are insignificant. Although there is nothing to guarantee that greater cultural pride will improve school performance, Ravitch underemphasizes the role that pride can play. High performance in any field requires a sense that this is the kind of activity that people like me are able to accomplish. If I believe that "people like me" are not made for this kind of activity, then I will see little reason to try to succeed. If I am more optimistic and believe that people like me can master this activity, then the significance of my temporary difficulties and failures may fade, and I may well come to master the activity. This has been one of the key insights behind affirmative action, for example. If one wants, say, more women doctors, then it is important to increase the opportunities for women and to spotlight the achievement of women in medicine. This is the significance of an episode in Malcolm X's autobiography in which he reports being stunned the first time he saw a black man flying a jet plane.

From the pluralist perspective cultural pride is a problematic goal for public education because it requires that children's attitudes be shaped in a predetermined direction and that schools assure that students develop a favorable attitude toward the practices of their own cultural group. To the pluralist a line has been crossed between encouraging a sympathetic understanding and encouraging a posture of advocacy.

To see the distinction, consider a social studies class where students are studying cultures that practice polygamy. The teacher is not expected to require that students develop favorable attitudes toward the practice, even though it is important for her students to entertain the culture sympathetically. To approach the topic of polygamy in a sympathetic way is to seek to understand from the inside why it is practiced. Yet seeking this type of understanding is not the same as having a favorable attitude toward the practice in the sense that one must approve of it or become an advocate for it. Indeed, once the practice is understood from the inside there are many different attitudes that may be taken toward it. One may accept or reject it totally. One may want to defend it within certain environmental and social contexts. One may believe that it would be a good thing for other cultural groups to adopt as well, or one may believe that it once served a purpose, but that it no longer does so.

To the pluralist it appears as if the multiculturalist is violating the boundary between sympathetic understanding and advocacy in one critical instance, namely, where the practices of the child's *own* cultural group are concerned. The questions that the pluralist's objection raises are whether there is ever a good reason to use different methods in teaching children about their own culture than in teaching them about other cultures and whether there is reason to evaluate the success of such teachings differently — one by the amount of pride developed, the other by the level of understanding.

The answer to this question differs considerably from group to group, depending on the educational needs of children in different situations. The general answer rests, however, on a distinction between cultural understanding and cultural competence, where cultural understanding involves coming to know what a certain practice means and why it developed and cultural competence requires that we become able to perform the practice in the right setting and in the right way. To teach about another culture is to teach cultural understanding. Here the student learns about various cultural practices and why they are performed. To teach cultural competence is to teach a student how to function in a certain cultural setting. Competency is related to many different things, of course, but one's culture, as a center of experience, is primary — it provides the basic interactive instruments, such as gestures, expressions, language, and meanings, that are required for collective action of any kind. When these instruments break down in certain kinds of situations, and when the breakdown brings about certain undesirable results, then the development of cultural pride becomes an educational concern.

CULTURE AS MEANS AND END
Culture entails a series of historically transmitted practices that involve many different skills. Language is the most obvious, and as with other social skills, its effectiveness depends on its recognition by others. Imagine that tomorrow morning you wake up in a place where only you speak and understand English and where no one shares your assumptions about what is normal social practice and what is not. In other words, imagine that the world in which the

tools given to you by your culture, tools that work because others understand and accept their meaning, suddenly have no use. What you would have lost is not only your specific competency—how to order a meal or stand in an elevator—but your general competency to recognize which of your behaviors are working and which are not. Imagine what such a loss might do to your understanding of yourself and your capacity to think, understand, and feel. Eva Hoffman, who, as an adolescent, immigrated to Canada, explains the problem of one whose language—in this case Polish—no longer comprises the linguistic environment:

> Polish, in a short time, has atrophied, shriveled from sheer uselessness. Its words don't apply to my new experience; they're not coeval with any of the objects, or faces, or the very air I breathe in the daytime. In English, words have not penetrated to those layers of my psyche from which a private conversation could proceed. . . .
>
> I have no interior language, and without it, interior images—those images through which we assimilate the external world, through which we take it in, love it, make it our own—become blurred too.[11]

CONDITIONS FOR DEVELOPING CULTURAL PRIDE IN SCHOOL

Membership in the dominant culture has certain natural advantages even without a history of minority oppression and domination. The most important of these advantages involves the simple fact that one's cultural tools work well. When one speaks, others understand. When they speak, one understands. When a certain feeling arises, language allows it to be expressed, understood, and shared. One does not constantly have to explain a certain practice or custom because others find it odd or strange. One does not need to be reminded of the worth of one's everyday habits of interaction, just as we need not be reminded of the worth of a well-tuned car.

They work just fine. The development of cultural pride may mean something as simple as being reminded that one's once taken-for-granted cultural tools are working poorly because one is now in a different social environment, not because of some inherent defect in one's character.

The systematic and conscious development of cultural pride by schools is required when the tools of culture are in question as social currency. When one finds that people respond nervously because they feel that one is standing too close, or that they feel slighted because they perceive that one is standing too far away; when they object physically because one has shaken their hand too hard, or are embarrassed because one has complimented them too much, one's social network can disintegrate, opportunities to grow and develop may be lost, and one's self-esteem may suffer. One loses confidence in oneself much in the same way that one loses confidence when a formerly effective tennis swing no longer works in the way that it once did. To be at home in a culture is to be comfortable with one's own taken-for-granted habits and practices and to experience a social world that, because others acknowledge and respond to these same taken-for-granteds, can be made to work in the intended way. To be a stranger is to be in a social world that does not respond in the way one anticipates.

This strangeness is different for foreigners than it is for marginalized minority groups. The foreigner often enjoys a certain subjective advantage because of the understanding that the cards might have been reversed and that those who are now at home with their practices could, at some other time and in some other place, become foreigners. Foreigners know that were the situation reversed the cultural tools that are working so well for others would become as awkward and inefficient as their cultural instruments are now.

This is not an advantage easily enjoyed by members of marginalized cultural minorities in their own "homeland." In these cases the history of domination and oppression has been justified by narratives that deny the value of their cultural practices. For members of these groups the social context is not simply a lock that cannot be opened by their particular cultural key. Rather, the social context includes the persistent message that theirs is an inferior key, one made of substandard material.

Cultural pride is not much of an issue when a child has the skills that provide effective social interaction, and in these cases, schools have no reason to be concerned about the child's attitude toward her group. A child who possesses these skill is in a position similar to that of children who enter school able to name their colors. Given the ability to name colors, the school has no reason to teach such knowledge and can immediately engage the child in painting or drawing. If the child has not learned the colors, however, then the school has a responsibility to teach them. The difference between cultural and color-naming skills is the difference between having a perfectly adequate tool that is wrong for this task and having no tool at all. To lack a cultural skill is not like having no names for the colors. It is like having different names, names that are perfectly understandable in some social settings but not in this one.

THE MEANING OF CULTURAL PRIDE

The discussion above suggests that there are situations in which a student's home culture does not adequately prepare the child for school and that where this is the case educators need to teach some students cultural skills which others learn at home. It is one thing to be concerned about developing the skills required to interact in an unfamiliar social setting, however, and it is quite another to believe that the public school has a responsibility to teach children to be proud of their cultural heritage. A gap between the cultural tools that the child brings to school and the preschool cultural understandings that are preconditions for school learning is a technical issue and has but one technical implication—teach children the cultural understandings that are required for success in school. The responsibility to teach children to have pride in their cultural group requires something more than simply an obligation to fill the gap between the two.

To develop cultural pride requires more than teaching children how to interact within the mainstream culture. It also requires teaching children to feel partial toward members of their own cultural group. Students who have pride in their culture will have a strong identity with the accomplishments of people like themselves, and they will be especially concerned about the plight and suffering of those from their cultural community. They will want to know more about their own cultural heritage, and they will come to believe that there is a special bond between people who share their cultural history and background. In a pluralist society, there is no special problem with this kind of identification, and it is enabled by the principle of freedom of association. It is more difficult, however, for many people to see why the public schools should advance this goal, and the pluralist critic will ask: Why should *my* tax dollar be used to teach *your* children to favor people like you and not people like me and for no other reason than that they are *like you* and *not like me*? The critic is right in this sense: unless the development of cultural pride has some other basis than a simple technical mismatch between the skills developed by the local culture and those assumed by the school, there is no justification for supporting it as an educational goal for the public schools.

This, however, is only part of the story, and there are at least two conditions that, if both are present, legitimize cultural pride as an educational goal. The first is the technical condition, mentioned above, under which the meanings and practices of the home community are ineffective in the school and, as a result, children grow up unable to fully participate in the larger society. When this condition exists alone, then, as I suggested, the school needs only to develop programs that will help the children learn better the ways to interact in the larger society. Bilingual programs that aid children to make the transition from the language that their parents speak to English is an example of a program that would meet this need. When this need exists alone, it is necessary not to help children maintain proficiency in their parent's language but to use that language as a bridge into the common language or languages of the nation. This is a necessary condition for justifying the focus on cultural pride by the public schools, but it is not sufficient.

The second condition is that the prevailing explanations for these failures target local cultural practices, meanings, and interpretations and delivers the message that they are inherently deficient and inferior to the dominant cultural practices. Rather than viewing the problem in terms of a mismatch between local meanings and officially privileged national practices, it is viewed strictly as a problem with the local practices and with those who maintain them. These explanations are the effects of oppression, and they need to be corrected by a clearer understanding of the reasons for the development of certain oppositional practices, meanings, and interpretations. What then appears to the outside observer to be an unwarranted emphasis on developing a favorable attitude toward one group is in reality the result of a pedagogical reinterpretation of a cultural rupture and its pedagogical implications.

WHY CULTURE MATTERS: THE ISSUE OF CULTURAL RESPECT

This brings us to the second goal of multicultural education — the requirement that we respect other cultures. This goal too is problematic and in need of interpretation. Why should we respect other cultures, and what does it mean to do so? Consider the problems raised by the following: children in grade schools in the 1940s used to sing a little chant as a way to learn about the pluralistic character of America. It went:

> Their fathers, may be English, German, French or Dutch
> but if they're born in Yankee land,
> the rest don't count for much.

The chant was not a way to teach children to respect other cultures. It was, rather, a way to teach them the desirability of transcending all but the predominant culture and of participating primarily in "Yankee land." Children were being taught to respect one another not as members of a culture but as individuals and as citizens of the nation. The song was intended to teach children that regardless of the conflicts that once governed the lives of their ancestors in Europe, they now were all Americans and needed to begin anew. The song was asking that they take on a new identity and relate to each other, not as Germans, French, or Dutch, but as American citizens, as individuals who could think and live beyond their local culture.

Today some may think this song quaint, as if America did not have a cultural bias, or even as misguided or possibly dangerous, a potential license to alter cultural formations that do not accommodate to the modernization program. Nevertheless, the song and its critique pose a fundamental question about multicultural education: Just what is cultural respect, why should it matter, and does it have any limitations?

The song, which was praised by progressive educational groups in the 1940s, expressed a certain kind of respect, namely, that no one should be ashamed of his family background because in America anyone could become American. Respect carried a kind of negation — it meant nonshame. Yet why, today's multiculturalist would ask, is there even the suggestion that one might be ashamed of one's own heritage? Is not the problem with the song that it is premised on an insult?

HOW CAN MODERN SOCIETY RESPECT TRADITIONAL CULTURE?

This question about traditional culture provides a way to examine contemporary issues of schooling and identity. Modernist literature describes traditional culture as fatalistic. It links past, present, and future in a way that largely excludes the efficacy of individual choice. Such cultures are said to be "informed by belief in established, timeless orders."[12] They root themselves in the past and are "highly authoritative."[13] As the editors of a book on issues of tradition describe traditional societies as depicted in the sociological tradition:

> The tradition-informed way of life is hierarchically differentiated: both within particular traditions, and with regard to how other ways of life are evaluated. Little or no validity is accorded to those who might speak with their own, out-of-place voice. Identities are inscribed, rather than being at stake for discursive controversy. Indeed, the authorial taken-for-grantedness of identities precludes the necessity of questioning those discourses which serve to legitimate the order of things.[14]

I am cautious about adopting one description for the many cultures that we call traditional. Assuming, however, that this description of traditional culture is accurate for some set of cultures that are called "traditional,"[15] then what if any grounds exist for schools to teach respect for these cultural forms when one of the goals of modern education is to teach children to think for themselves, and not just to accept the word of authority?

The answer to this question involves a consideration of the character of the present conditions in which respect is being requested. Multiculturalism is not respect for cultural formations under any and all conditions. Rather, it is respect for such formations in the context of modern social conditions. Under these conditions, certain possibilities for choice are present that were not present under earlier situations dominated by traditional social forms. Today a given traditional society shares a certain political and social space with members of other traditional societies and with people who are unambiguously modern. Hence respect is asked not for a group that dominates its members' thought and action without alternative forms available. Rather, respect is asked for traditional cultures whose members are often at the edge of a commitment and who are constantly renewing or rejecting the hegemonic dominance of their cultural authority. To understand cultural respect in this context is to view it as an element within a modern, *liberal* framework and not as an element within a traditional one. It is a way of celebrating and preserving opportunities for choice, even opportunities that, once chosen, constrain choice in the way that some traditional societies do.

Yet this suggests too that the standard description of traditional society as noted above is not completely accurate, either. A traditional cultural group that exists within the context of modernization is different than one that stands alone. In the latter, choice outside of that tradition is but a remote possibility. Within the context of modernization, however, traditional culture is itself an object of choice, and its members must establish and renew their identity within such a framework.

Thus part of the question of what it means to respect traditional culture must be answered within the context of modernization. This respect is grounded within the liberal tradition of individual choice. It is a minimal conception of respect. We do not respect a tradition as such. We respect the availability of a tradition given a situation in which the individual has the ability to choose otherwise. Traditional authority may want more. It may want respect for its way of life because it expresses basic human concerns and does so, in its eyes, more adequately than any other way of life. Is it possible from the outside to provide this kind of respect and to respect not just a person's right to choose a tradition but the tradition for what it itself does? This question requires some exploration of the way in which culture and tradition are implicated in education.

THE IMPLICATION OF TRADITIONAL CULTURE IN EDUCATION

What is required here is for outsiders to respect a tradition not just as one among many alternatives but also for the value it holds for those who practice it. One way to do this is to think about the role that culture plays in personal development. Language provides the easiest example. An infant has the potential to learn any natural language. Only one of these languages will become the child's first and primary language, however, and on this language the child's future growth and development will depend, including the growth and development of second and third languages. Thus, whereas all natural languages exist as potential first languages for the child, she must only take one of them as her own. Jonathan Glover captures the similar relationship that exists between the development of personality and culture. He writes:

> Just as a species may flourish in a particular ecological niche, so the development of individual personality may depend on the support of a group. Like climbing plants searching for something to hook on to, we look for such support even where, as with the random allocation of the psychological experiments, the group has no shared basis. But, as climbing plants flourish where there is support, so our sense of ourselves flourishes in groups with enough in common to take on a life of their own. This dependence on the shared understanding of a group is brought out by differences of language. When you speak a foreign language poorly, you have to say simpler things than you would like. In doing so, you present a simplified version of yourself. (This does not only apply to talking another language. It can also hold in another country where they speak a

version of your own language. Turns of phrase, humor, and tone of voice are part of a "language" which may be different. One way of drawing the boundaries of a culture is to take the region where such signals are understood.) [16]

Culture involves a set of material and symbolic codes that provide a group of people, including children, with the means for practical action and communicative interaction. The elements of culture are many, including a common language and set of traditions, shared historical experiences, and an "intuitive" understanding of gestures, body movements, and speech fragments. Each of these elements in turn requires further elaboration. For example, symbolic codes include scientific communication, artistic expressions, music, dance, and stories, as well as rituals. Discursive languages and traditions differ depending on how communication transpires. One reason written and oral traditions are classified separately is that they enable people to think and do different kinds of things.

"Our" culture or cultures therefore have much to do with (how we become) the person or persons we are. They provide both the scaffold for our development and the initial conditions — the other who is the same as us — for self-recognition. They allow us to think of ourselves, in Glover's term, as an "I" and to understand that this "I" entails a certain unity of consciousness, that it is a person.[17] It does more than this, however. It also plays an important role in constituting that person and in determining that she is *that* person rather than some other *possible* but in fact *nonexistent* person.

Culture constitutes selfhood in many different ways. Take, for example, the fact that part of who I am depends on the beliefs that I hold and that those beliefs are often a part of my cultural background.[18] Although it is probably true that there is no one single belief that makes me the person that I am, the constellation of beliefs and how they are held is certainly a major factor in this determination. Imagine, for example, my clone, a biological configuration that is me except that it not only holds radically different beliefs than I do, but also entertains beliefs about radically different things, as, for example, might be the case if the biological me were born in a different time or in a radically different cultural formation. The present me ponders whether to borrow money to buy a car. The biological me lives in a place where automobiles have not been invented and camels are the major means of transportation. The present me lives in a world of money, banks, and interest. The biological me lives in a world where these do not exist. To hold that the present me and the biological me are the same person is a hard claim to understand.

Hence, part of what is involved in respecting different cultures is what is involved in respecting persons and personality. In the case of cultural respect, we respect the conditions for personality formation. In respecting traditional culture, however, something else is required, and that is that we are asked to respect, in Nelson Goodman's phrase, *different* "ways of world making"[19] or of coming to an understanding regarding the way the world is and different ways of relating to it. We respect a certain way of learning, what I called in chapter 3 learning-through-culture.

Learning-through-culture is to be distinguished from simply learning about cultures other than one's own. It is a concept that recognizes that there are distinctive ways in which cultures constitute both the process and the product of thinking and that these in turn become distinctive elements of learning. It is important not to confuse the fact that there may be culturally different ways of learning and culturally different things to learn with the view that people from certain cultures are simply not capable of learning in the way in which we do.[20] Nor should the analysis be taken to mean that traditional culture forever limits people from thinking in certain ways, say, by inhibiting abstract reasoning.[21]

Luria, among others, shows that the individual's cultural frame can be altered and that one culture is not a cell to which we must be forever confined. Members of different cultures may differ in their initial appropriation of modernist conceptions of rational thinking, and this poses a paradox for the modernist advocates of cultural respect. Must a culture always be respected as if from the inside, even when its forms of learning are incompatible with the requirements of modernity?

I cited an example of this difference in chapter 2 when I referred to Luria's research on peasants who seemed unable to respond accurately to a standard syllogism such as "In the north, where there is snow all year, the bears are white. Town X is in the north. Are the bears white in that town or not?" Recall that he received answers such as "How should I know what color the bear was? It was your friend that saw him, ask your friend." [22] What such responses suggest is a certain way of learning, one that demands attention to primary experience and a possible inability or unwillingness to engage in binary or universal reasoning.

Interestingly, the response of the peasant is similar to the answers that female subjects gave to Carol Gilligan regarding a moral dilemma about whether it is right for a man to steal a costly drug to save his dying wife.[23] In their responses, female subjects often refused to accept the premises of the dilemma and offered practical suggestions on how to get around it, such as talking to the druggist who refuses to sell the cure at an affordable price about the seriousness of the situation. One important difference, however, is that Luria relegates this way of thinking to a less-developed culture, whereas Gilligan views it as just a different mode of moral development.

Gilligan, however, is an exception, and researchers and public schools have tended, like Luria, to relegate this kind of response to lower-order thinking skills and implicitly resurrect the hierarchy promoted by assimilationists and segregationists alike.

This way of labeling demeans the group. Liberal tolerance is sometimes seen as a way to avoid such demeaning, but it only addresses the promise of the individual person to overcome cultural limits. It does not address the value that the culture contributes to thinking and understanding, and it leaves the issue of cultural respect a matter for liberal toleration alone. The concept of toleration, however, suggests the value difference that is implied. We tolerate our inferiors, not our equals.

An alternative is to view both "traditional" and "modern" modes of thinking in terms of different purposes without rejecting the possibility that traditional people likely already know something about abstract thought, even if it may be difficult for mainline researchers to probe. As one researcher noted, "If primitive [sic] peoples thought according to a radically different rule of logic, man would probably be extinct. Imagine what would happen . . . if a primitive hunter were to reason thus: a rabbit has four legs; that animal has four legs; therefore, that animal is a rabbit." [24]

The modern ideal of abstract reasoning is best understood in terms of the specific purposes that it is able to serve. Purely logical reconstructions are rare in the modern world and are most useful in mathematics and highly technical scientific fields — and even there often only when explaining or reconstructing a complex process. Most of our day-to-day life is carried on in terms of hunches, past knowledge, reasonable guesses, and imprecise definitions, all of which serve quite well in most circumstances. And often, abstract logic or scientific reasoning is inappropriate to the situation, interrupting the flow of meaning by requiring an inappropriate level of precision. [25]

When high levels of predictability or control are required, where the consequences of behavior are uncertain, and where universal laws can be developed to express useful relationships between phenomena, then abstract logic and scientific reasoning are important tools to increase predictability and control. These are important thinking skills to have in cases where it is unlikely that future conditions will be like past ones, where rule-of-thumb procedures are unlikely to work, and where the meaning of highly ritualized performances is unlikely to be shared. Not all situations are like this, however, and respect for traditional forms of culture requires that scientific thinking be viewed within a certain context with certain purposes and that different forms of thinking be understood in terms of the goals and conditions that render them appropriate.

This way of thinking about thinking provides the space for traditional cultures to speak for themselves and to be evaluated on their own terms and not on exclusively modern ones. It requires that we "outsiders" allow cultures to speak for themselves and appreciate the groups' practices and meanings on their own terms. Such understanding is more aesthetic than practical and more passive than active. We seek to appreciate, not to change. Just as coming to understand another language involves understanding the distinctions and frames that are internal to it, understanding the practices of another cultural group involves seeing its members as they are, connected from the inside to a way of life that advances certain modes of communication and interaction that are foreign to us.

This kind of respect, as important as it is, is also limited. It places us outside of culture as observers. We stand in front of a window that allows us to look in on the unfamiliar practices of others and then to understand them in terms of practices that are commonplace to us. When we take this position, we place ourselves beyond culture, assume that our own practices are taken as natural, not cultural products, and therefore assume that they are in no need of explanation.

Another way of respecting other cultures involves seeing ourselves as cultural products and allowing that our own practices are formed through the inventions of other cultures. For example, to teach students about the important institutions that arose out of Africa—language, family structures, economic and social communities[26]—is to teach them that our own society is multicultural at its foundation. This form of respect enables students to turn lessons taught about other cultures back on their own and to understand their own cultural practices as social constructs, the product of long strings of cultural interaction.

INFORMATION ABOUT OTHER CULTURES

The final goal of multicultural education—to inform children about other cultures—also presents problems of interpretation and execution. Information is not neutral. It serves certain purposes and issues from certain centers of experience and not others. Critics of multicultural education are concerned that the information will be filtered in such a way as to highlight only the positive features of a cultural group while overemphasizing the negative factors in the nation's response to that group. The question that needs to be addressed is, What should be the educational aim of such information?

There are at least two competing scripts in our present-day discourse that often frame the information, and each provides a competing interpretation of the relationship between a nation and the cultures that comprise it. The first script is organized around the dyad advantaged-disadvantaged and the second around the dyad dominant-subordinate. Each script acknowledges the fact of inequality and links it to cultural variation. The second, however, implies an agent that advances the inequality for the sake of arbitrary and undeserved gain, whereas in the first the question of agency remains open and the script allows for a benign reading of cultural position and status.

Multicultural Education and the Issues
of Dominance and Equality

In all nations, including democratic ones, certain cultural forms dominate business, education, and legal institutions.[27] People who use these cultural forms have advantages that others do not. Given that there is always a certain arbitrary factor involved in the assignment of cultural dominance, some advocates of multiculturalism believe that it is unfair to assign advantage and disadvantage on the basis of cultural style. Their concern is warranted in cases where cultural style is viewed as a signal of intelligence or ability and opportunities are distributed according to this signal.[28] Not all inequalities that arise because of cultural difference are arbitrary or irrational, however.

Disadvantages have different causes, some of which may be morally neutral. Consider, for example, the fact that almost all Americans speak English as their first language and only a relative few speak Russian or Japanese as their first language. This means that in this country native speakers of English will have large advantages that native speakers of Russian or Japanese will not have or will need to work harder to obtain. People who wish to become lawyers will have an advantage if they are raised either in the United States or in England rather than in the former Soviet Union. The advantage will have as much to do with habits of thought as it will with language differences. The same would hold for children raised in the United States or in England who wished to practice law in Russia.

Culture matters, and it provides those who are favored with positions within the dominant culture with certain advantages that those raised in other cultures do not have or will have to struggle hard to obtain. Anyone who thinks that this result by itself is wrong or unjust has a burden of proof to satisfy.

This is obvious except to those who mistakenly believe that societies can and should be culturally neutral. Were it really possible for nations to be culturally neutral, and should they actually become so, it would remove from them any distinctive quality. To judge nations on this standard would, ironically, be hegemonic in the extreme. Inequalities are unjust if they are caused by morally impermissible acts or if such acts remain unaddressed over a number of generations. In cases where large cultural differences contribute to inequality, the important issue is whether reasonable educational compensation is provided to children who, through no fault of their own, are placed in a disadvantaged position. Yet this concern, which presupposes an ideal of equality of opportunity, arises not out of traditional culture—which may well hold that we should be partial to people like us regardless of issues of merit—but out of the principles of advanced liberal society.

When children learn about other cultures under the advantaged-disadvantaged dyad the object is to reinforce this principle by demonstrating that the society is open to many different people and that the route to achievement begins in many different places. This is the script of many voluntary immigrants, and it is the one pluralists advocate. Under this script there is a nesting of cultural and national goals. Although the struggle of immigrant groups and the resistance to their advancement by more established groups are not absent from this model, the struggle is presented in terms of a hardship overcome and victory achieved. In the more liberal and progressive models, an American identity has not been substituted for a local cultural identity; it has simply been added onto it.

There are a number of advantages to this representation. It stresses unity amid difference. It allows children to maintain an identity with their parents' local culture while also identifying with the national culture. It thus provides a way both to acknowledge differences from members of other cultural groups and, when necessary, to overcome them. It is also inspirational for some children who might otherwise feel that their futures are limited because of their parents' background. And, finally, it provides a strong ideological reason to favor people because of their contribution rather than their sex, skin color, or religion.

Yet the script does not allow for a full examination of social class, race, or gender issues and only allows for one explanation of failure—inadequate intelligence or motivation. Its uncritical acceptance of individual competition advances a political project in which solidarity and alternative forms of social organization have but a small role to play. And, finally, it ignores the power of the dominant-subordinate dyad in describing the experience of African Americans and other non-European peoples.

Multicultural Information and Education
Culture, as I argued earlier, provides the categories for self-understanding. Multicultural education provides the conditions for revising these categories and the sense of self that they frame. The dyad advantaged-disadvantaged serves as a cultural script that rings true for many. Yet it also neglects the experience of many others. The dominant-subordinate script fits the historical experience of many African and Native Americans more closely than does the advantaged-disadvantaged script. For African Americans, it fits the involuntary sundering of their ancestors from their African roots, their coercive subordination, the forceful and violent appropriation of their labor, and the continuing devaluation of their contribution to the American nation. For Native Americans, it fits the destruction of their economy, the plundering of their land, and the genocidal killing of many of their people.

Both the multicultural educator and the pluralist believe that the schools must select the right script, the one that best fits the American experience and the experience of its people and cultures. Their argument is about which is the right script. Yet in reality no child fits either script totally and absolutely, and the struggle between them is as much about future identities as it is about past experience. Children are in the process of taking on a cultural and national identity, but they are also in the process of taking on other identities as well — racial, gender, and class; and increasingly they are identified by their sexual orientation. These other facets of identity provide alternative possibilities, different standpoints from which to draw identity and to interrogate the different scripts one is handed.

The error is to think that children must locate themselves exclusively within one or the other of these scripts. Rather, multicultural thinking skills ultimately entail students coming to understand the various stories about cultural and national identity *as scripts* that are presented for them to validate, challenge, negotiate, and rewrite. For example, at some point in their educational career students should be able to understand how the advantaged-disadvantaged script relies on a certain conception of national identity that the dominant-subordinate script rejects. The dominant-subordinate script can be examined in terms of the way it shifts the status of some Europeans from disadvantaged to dominator by classifying them not by nation but by continent. Hence, Irish Americans or Italian Americans who once viewed themselves as the victims of Anglo-Americans are recategorized under the opposing script as "Americans of European background."

The change is important for students to see because the immigrant story and the advantaged-disadvantaged script depend on the view that certain groups were in fact able to overthrow the roadblocks that were put in their way. Although there clearly were attempts to establish dominant-subordinate relationships, according to the script, the determination of the immigrant, coupled with the comparative openness of the country, did not allow this relationship to become permanent.

The script change from advantaged-disadvantaged to dominant-subordinate thus revolves on the shift from a national to a continental (and quasi-racial) identity. When reclassified, Italian Americans, French Americans, Irish Americans all become European white Americans who, as the script continues, arrived here, perhaps not sharing the language and the practices of the dominant group, but with features sufficiently like theirs to allow progress. Thus within a few generations their offspring inherited a portion of the privilege that had been extracted from Africans and Native Americans.

Students need to read the scripts not just as means to locate themselves and others in terms of their understanding of the American experience but also as proposals for commitment and action that require careful criticism and reflection, as well as a close reading of different historical possibilities. For example, students might interrogate the dominant-subordinate script in terms of colonization in Europe, both from without by Mongols, Tartars, and others and, more important, from within as regional populations were subdued in the process of nation building. And there is also need to interrogate this script in terms of postcolonial nation building in different parts of the world and the various ways, both peaceful and violent, in which peoples have been unified within national boundaries constructed by dominant powers.

And both scripts need to be compared for points of similarity as well as points of difference, including the way in which elements of innocence, struggle, and redemption function within each script. Scripts serve as occasions for students to reflect on their own experience in terms of its fit with the different scripts. Where do women fit? Does either of the scripts fit the experience of Asian Americans? What happens when the comparison of privilege and well-being shifts from an inter-American context in which European and non-European Americans are the principal players to an international context in which the privileged north and the poorer south, or first- and third-world peoples, become the principals? And just as the European American story is in the process of redescription, students may be asked to consider what the elements are that may cause the newer version of the American story to be retold.

Students need also to be aware that scripts help locate people but do not define them and that people may occupy different roles within the same script at different times. Consider, for example, the category "speakers of Spanish in the American hemisphere." Here is a category that once applied to a dominant, oppressor group and now applies to a dominated people who believe that it is critical that "their" language be provided special recognition. To acknowledge the irony involved in this shift is to soften some of the edges of the debate and to allow students to see that their own future identity is still in part an active self-creation.

The full educational value of the two scripts is realized when they are used in contrast with one another as tools for reflection and understanding and not as the choreography of an old dance. Information about cultures is educational insofar as it enables students to understand the way in which these scripts operate and the extent to which each of them is bidding for their allegiance and commitment. It is educational insofar as it leads to informed allegiance and a reasoned commitment. It is also educational insofar as it enables students to understand that although certain circumstances may require that they commit to one or another script as it is handed to them, scripts best serve as tools to develop their own identity—and that their own personhood is never fully exhausted by a single script. William E. Connolly puts this point very well:

> The human animal is essentially incomplete without social form; and a common language, institutional setting, set of traditions, and political forum for enunciating public purposes are indispensable to the acquisition of an identity and the commonalities essential to life. But every form of social completion and enablement also contains subjugations and cruelties within

it. Politics, then, is the medium through which these ambiguities can be engaged and confronted, shifted and stretched. It is simultaneously a medium through which common purposes are crystallized and the consummate means by which their transcription into musical harmonies is exposed, contested, disturbed, and unsettled. A society that enables politics as this ambiguous medium is a good society because it enables the paradox of difference to find expression in public life.[29]

Instruction in a multicultural setting need not be educational. If it simply works to fix a child's identity but does not provide insight into the techniques and the issues involved in fixing that identity one way rather than another, then it is something less than educational. This is true even if that instruction is intended to enhance a child's identification with people who look like her and share the background and outlook of her parents and her parents' community. Socialization of this kind is often preparatory for education, but it is only preparatory. It becomes educational when it enables a student to understand that her identity is potentially more than the cultural and national forms that enfold it, that it involves a process of self-creation and growth that neither culture nor nation can claim fully.

6.   Uncommon Identities:
Hard Cases

In this chapter I address two questions: When should a public school be obliged to recognize group differences? And how should it do so? The complexity involved in addressing the issue of difference can be illustrated by two different court cases. In the first, decided by the United States Supreme Court in *Wisconsin v. Yoder*,[1] the Court allowed a group of Amish parents to remove their children from the public schools after the eighth grade. The parents had argued that schooling beyond the eighth grade was disruptive to their communal life, and the Court agreed on grounds having to do with the uniqueness, isolation, and peaceful nature of the Amish community. The dissenting justice argued that the decision disadvantaged individual Amish children and denied them opportunities that were due every American.

In the second case, *Mozert v. Hawkins County Board of*

Education,[2] a group of parents requested that their children be allowed to absent themselves from a classroom because they believed that the required text presented sinful material that threatened their children's religious identity. This case was decided by a federal court against the parents on the ground that exposure to another way of life did not constitute a direct challenge to the parent's religious beliefs.

These decisions are both compatible with the values of liberalism, even though they seem inconsistent with each other. On one hand, parents have a right to form and enter communities, to live without interference from state officials, and to pass on their values and beliefs to their children. On the other, schools have an obligation to promote children's right to freedom of association, personal growth, and equal opportunity. This obligation requires teachers to provide students with the information and insights that will enable them to reflect on the values and beliefs of different communities and to accept or reject these values for themselves.

Both cases tested the extent to which the school must go in facilitating each of these rights and addressing the question of which should have priority when they conflict. The *Yoder* decision suggests that there are instances in which the school must refrain from its normal obligation of promoting individual growth in order to facilitate the right of a community to reproduce itself. The *Mozert* decision suggests that there are times when the school must not honor the preferences of the parent in order to facilitate the child's intellectual growth and development.

Although the courts needed to sort out the specific factors that enabled them to rule as they did, the cases are similar in one critical respect. The plaintiffs did not ask the school to do anything to advance their communal identity. They simply asked it to refrain from doing something that they believed threatened to disrupt it. Moreover, in both cases, the court felt that to permit such restraint under existing conditions would predictably lead children to accept the belief system of their parents and to do so without the benefit of exposure to alternative views.

As complicated as these cases are, the fact that the parents were not asking schools to do very much that was different from what they would normally do limits the considerations that the courts needed to address.[3] Parents were asking that schools take a passive and neutral role regarding identity and that they do nothing that would provide children with material that would lead them to question their parents' commitments. The problem arises because "neutrality" in these cases cuts children off from certain opportunities and narrows their understanding of the larger society. It also arises because the effect of neutrality in these instances in all likelihood is to *propel* the students without due consideration into the one secure belief system that is available to them—their parents'. The courts' differing responses in the two cases illustrate that the nature of the particular group and its relation to the larger society are important considerations in determining how to apply liberal principles of noninterference and equal opportunity.

In both cases the same principles were at stake. The parents were appealing to the classical liberal ideal of noninterference and arguing that they should have the primary say over their children's beliefs and education. The state was assuming that the basic authority of the school to teach civic virtues, to provide for intellectual growth and, especially in *Yoder*, to encourage equal opportunity limited the parents' rights. Neither set of parents was asking that public resources be used to support their communal identity. True, the *Mozert* parents were asking that alternative material be made available that would not violate certain religious concerns, but they were not asking that this material explicitly support those beliefs.

These cases and the understandable controversy surrounding them continue to influence the way the issue is framed. It is generally assumed that schools should have no role in promoting the agenda of a specific group and that they are allowed only a passive part in subgroup identity formation. I have challenged this assumption in one instance that I addressed in chapter 5, where I argued that the development of group pride was justified in certain cases as a way to advance individual self-esteem and achievement. Yet even in that challenge the focus of the argument was the benefit and academic achievement of the individual child.

Although the courts and liberal politicians and educators have gone in one direction on this issue, arguing in ways that allow only *individual* benefits to be considered, many advocates of multicultural education have moved in the opposite direction and have assumed that any claim to cultural status should automatically entitle the *group* to special educational recognition and support.

Advocates of multicultural education hold that the school has a responsibility to recognize group differences and to encourage children with certain racial, ethnic, or sexual characteristics to express their distinctiveness from the mainstream by supporting a primary affinity to people who are most like themselves.[4] Yet this view assumes that children are already identified with a culture and that they are identified with a single one, and it also assumes that all cultures are equal in terms of their claims on educational resources. Both of these assumptions are problematic. Although most of this chapter addresses the question of cultural claims on educational resources, I want to briefly return to the question of identity and to the claim, expressed above, that schools should support children's affinity to those most like themselves.

MULTIPLE IDENTITIES

Identity is the name we give to a subject, that is, to one that has the capacity to organize experience and to be experienced as a coherent whole. Human beings have identities. We *experience* ourselves as ongoing, organized, and organizing centers of experience — as selves. We remember our past, anticipate our future, and connect both to our present. Moreover, we also have *identities as*—we experience ourselves related to some, but not all, other human beings. We believe that these people share our memories, present interpretations, and aspirations. The question whether they really do share these things is important, but more important is the shared perception that these are held in common. For one does not check each and every memory when affirming one's affinity with another. Rather, the perception of common memories, interpretations, and aspirations is sufficient to create a bond with people, some of whom may be distant and physically unconnected to one another. Yet this *identity as* is, to varying degrees, open and fluid, and there is no a priori reason why we should accept our connection to only one group.

From an abstract point of view identity is fluid. There is no single racial, class, or gender identity, and there are many examples with regard to race and class, and even sex, in which individuals change categories. Some "African Americans" found that they could "pass" for "white," and within a few generations their children saw themselves as, and were seen as, white. People change their social class and then their children experience life through the framework of the new rather than the old class. The same is true of religion. Gender is experienced in so many different ways that the traditional idea that there are only two sexes is more controversial than it appears. Alternative sexual orientations and preferences, cross-dressing, sex-change operations, and so on all suggest that sexual identity is somewhat fluid.

People may move from one to another category as individuals; the categories themselves may allow for a great deal of gradation, which then blurs the sharpness of the distinctions between them; and some categories are important for a while and then they fade, to be replaced by others. For example, whether one was a first son was, but is no more, a major category of social and economic distinction in the West, and it is still so in many Asian countries.

Identity labels do not indicate any fixed and stable position. There is no one way to be "female" or to be "male," and there are many ways in which conventional males exhibit female behavior and in which conventional females exhibit male behavior. And the same is true of class. Moreover, the entire concept of race as a biological given is highly suspect, and to establish an identity on the basis of a fictive biological category can be a mistake of large educational and social proportions.

If race means anything, it is a cultural and historical category, but cultures are notoriously fluid; they signal evolving cores of meaning, and the whole concept of cultural identity only makes sense in relation to other cultural identities. Hence, for example, when I am abroad I am American, when I visit my friend's church I am Jewish, when I take the bus through the black neighborhood, I am white, and when I need a bathroom, I am a male. Identity, it may be argued, is much like the bubbles in champagne: they come into play at different moments and then fade. Only they do not fade forever. They remain inactive until circumstances stir them again, and it is the very specific play of all our identities—together with our internal experience of the interaction of our self with others—that gives each of us our specific character.

This is not to say that identity is completely free-floating. After all, when I am in Europe I am a U.S. American, and I am never a Korean or a Mexican. Moreover, others respond to physical characteristics, posture, complexion, dialect, and so on as if we were one kind of person and not another. And if that response is consistent with a social, cultural, or biological heritage, it will often reinforce that affiliation. Traits cluster together in ways that produce certain expectations that when disappointed provoke sharp reactions of surprise or shock. These reactions bring into relief the belief that these traits belong together and provide an occasion either for anger and rejection or for reflection about what to count as identity.[5]

The complexity of identity suggests that the idea that schools should support children's affinity to those most like themselves is a more difficult injunction than it appears, because it involves strategic decisions about who a child is most like. This is not to argue with the basic point of the injunction — that children should care about their identity and that they should be aware of the way it is shaped though culture. It is simply to note that there is nothing automatic about this process. Decisions are made all along the line about what cultural entity a child belongs to and whether it is appropriate for the schools to support an identification with that particular entity. These decisions are never clear-cut but are based on different factors.

When an attribute becomes a formative feature of identity, a number of things happen. The attribute is taken to signal something larger than itself. It becomes a sign for more complex historical, social, and political formations. To take on an identity means to take on those larger formations as well. It is not sufficient, for example, to have a dark skin in order to receive recognition as an African American. One must also be seen as, and see oneself as, a part of a certain historical formation.

WHO CARES ABOUT CULTURAL IDENTITY?

Different people care about cultural identity for different reasons. Mature members of a culture care about an identity precisely because to be a mature member of a culture means to have been shaped by it, to participate in it with ease and to enjoy doing so, to understand that such enjoyment is dependent on other people enjoying it, and to accept a commitment to reproduce that capacity in new members. Those outside of the cultural formation may also care about it, but in a different way. They may enjoy the culture as observers of its practices; they may delight in being in the midst of a diversity of cultural expressions; or they may feel that their own culture is more secure because the principle that enables recognition of the importance of this culture also enables recognition of the importance of their own.

Yet those outside a given cultural formation may also be indifferent or even hostile to another cultural grouping, feeling that its fate is no concern of theirs. From the point of view of this indifference, there is still a minimal liberal principle in play. All people have a right to their own cultural formations as an extension of the right to freedom of association. They would not necessarily have a right to use the resources of public education to reproduce themselves.

THE ARGUMENT AGAINST MULTICULTURAL EDUCATION: A RECONSIDERATION

Critics who are concerned about the social effects of structuring public education around specific identities are uneasy about using schools to heighten children's awareness of the importance of certain attributes—skin color, sex, ethnic background, parental income—that they happen to share with some but not all other citizens. They object to schools' contributing to a heightened sense of differences, differences that are constructed within the context of public political formations, and they are concerned that active recognition of the "child's group," instead of broadening the child's awareness of different forms of the good, narrows it.

Some object that since public schools are supported with resources to which everyone must contribute, it is illegitimate to use these resources to encourage children to think of themselves in narrow and particularistic terms. Others are concerned that if public schools teach children to differentiate themselves from one another on the basis of cultural difference, they will not identify themselves with the nation as a whole and will not develop the wider scope of sympathy that national unity and collective welfare require. The fear is that more assertive forms of cultural expression will lead to a rejection of the common identity and that a child who is educated in a narrow cultural framework will not develop sufficient sympathy toward members of other cultural groups.

There is an additional concern that, were the schools to advance the multicultural platform, there would be an endless splintering of identities. Hence, if today blackness is a category for special treatment, tomorrow it may be Cuban blackness versus Haitian blackness, and so on. Or if today schoolgirls are encouraged to assert their identity as women, tomorrow working-class schoolgirls may be encouraged to reform their identity in opposition to middle-class ones.

In addition to these concerns there is the danger of over-defining the individual child and fixing her identity too early. After all, people are not just one thing. True, they may be *identified as* a this, but they are also *identified as* a that and another that and another. The fear is that if public schools recognize children in terms of a single identity group they will do them an educational disservice because they will ignore other potential identities. (This is perhaps one reason for the sometimes scorned remark made by some teachers that they do not see black children, Asian children, or Hispanic children. They see only children.) The concern is that active recognition fixes a child's identity to a given group on the basis of otherwise relatively inconsequential attributes such as skin color, gender, or parental background, and it rejects the idea that a school should attempt to set a child's destiny simply because the child shares with others a certain attribute.

This is an important criticism. Children do not have a choice about possessing certain attributes, and as the critic rightly understands, attributes alone do not identities make. Whether one is born a girl or a boy, dark-skinned or light, to rich parents or poor is not a matter of choice for the child. Children come to school with a certain color skin, from a certain ethnic or class background, and with certain sexual characteristics. What is a matter of choice is the significance that is granted to this attribute and whether schools and society at large decide to view it as a source of affiliation and a center for identity formation. No one attribute, including the beliefs and practices of one's parents, automatically carries with it an identity, but children can be treated in a way that encourages or discourages them to form their identity around certain features that they share with specific others.

What some critics of multiculturalism fear is that identity recognition forecloses certain options that should be the child's alone to foreclose. In other words, the critic of multiculturalism fears that when the school takes a certain attribute and uses it to advance a certain targeted identity, it is presupposing the child's affiliation and in doing so it is seriously miseducating the child. The fear is that this is miseducative because one of the key goals of education is to develop the child's capacity to eventually choose her own affiliation.

Yet the schools cannot keep all options open, and it is not as if children do not come to school with certain directions, patterns, and identifications already marked.

TWO FORMS OF RECOGNITION

All children deserve respect as persons, and this involves respect for those features of the self that relate them to others, including religion, sex, parental beliefs and practices, and race. This basic respect is a form of collective recognition, for it acknowledges more than just the individual child and his or her intellectual or social potential. It also acknowledges that the child is already identified with certain groups. This kind of recognition is minimal. It requires teachers and others to allow children to express their differences as long as they respect the rights of others to do the same. It does not require that teachers encourage students to express their differences, nor does it require the teacher to do anything to raise a child's awareness of her or his own group identity. Minimal recognition is generally uncontroversial. There are exceptions, however.

Consider, for example, when children wear cultural items that are offensive to children from other groups or when certain symbols or items of clothing may be taken as challenges to legitimate educational authority. If the intent of wearing a certain symbol is to intimidate members of other cultural groups in a context in which it is reasonable to expect that they will be intimidated and thus inhibited from expressing their own cultural forms, then passive acceptance is something different than minimal recognition and is educationally irresponsible.

Minimum recognition is something that should be granted to all students. It is a part of the liberal ideal of respecting each individual and is an important component of teaching children about different conceptions of the good. There are, however, as I will show, cases in which more than minimal recognition is required and in which the school has a responsibility to take an active role in advancing a child's identity and sense of belonging to a certain group.

What a person becomes, how she experiences her connections to others, is related to the categories in terms of which she is seen by others. She is not just an abstract person with abstract rights but stands as a certain kind of self. This certain kind of self is a part of her *identity as*. This *identity as* is dependent on many factors, including both how the self is recognized by others and the categories of recognition that are available in a given society. For example, a first son is accorded public recognition in Japan, but not in the United States. Or, if you are the seventh son of a seventh son born to an Irish family you may find that people have unusual expectations of you.[6]

Minimal recognition involves respecting a person as an individual without necessarily calling attention to any special feature of identity. It also requires showing respect within the constraints that are appropriate for a person who occupies a certain role or who has an identity as a member of a certain kind of group. Hence, for example, in cultures where there are strong markers between men and women, between people of different occupations, or between first sons and every other sibling, minimum recognition entails showing respect within the constraints and forms appropriate to those distinctions.

In liberal societies, minimal recognition in the classroom requires that a teacher understand children's cultural background and the way it influences their responses to certain situations. Here minimal recognition might entail fitting one's teaching into the style of the cultural group with which one is working, dressing as they expect a teacher to dress, and allowing their meanings to be reflected in discipline and classroom management. If the group does not value competition, for instance, the teacher might decide not to use it as a way to encourage achievement.

Minimal recognition often requires a passive stance on the part of the teacher. Children may be allowed to bring in items that are important to their own identity as members of this or that group. And, if a student felt bad because classmates looked down on her because of cultural or racial affiliation, the teacher may become more active in promoting the self-esteem of the child. This could entail encouraging her to bring in cultural items that speak to the accomplishments of the group. Recognition here is still minimal, however. It is provided in order to aid the child's performance or comfort in the classroom, and it may or may not have any importance for the culture itself.

A second kind of recognition, robust recognition, is different. It requires the teacher to take active steps to engage the child in a way that will strengthen her affiliation to a given cultural group. In other words, robust recognition requires the teacher to steer the child toward a certain kind of membership and help her develop an *identity as a person of this kind.* It requires, for example, not just that children be *allowed* to bring cultural symbols into the classroom but that they be *encouraged* to do so (assuming that the group wishes to display their cultural heritage). Robust recognition also involves directly teaching children outside the targeted group to understand and appreciate cultural practices that are specific to the culture of the marginalized student.

For example, questions have been raised about whether ebonics, a form of speech used by many African Americans, should have a role in the instruction of African American children. Although the debate over ebonics is usually about what is required to effectively teach black children — and whether ebonics is a true language — it should also be a debate about the requirement for robust recognition. Given the view that many linguists hold that ebonics is a coherent nonstandard English dialect, the argument from robust recognition would allow that it is a critical component for encouraging group identification. In addition, if the group has been stigmatized in part because of a devaluing of the dialect itself, then additional steps may be needed to inform those outside of the group of the way the dialect works, the distinctions it allows, the grammatical structure it exhibits, the meanings it can convey, and the history of its development. They need not be taught ebonics, but they may need to be taught about ebonics.

It should be added that there is nothing in the example used above that would deny the importance of teaching standard English to African American students. The argument for doing this is obvious from an economic standpoint as well as from a literary and cultural one. Children have a right to all of the linguistic forms available, and anything that prevents them from participating in the activities of the larger society is suspect. To provide robust recognition through ebonics is different, of course, from what we do when we teach a foreign language such as French or Japanese. But there is an important similarity. We do not ask children to choose between French and standard English. We ask them to enter into another way of speaking and thinking.

When the distinction between minimal and robust recognition is applied to different groups, it can help us to sort out some different claims. For example, children of voluntary immigrants certainly have every right to minimum recognition, but their case for robust recognition is usually weak. If people have chosen to leave a country to seek a better life elsewhere, there is often an implicit waiving of their right to have the group identity maintained through public resources.

There are exceptions to this waiver, but for most people claims to cultural resources are most effectively advanced on the basis of individual rights to free association or educational rights to cultural resources in order to serve individual educational needs. It is on this basis, for example, that bilingual education is reasonably justified for many groups. It is necessary as a bridge into American society. Nevertheless, there is a reasonable expectation that public resources will be used to make such children somewhat less like those in their original country and somewhat more like those in their adoptive one. Minimum recognition is certainly due them, although even here, as with groups that may command robust recognition, certain cultural practices that are viewed, say, as sexist or as abusive to children may be legitimately discouraged by the schools.

ON THE QUESTION OF ROBUST RECOGNITION: THE EXAMPLE OF DEAF EDUCATION

There are some who believe that more than minimal recognition is due, especially to endangered cultural groups. They hold that because modern society actually threatens their solidarity, schools have obligations to provide them with robust recognition and to provide the teaching required for the culture to continue. As we have seen, there is something to this claim, and the more potentially new members are dissuaded from participating in a culture, the less appealing the culture is likely to become. This may create a downward spiral: the failure of new members to participate in the group makes the group less attractive for new members to participate in. Moreover, it is probably true that modernity contributes to this condition by providing alluring opportunities outside of the traditional cultural formation. The question is whether these two factors alone are sufficient to oblige the school to extend robust recognition to a group. There is a controversy raging among deaf educators today that can be used to test this claim, and it illustrates that the implications of an educational policy that focuses on individual "need" can differ from those of one that focuses on "cultural integrity."[7]

Deafness has been treated alongside blindness as a disability and, as with other "disabilities," the recent tendency in education has been to mainstream deaf children into regular classrooms. The idea has been to provide these children with what is called "the least restrictive environment." Thus, rather than place these and other children who are perceived to have some kind of learning problem in special settings of their own, they are provided with the extra aid that they need to function in a regular classroom. Hence blind children might be provided with Braille textbooks or with readers, and physically disabled children might have an aide who would help them to walk or go to the bathroom. And deaf children might be assigned someone who would sign for them and would aid them in other ways to access the world of oral English. This includes the use of sign language that mimics English, as opposed to American Sign Language (ASL), which is distinct in terms of word order and other linguistic traits and which is viewed as a product of deaf people themselves.

Those who accept the deficit view of deafness believe that the goal of education should be as high a level of integration with hearing children as is possible and that education for the deaf should enable them to take advantage of the opportunities provided by the larger society to all people. Deaf children are to be taught that, with the exception of the absence of hearing, they are just like other children.

This approach to deaf education is viewed by certain advocates of the deaf as both misguided and extremely harmful. The critic objects that the goal of deaf deficit education — the label they give to the present form of deaf education — is to assure that deaf children can function in a hearing world even though they claim that functioning is destined to be at a very low level for most.

A considerably different understanding of deafness and of language is found in the cultural view of deafness, which the critic of the deficit view advocates. According to this view deafness constitutes a unique culture, and because it is unique it has its own language. Hence, signing that mimics English is an inadequate substitute for the signing that arises as the product of that culture and as such constitutes its own language. Deafness is not, according to this view, a deficit to be overcome, and signing is not just one among many modes of representing English. Deafness is no more a deficit than is Frenchness. It is a way of being and of connecting to others who share the same way. To try to "change people" so that they are better able to communicate with hearing people is likely to cut them off from those with whom they already share an identity and with whom they have the greatest possibility of developing a rich cultural life.

In this argument the objection that was raised earlier — that educating a child into a specific identity presupposes a choice that should be made as a result of education, not prior to it — is answered bluntly. By being born deaf the child is already connected to a system of meaning and meaning making! If the schools fail to recognize this, they are not enhancing the child's ability to choose. Rather they are cutting the child off from the meanings that allow choice to take place.

The educational goal that is attached to the cultural view of deafness includes maintaining solidarity with the deaf community. Thus, for example, the teaching of lip reading is largely frowned on, not just because it is said to be ineffective by these critics but also because it is a signal of cultural ambiguity that creates identity problems for the individual child. Integrative education is rejected in favor of separate schools in which children are taught ASL. Advocates for ASL hold that "it is a language in every sense of the word, relying on visual, rather than auditory, encoding and decoding. ASL has a complex, rule-governed phonology, syntax, and morphology."[8] Thus, according to this view, the proper way to look at deafness is not as a deficit but as a culture, and given its status as a culture, it is believed that there is no way to evaluate it from the outside:

> To evaluate the world of the deaf community, extrapolation from the hearing world is of no use at all. Is it better to be deaf or is it better to be hearing? . . . Of course, the answer makes no sense except in relation to a "cultural frame." To know what it is to be a member of the deaf community is to imagine how you would think, feel, and react if you had grown up deaf, if manual language had been your main means of communication, if your eyes were the portals of your mind, if most of your friends were deaf, if you had learned that there were children who couldn't sign only after you had known dozens who could, if the people you admired were deaf, if you had struggled daily for as long as you can remember with the ignorance and uncommunicativeness of hearing people, if . . . if, in a word, you were deaf.[9]

The advocates of this view are reluctant to allow any project—including surgical implants to aid hearing—that would weaken the deaf child's identification with other members of the deaf culture. Lane writes:

The decision to surgically implant a young deaf child is ethically unsound for a reason yet more fundamental than the several I have given. There is now abundant scientific evidence that, as the deaf community has long contended, it constitutes a linguistic and cultural minority. I expect most Americans would agree that our society should not seek the scientific tools or use them, if available, to change a child biologically so he or she will belong to the majority — even if we believe that this biological engineering might reduce the burdens the child will bear as a member of a minority. Even if we could take the children destined to be members of the African-American, or Hispanic-American, or Native American, or Deaf American communities and convert them with bio-power into white, Caucasian, hearing males — even if we could, we should not. We should likewise refuse cochlear implants for young deaf children even if the device were perfect.[10]

Lane makes the case for separate schools for the deaf on the same grounds: minority cultural status provides a special entitlement.

WHY CULTURAL UNIQUENESS FAILS AS AN ARGUMENT FOR ROBUST RECOGNITION

My concern in this section is not whether there should be separate schools for the deaf. There are technical issues that will need to be addressed by deaf people and those who educate them before this question can be answered definitively. Assuming that these are resolved in a certain way, much of the argument presented above is compelling in terms of the needs of deaf children. Lane goes beyond the needs of individual deaf children, however, and offers an argument for the robust recognition of deaf culture. That is, he seems to think that our educational programs are obliged to preserve deaf culture even if the technology were available to enable all children to hear. In invoking minority status as an argument for cultural entitlement, Lane is supporting his case by implying that it is wrong to interfere with the reproduction of a cultural group by altering a child's orientation even if such interference (1) is inconsistent with the parent's desires, (2) will do no harm to the child and (3) is not objected to by the child.

Consider, however, a slightly different situation than the one described in the quotation. Suppose there was a way to determine whether a fetus would be born deaf and also that there was a pill that the mother could take prior to birth that would allow the child to hear by raising the level of a certain hormone. Assume too that the pill has no undesirable side effects for either the child or the mother. Given these assumptions it would be hard to say that there is something wrong with taking the pill. Yet, if it is not wrong for the mother to take the pill, why is it wrong on the day the child is born to have the child be given a droplet of medicine or a surgically implanted device that would have the same effect? To do so, of course, would be to perform a biological intervention, and it would change the child's cultural destiny. Yet is this so different from the change to a child's cultural destiny effected when a family immigrates to a country where the children will learn to speak a different language? Indeed, if anything, it seems less intrusive because by being enabled to hear, an otherwise deaf child of hearing parents is being brought closer to her family's culture. Immigration, on the other hand, often leads to cultural separation and alienation.

Given the availability of an alternative, I am hard pressed to think of a good reason why a woman should be forbidden to take the medicine. True, as mentioned before, every person who leaves a community makes it harder for those who remain. Over time, if enough people leave, the incentives for maintaining the language and the customs diminish, and given this diminution even fewer people may choose to remain in the community. When this happens it is a cause for much sadness on the part of everyone because the loss of a culture is the loss of a unique mode of human expression. Nevertheless, the prospect of loss is not sufficient to force new people to enter the culture, to prevent older members who wish to leave it to do so, or to constrain the right of parents who are in a position to select a culture for their children.

There is something misleading about the linkage between African, Hispanic, and Native American cultures on one side and deaf culture on the other. One need not reject the idea that deafness constitutes a culture or that there has been a history of deaf oppression that resembles that of other groups — a point that Lane goes a long way to make and makes rather passionately. The problem is that in the case of deaf children with hearing parents — which is the group being addressed — there is often no intergenerational carrier of this oppression.

That by some accident of birth I am born deaf to hearing parents does not mean that the history of oppression by hearing people toward deaf people incurs a special obligation to me. It only means that there is an obligation not to oppress *me* now. Yet it may be as oppressive to force a deaf person, especially were the technology available to allow her to hear, to participate in deaf culture as it would be to require that she have nothing to do with that culture. The fact that there is a deaf culture will not solve this dilemma, and, given a choice between effective hearing technology and education into deaf culture, hearing parents of otherwise deaf children would have strong reason to bring children up within their own hearing culture.

The obligation to people who are presently deaf is not owed because some unrelated deaf person was discriminated against a hundred years ago. It is owed simply because society has an obligation not to discriminate now. If mainstreaming deaf children is discrimination, then that is reason enough to end the practice. This has little to do with an obligation that the larger society has to cultural preservation, however. It has to do with the obligation society has toward individuals who happen to share a certain characteristic. What we owe is owed to the children themselves. It is not owed to their families or to members of a group who share that characteristic.

Indeed, to suggest otherwise in this case is to allow that we use children without good reason for the advancement of a culture's good, not for their own good. (I use the indefinite article rather than the possessive to indicate that the choice in my example is not to support *their* culture, but rather to determine *which* culture will become theirs.) One can accept the idea that deaf people constitute a culture but still question whether this fact *alone,* regardless of the potential for hearing or the wishes of the parents, should direct children who are born unable to hear, but who yet might be enabled to hear, toward that culture. And, one can still raise this question without rejecting the potential value of separate schools under present conditions.

The more general mistake is to believe that any successful argument that establishes an entity as a culture is sufficient to establish conditions for special educational consideration. Yet to take cultural integrity alone as sufficient for robust recognition would require that virtually all cultural groups receive such recognition — even those whose practices mutually exclude the recognition of the other. Cultural integrity is often a necessary condition for robust recognition, but it is never sufficient.

WHAT WE OWE TO ENDANGERED CULTURES

There are reasons that can be used to support the claim that robust recognition is owed to members of a group whose culture is in danger of passing out of existence. Although this claim is valid with some endangered cultures, it is not so with all.

One difficulty is that it is also often difficult to know what it means for a cultural group to "pass out of existence." We can understand, for example, that the Shakers passed out of existence because they simply could no longer reproduce themselves. When it comes, for example, to Polish-American-Jewish culture, however, it would be hard to say whether it is passing out of existence or whether it is being amalgamated into wider streams of Jewish-American culture, say, Eastern European Jewish culture, and whether today most American Jews of Polish origin had any real interest in sustaining it.

There are a lot of reasons why one might want to try to preserve an endangered culture, but only a few of them entail an *obligation* on the part of the public to do so. Certainly, for example, a commitment to diversity is one of these, but diversity alone is not sufficient to tell us which cultures to preserve. An argument for robust cultural recognition as a public obligation needs a stronger basis than preservation of cultural integrity.

There are two ways in which this basis may be strengthened. The more common is as a side effect of aiding individual children who *because of denigration of their culture* are considered at risk. Here the argument is that without robust cultural recognition, the child will suffer certain serious deprivations or the child will be denied certain opportunities that it is generally reasonable to think that all children should have. Here the active engagement that is associated with robust recognition is acceptable, but only to advance the position of the individual child. This differs from minimal recognition. Here denigration of the culture is the cause of the child's being at risk. In minimal recognition the cause is irrelevant. What is important is that cultural recognition will aid the achievement of the child.

The other argument relates to the issue of cultural endangerment, but it is also concerned about the source and the conditions of such endangerment. I believe that if a case is to be made for deaf education along cultural lines, it will be made successfully only in terms of the first of these arguments. Other cultural groups better represent the second.

To say that robust recognition for deaf children is better argued on the ground of individual need or of denied opportunity is not to suggest that culture is irrelevant to the success of these arguments. Indeed, the fact that the conclusion to a successful argument should lead to robust cultural recognition suggests that culture does matter. What is important in these cases, however, is that it matters that it makes a difference to the life of the individual child. As Lane writes:

> How does the deaf child's sense of self develop in a hearing family? He observes that commonly one adult will approach another and move his mouth rapidly for a long time, and the other responds likewise, or perhaps engages abruptly and inexplicably in some activity. If there are hearing children in the home, they will behave in the same way among themselves, and they will perform this seemingly dumb show with adults. "I noticed people watching each other's faces," a deaf educator has written, recalling her childhood, "but I saw only a blur of lipshapes, mouths opening and closing, stretching and puckering into lines and circles. Why were mouths so interesting? Mouths bored me." "Lipshapes" are rarely directed at the deaf child, and when they are, they are indecipherable; his own mouthings go unnoticed. Sometimes the family seems able to presage events: they open the front door just when people are waiting there; they arrive from another part of the house just when the child has hurt himself and cried. These may be some of the first inklings that *something is wrong*. If the child is the object of excessive oral drills, which are painful and frustrating, the concept emerges: *Something is wrong with me.* [11]

What makes the argument so forceful is not any obligation that might be owed directly to deaf culture but rather that without an engagement with deaf culture the child will have a stunted life. She will not be able to enjoy the richness of meaning that deaf culture could otherwise provide. If the author is right and neither existing technology nor the understanding of the hearing community is adequate for meaningful cultural integration, then surely the child should be brought up in a way that will enable her to communicate with people who have a meaning system that she can access and enjoy. If the argument for teaching children who cannot hear through the ways of deaf culture is successful, it will be because there is an equivalence between what nonhearing children need and how they are to think of themselves in terms of language, artistic modes of expression, and a community of affiliation. True, this is a more generalized conception of need than the one commonly employed. A hard-of-hearing child may simply need a hearing aid to enable her to access the prevailing cultural forms. Other children may need eyeglasses. In the present case, what is needed is a way to access and create meaning. The success of this argument will have to do with issues that are addressed to the benefit of the child. Beyond this it is hard to see that anything is owed to deaf culture as such. Yet this is not true in all cases in which claims are made on behalf of cultural groups.

WHAT ARE GROUP RIGHTS AND WHY ARE THEY PROBLEMATIC?

Will Kymlicka notes that group rights consist of three factors. First, the members of the group have certain claims that they can rightfully press against the larger society, and they do so as members of the group. Second, the group has authority to control the behavior of individual members. Third, the larger society can treat individual members in terms of their membership in groups.[12] Those who support liberal democratic education are rightfully suspicious of educational claims based on group benefits and group rights on the grounds that individuals need to be free to associate with each other on their own terms and that notions of group rights would interfere with such association.

Indeed, much of the history of group rights is an overly

restrictive one. It includes occupational classifications handed out and enforced according to religious affiliation, marriage restrictions based on race, and educational opportunities restricted according to family position and limited to males. Hence there are reasons to be concerned about an educational system that is constructed on the basis of group difference, however well intended the argument for it may be.

Nevertheless, I have already presented one case — Yoder — which appears to be an exception to the rules, and I have suggested some reasons why this exception may be justified. True, this decision is a little off-center of our concern because it does not advance the use of public educational funds to support the reproduction of a particular cultural identity. Instead it supports the nonuse of educational funds to *allow* unabated the continuation of cultural identity. It judges cultural reproduction on a par with equal opportunity.

In other words, the court ruled that Amish culture and the solidarity of the Amish community were of sufficient value to overrule normal expectations that schools should advance individual opportunity. Granted, both *Mozert* and *Yoder* were argued within the constitutional guarantee of religious freedom, but the overall argument had to do with the place of the group in the larger society. For the Amish, the group's relative isolation was an important consideration in the decision, whereas in the *Mozert* case, the fact that the group otherwise participated in the activities of the larger society was a consideration against their claim.

These rulings suggest that although there is a good reason for placing a heavy burden of justification on group rights, the appropriateness of lifting some of this burden needs to be determined with attention to social and historical contexts that will differ from group to group. It is with this difference in mind that I want to take a look at the way in which need, group standing, and historical injustice create special categories of educational obligations. These categories differ from most cases of educational entitlement in that they identify certain kinds of people for special treatment. They also differ from each other in terms of their recognition of a group, as opposed to an individual, right.

NEED, STANDING, AND HISTORICAL INJUSTICE AND THE CREATION OF SPECIAL EDUCATIONAL OBLIGATIONS

Need

Within the context of a liberal, individualistic society such as the United States special entitlement arising out of economic need is consistent with the commitment to the ideal of equality of opportunity. It fits with the belief that no one should be held back simply because of the economic position of her parents or because of other artificial roadblocks. Hence the argument that a talented, motivated child should not be held back because her parents cannot afford to provide the kind of education appropriate for a person of her ability is acceptable to many in terms of their general understanding of fairness and merit. This understanding, which forms the basis of programs such as Head Start, is reinforced in many ways and is imbedded, for example, in the folklore of the country as one of the reasons people come to America.

The category of need is not, however, a category of group entitlement and does not usually call for robust recognition. People are placed in the same category for administrative purposes. From the point of view of the administrators of the system they are related only in terms of what they have not—educational resources. Their entitlement is not granted because their need is accompanied by a strong class consciousness that bonds them to others with a similar need. Nor is the entitlement provided because anyone might believe that they should be so bonded. Rather, for these purposes each has his or her own separate history, meanings, projects, interests, and so on. This administrative category is, of course, available for those who do share an identity, racial, class, or otherwise, and the participation of cultural minorities in programs such as Head Start or Upward Bound indicates that people otherwise identified with one another do use them. Nevertheless, in these cases it is not ethnicity, gender, or nationality that forms the basis of the recognition. It is economic position and the chance that without aid certain deep-seated liberal principles of fairness will be violated.

The acknowledgment of need is perfectly consistent with liberal individualism. It focuses attention on the individual child while allowing that certain categories of individuals may require extra aid. There is, however, another step in this progression from individual to group entitlements that, also consistent with liberalism, focuses attention not on individuals as such but rather on individuals as members of certain identity groups. This progression can be seen in the notion of standing.

Standing

Economic position is only one of a number of factors that could limit a child's ability to develop and express her talents and ability. The reduced level of opportunity for women is a clear instance of the way in which cultural factors can reduce opportunities as much as economic ones. Women have been raised in the same families as their brothers but have been systematically placed in positions with less public status and authority. This suggests that economic disadvantage is not the only roadblock to achievement. Cultural bias and reduced educational and economic opportunities reinforce each other to produce a lowered standing. And what may begin as a cultural or an educational difference results in an economic difference that in turn reinforces the ways in which women (and other classifications of people) are treated both culturally and educationally. The problem is not simply one of individual merit denied. It involves the fact that certain attributes, here related to sex, have been elevated to the status of a group identity, and that identity has been assigned a lower standing which in turn affects each individual who shares that identity. It is not exactly need that is denied but something like the stature and status that would otherwise be due had women been truly considered equal to men.

In order to address the issue of standing it is important to focus attention on those who share certain "innate" characteristics, such as sexual attributes and skin color, and who, because of this characteristic, have been assigned a lower status.[13] In this case, robust recognition is a significant factor in addressing lower standing. Unlike need, with respect to which the group classification is addressed, if at all, as an accidental feature of the problem, here the classification is acknowledged to be its primary cause. Yet because the problem of standing is still viewed as a problem of individuals *of a certain type,* this recognition is often indirect, seeking to improve opportunities and role models for this type of *individual.*

Because reduced standing negatively affects not only opportunities that are made available by institutions but also the way in which individuals come to think about themselves, as well as the aspirations they hold, and because standing defines "ordinary" institutional practice, a systematic and extraordinary effort is needed to effect the desired change. Robust recognition does this, but only by providing opportunities for individuals that will enable other members of the groups (as well as those outside of such groups) to see themselves in a different light and to develop higher aspirations and skills. In other words, here robust recognition works to allow individuals to see themselves as members of a group. It does not, however, work to increase the solidarity of the group itself, although this may be an unintended consequence.

Although recognition here still works to address the concerns of individuals, it is different from the need-based approach.

The need-based approach functions to eliminate the one characteristic that is shared by all of those who are selected — poverty. An approach that deals with lowered standing requires students to be addressed in terms of attributes that will persist even after a change in educational and economic status has occurred. Because low standing is reflected both externally — in reduced opportunities — and internally — in rechanneled and lowered motivation — and because these reinforce one another, it is important that they be changed at the same time.

Lowered standing, however, does not call forth a group right but rather a group-*based* entitlement. The latter results when some people have been wrongly denied the treatment that should be afforded to individual, rights-bearing citizens because of a characteristic that they all share and when steps are initiated to correct this problem. The characteristic may be blue eyes, black skin, short stature, or the physical apparatus needed to bear children. The people who have this characteristic may or may not share a lot of other things, and they may or may not care about each other's welfare or think of themselves as sharing an identity. All of this is irrelevant to the claim that they all have.

This entitlement is not a group right because it does not advance the coherence or the status of one group *over* another's — although it may use an existing sense of identification in terms of role models to enhance its effect; nor does it seek to provide recognition to members of one group *over* those of another. It does not *confer* special group status. Rather, it uses group membership to identify and correct past acts of discrimination, acts that have resulted in inadequate educational, economic, and social positioning. It allows special attention be provided to those who share the attributes that bring forth this entitlement. It does not, however, require that they renew their ties to one another on the basis of those attributes.

Historical Injustice

When the issue involves African or Native Americans there is an additional factor to be considered, and this factor establishes race and culture as categories for educational recognition. In these cases, the task is not only to correct inequality of opportunity and, as with white women, to increase standing. It is also to pay a debt that is owed as a result of unprecedented violation of human rights and liberties.

This debt arises not only because of systematic violations of the rights to life and liberty of individuals. It also arises because of historical violations of the cultural foundations through which meaning is constructed. In these cases the recognition of identity involves more than simply the fact that need and identity overlap. It involves an independent component that would remain even if the material well-being and the standing of the group matched those of other individuals.

To see this point, consider the various ways in which individuals from different cultural background might be represented on certain holidays. For example, when Columbus is recognized, what is being remembered is the (European) discovery of America. The fact that Columbus was Italian is incidental. Although Italian Americans may feel a special connection to the event, their identity as Italians is not an essential part of the public recognition. If Columbus had been Austrian or Irish the public meaning would be the same. There are other public symbols — the Statue of Liberty is the most famous — that serve to recognize the pluralistic character of the country as such. In this case what is being recognized is a general ideal rather than any particular manifestation of it.

Martin Luther King Day is different from both of the above. Its importance as a national holiday cannot be separated from the historical experience of a specific group of people. Martin Luther King Day represents the ideal of freedom as embodied in the civil rights movement and the people from all races who worked for that ideal. And through that movement it represents the long-standing struggles of the African American people for freedom and dignity. The very meaning of this symbol is constituted in the people who are recognized through it. It is not, as with the Statue of Liberty, the quest for liberty of all ethnic groups that is being celebrated. It is the struggle for freedom of a particular group with a very specific history that is being celebrated by all. At the same time Martin Luther King Day, as the symbol of hope and liberation of this group, is the most important representation of the possibility of national redemption. The holiday expresses the journey through slavery of black Americans while it holds out hope for the unity of a nation of black and white alike.

Native and African American people have special claims that their struggle, their suffering, and their achievements be recognized.[14] The institution of slavery and the assault against the American Indian not only violated individual lives, they violated essential elements of collective and individual development.[15] These violations and those that followed from them are accountable for many of the problems confronting these communities today.

The forceful rupture of a culture has real consequences for living people, both in terms of truncated expectations and opportunities denied and overlooked, and in terms of a general social attitude of accepting as part of the natural state of affairs lower levels of material well-being. Recognition of these crimes requires that the experience of these people not just be subsumed under that of minority groups in general nor used as an illustration of the success of pluralist policies and liberal ideals. The historical record speaks of an experience that is different in kind and of an initial violation in which pluralism and the right to maintain one's own culture on one's own terms using one's own resources was not even a recognized alternative.

What is now at stake is not just the child's affiliation and identity as an *American* Indian or an African *American* but the nature of that identity in the American context. The story that African and Native Americans are peoples whose lives and histories make up a significant part of the American experience (along with those of other minority groups) is not sufficient and does not reflect the truth of their experience. They are separate chapters in the American story, and they offer compelling and competing narratives to the dominant account. Here robust recognition involves shining the spotlight on these separate chapters, enabling those inside to hear them acknowledged by those outside and enabling those outside to hear them told by those inside.

7. On Robust Recognition and Storytelling

Robust recognition means that a group has a special right to have its story told both to its own children and to other people's children. But what does this mean for the public schools? Is there only one story to be told, and if so, who should be empowered to tell it? Should only those within a group be allowed to tell the story of the group or to write a history of it? And finally, what educational benefit do children from various groups gain when they hear the stories of other people, including those who cannot command robust recognition? In this chapter I address these questions.

TELLING STORIES

Some people feel that only members of their group should have the authority to represent its story to those outside it. Those who assume that authority should reside only within the group may believe from past experience that if left to outsiders, the story of the group will be distorted and misrepresented. The belief may arise from the humiliation of certain groups such as Indians when they have been caricatured as sports team mascots or in political cartoons. Thus, for example, there are often heated disputes where Native Americans are used to represent sports teams, and some people argue against this use not only on the ground that it is demeaning, but also because others do not have a right to represent the story of the American Indian.

I agree with those who find the use of such symbols offensive. My agreement, however, is not based on the view that only the members of a group are in a position to represent their own experience, although there may be cases in which this is true. I agree (1) because the symbol is usually a demeaning caricature, positioned within a field in which most other signifiers are either mascots or fetishes, for example, bears and socks; (2) because of the history of the oppression of Native Americans; and (3) because the symbol isolates and distorts one feature of a group, such as its warriorlike quality, to the neglect of all others.

Something similar can be said about attempts to tell the story of a group. Authenticity and respect require that voices from the group be represented in the story. Indeed, this may be a more accurate way to hear the concerns of underrepresented groups who complain that history is *his story,* meaning the story as told from the white, male, middle-class standpoint. The concern may not be just that others are telling their story but that the insider's voice is not included in the telling. It is best perhaps to take the objection that others are telling our story not as representing a general principle that outsiders can never tell insiders' stories but rather as an objection to specific cases in which the insider's voice has been overwhelmed by the tellings of the outsider. There is, however, a stronger reading that can be given to this objection, and it is this stronger reading that I address below. It is that only the insider should be empowered to tell the story.

One of the reasons that I object to the idea that only the insider should be empowered to tell the story is that it implies the right of some kind of censorship on the part of the group itself. Although the implication does not necessarily call for legal censorship, it certainly calls for moral self-censorship on the part of those from the outside who want to research and write about the group. One manifestation of this is the norm that researchers and storytellers are obliged to clear what they write about the group with its representatives.

Although members of a group certainly have a right to assert such authority as their condition for cooperating in a study, the researcher should choose to accept it only where matters of privacy, confidentiality, accuracy, and good judgment are concerned. Otherwise, the audience has reason to distrust the research, and all such work should carry a warning that "this material may have left out critical information because of the subjects' objections." Researchers and writers have an obligation to their audience to be truthful, and censorship, even by members of the group under study, raises questions about how well this obligation is being met. If a group is given the right to censor material, the researcher should be obliged to state that this right was given, even where it was not exercised. This is because providing the right of censorship to another may exert a subtle pressure that leads to self-censorship. Views or observations that one expects will be rejected or that may jeopardize the relationship with the group are never expressed. Obviously, this does not mean that research is unbounded. Rights of privacy, confidentiality, and human decency, as well as comprehensiveness and accuracy, require good researchers to maintain close contact with members of the group they are studying and often to check their understandings against the understandings of the members. When this is done, however, it is to increase accuracy, not because of a special right that anyone has to "their own story." Of course, researchers who do study a marginalized group often have a special obligation to provide it with information about itself and its environment that can help its members make more informed decisions. Yet this is a matter of decency and should not be confused with a blanket obligation to clear the findings with the group, unless the readers are warned that the study was limited in this way.

Nevertheless, the view that only those from within a group should be authorized to tell the story of the group is not based on ethics alone. Some believe that an accurate representation of the group is possible only from the inside. Hence, some believe, to have the member tell the story is a matter of truth as well as ethics. This is not a new position; it was addressed as far back as the eighteenth century by the German philosopher Johann Gottfried von Herder when he speculated about language: "If, therefore, each language has its particular national character, it seems then that nature lays upon us an obligation only to our native language, since this is perhaps more commensurate with our character than any other and coextensive with our distinctive way of thinking."[1]

The idea of an inner uniqueness that is expressible only in a native language is found in the view that oppressed peoples have a unique center of experience that can neither be understood nor expressed from the outside.[2] Those who hold this position suggest that each term in a given language has its own cultural history, which ties it to other, similarly unique terms in that culture. Cultural meaning, this argument goes, can only be derived from experience within the culture, and therefore a story told by an outsider could only distort it.

The argument is supported by the view that has become prominent since Thomas Kuhn, in *The Structure of Scientific Revolutions,* advanced the notion that even in science there is an inherent incommensurability between paradigms.[3] This view also obtains support in the area of cultural and disciplinary knowledge by those who argue that many of our attempts to understand cultural difference wrongly presuppose an underlying similarity of concepts across different discourses. As Foucault puts it, referring to the supposed unity of discourse, "We must question those ready-made syntheses, those groupings that we normally accept before any examination, those links whose validity is recognized from the outset."[4] Yet both Kuhn and especially Foucault would be highly suspicious of providing ready-made priority to but one story, even one that somehow originated from inside the group. What is more consistent with their view is the position that all narratives, even those that are about other groups, must be told from within some group.

The more extreme view is problematic when it is fully articulated and examined. It not only holds that the story could not be told from outside the group without distortion, but it also implies that the story could not be heard without distortion by anyone who has not had the same experience as members of the marginalized group. Hence, given the extreme view, the reason for telling the story to people outside the group is unclear, and a strong point against this view is that the very telling of the story from the inside assumes that the possibility of understanding it from the outside exists.

Moreover, the extreme view implies that there is but one way within the group to tell the story, or that all stories within the group are consistent with one another and inconsistent with those outside it. This suggests that dialogue within the group is unnecessary and that across groups it is impossible. And it suggests that those within the group are always more able than those outside to tell the story accurately. None of these implications are invariably correct. People within a group differ in terms of their experience, and there is no reason to assume that a preestablished harmony exists within a cultural group across gender, class, or generational lines. Further, human beings across all groups share certain needs and certain experiences—birth and death, bringing children into the world and raising them, finding shelter and food—suggesting enough commonality that the stories issuing from one group should not be completely closed to people who belong to another.

Because different cultural groups in a multicultural society exist within the same political unit, often sharing the same language, they actually connect to each other's experience in many important ways, and the stories they tell must inevitably involve each other. The position expressed (and then modified and softened) by Herder provides an inadequate reason for restricting the authoritative voice to that which speaks from within a cultural group. Given that the stories and histories of one group usually involve the stories and histories of other groups, to tell one is to tell the other but from a different perspective, and it is arbitrary to restrict the telling of the story of one group simply to those who are members of that group. Moreover, there are groups who no longer exist. Yet it would seem arbitrary to assume that no one could ever tell their story. Nevertheless, anyone telling the story of another people has an intellectual, if not a moral, obligation to examine and try to understand the story as it was first understood and perhaps told by those who lived it.

If we are to accept the more moderate interpretation of Kuhn and Foucault, then "inside" and "outside" are not ways to identify different individuals or groups but ways to identify different perspectives. When I tell my story, I write as an insider, but when my story involves you, I write as an outsider, and the same must be said of the way in which you tell your story and the way it involves me. To understand the storytellers in this way may call for more contact and more negotiation, rather than an isolationist insistence on the priority of one or another telling.

In this negotiation, both the "outside" storyteller and the

"inside" one are disadvantaged in different but asymmetrical ways. The outside storyteller has to work hard to see the world from the inside, all the while carrying another story with her — her own and that of her audience. These stories make a difference in the register in which the first is retold. Her retelling of the inside story of another always points to the tacit understandings and frames of those who share her own story and are its intended audience. When the insider tells the story to the outsider he then has the opposite problem. He must be able to read those tacit understandings and frames in order to point his story in their direction.

A better reason that is sometimes given for the view that only those who live the story should be licensed to tell it is one of balance. Part of what oppression entails is the silencing of certain perspectives and the rejection of some centers of experience as invalid. If a story is told only by members of one group, we forget that there are other centers and we are seduced by a view that is partial and one-sided. The view is inauthentic, not because it is necessarily false but because it presents one center as all centers. To be silenced in this way has important psychological and spiritual consequences. People are unable to recognize themselves in stories that are about them and hence come to feel alienated from their own culture in its external presentation.

Yet the right conclusion here is not that *only* those who live the stories should be allowed to tell them, but that those who live the stories must not be silenced and that they must be enabled to tell their own stories. Yet enabling people to tell stories about themselves is not the same as excluding others from telling stories from other centers of experience. In other words, what is needed is an opening up, not a closing down. A softer and more defensible position than the extreme that I have represented is expressed by Paulo Freire, who writes that the oppressed have been silenced and that researchers must learn to listen in new ways if they are to hear and understand their experience.[5]

THE MEANING OF THE INNER AND THE OUTER STORY

The idea of an internal and an external story must be used with caution. The idea is misleading in two respects. First, it can be taken to imply that there is but one way of viewing the group's experience and that the insider's story is the "official" one. The problem here, as mentioned earlier, is that there are many stories from within and that if, in fact, one story became the *official* one it would function as an outsider's story to others—women, parents, gays— who would likely see it as slighting *their* experience. To speak in terms of an inner story should be taken as affirming that there are expressions of collective experience that originate from within and speak from a certain felt sense of authenticity. It is not just a single story. To be the outsider who is then in the position to select the most authentic inner story is, ironically, to be in a position of high and often inappropriate privilege.

Second, to speak of an outsider story should not be taken to imply that such a story floats unattached to any groups or that it itself did not originate as an inner story for some group. The story of immigrants overcoming the resistance of Anglo culture and, through hard work and persistence, fulfilling "the American dream" originated within immigrant culture, and it was never in great favor among, say, the Daughters of the American Revolution, who saw immigrants as inherently lazy and a threat to American virtues. *Internal* and *external* are place markers, and the stories that occupy these places will change, evolve, merge, be reassembled and rewritten.

Nevertheless, there are certain things that can be said about the internal and the external. For example, an internal story is likely to be more oppositional than an external one, and the external story will tend to nest the story about cultural groups within the story about national culture. The external story will also thematize the story of different groups as related to one another through the national story, whereas the internal story will tend to emphasize the uniqueness of the experience of this particular cultural group. And the internal story often will be told in terms of exclusiveness—explaining how "we" are different from others—whereas the external story often will be told in terms of inclusiveness—explaining how, despite our differences, "we" are the same. Yet this difference is not universal, as anyone who has looked at the story of black slaves by apologists for slavery knows.

BEING A PART OF THE INTERNAL STORY

Clearly, everyone is a part of some center (and usually more than one) of experience. Members who share centers of experience are often said to have almost an intuitive understanding of one another. They can finish each other's sentences, read each other's body language, and enter into each other's fears, enjoyments, hopes, and aspirations. They can hear each other's voices and find ways to express to each other authentic feelings, ideas, and concerns.

Yet to acknowledge this is also to amend one of the major arguments for developing cultural pride—that a group has been silenced and that its stories have not been told. There are few, if any, centers of experience that are silenced completely, although when domination is extreme, the voice or voices of those who have lived that experience may be officially filtered through more prominent centers, appearing as Freire powerfully but somewhat inaccurately identifies as "the culture of silence."[6] He is inaccurate because even in his own work, this culture—the voice of the peasant—is always available in everyday conversation. Yet here it takes an outsider such as Freire to thematize the message, to separate the inner from the outer story and to provide it space in a public discourse.

Hence, the problem is not that the "alternative" center of experience is silenced completely. If this were the case there would never be enough historical continuity to establish a voice in the first place. The problem is that the voice is silent (or silenced) within the context of a certain kind of setting, a setting that has possibilities for translating the collective voice into instruments for systematic, collective action and where it might interrupt and alter the taken-for-granted public story.

Telling of the story by "intruding" it into the dominant sphere is an accomplishment in itself. It communicates a sense of agency that, when one serves as the object of someone else's exclusive story, is denied.[7] Yet it is not *just* the telling of the story that is important. It is that the story is thematized in such a way as to reflect the agency that is entailed in its telling.

There are at least two themes that are expressed in this kind of telling. The first is a universal one, a sense that people like me can succeed in activities that are recognized by everyone as important. The universal side of cultural pride unites me with others and allows that people like me can excel in important human endeavors. It is this feature of cultural pride that is thought to be connected to motivation and school achievement. The other side of cultural pride is more particularistic. It involves a sense that as a people we have survived a unique set of obstacles and in doing so have added value to the world. This suggests that in certain cases the development of cultural pride may be a legitimate goal for education even if it is neutral with regard to school achievement.

Although the message is particular, its point is more general, speaking to the situation of oppressed peoples. If the story were only important for those within the inner group to know, there would be little need for the school to relate it. Its essentials would already have been told by parents, grandparents, bartenders, clergy, and other local storytellers. Rather, it is important within the setting of the school because others need to hear it as well. If the story should be heard by students from all groups it is because it enables a fuller understanding of dominant and subordinate cultural forms. The telling of the story may have a role in enhancing group pride not only because the story is being told—

unofficial storytellers do that all the time — but also because the internal story is being told in a setting where it is important for a reconstructed understanding of the external story.

Toni Morrison illustrates this point powerfully in her analysis of literary criticism in the United States and the field's inability to understand how certain silences regarding race influence the construction of literary texts. The incapacity to perceive these silences leads to systematic misunderstandings and an inability to fully account for the failure of certain American novels. Morrison's example centers around a novel by Willa Cather, *Sapphira and the Slave Girl*.

The story is about an invalid plantation mistress who incorrectly suspects that her husband is having an affair with Nancy, a young slave girl. To regain the full attention of her husband she arranges to have her "malleable lecherous nephew" visit and rape the girl. An escape is arranged by the mistress's daughter, who is an abolitionist sympathizer. Many years later, after the reunion of the mistress and her daughter, a reunion (described in a postscript) takes place between the two principal black characters, Nancy and her mother, Till.[8] Morrison describes the problem with the novel. Speaking of Nancy, she writes:

> Unable to please Sapphira, plagued by the jealousy of the dark-skinned slaves, she is also barred from help, instruction or consolation from her own mother, Till. That condition could only prevail in a slave society where the mistress can count on (and an author can believe the reader does not object to) the complicity of a mother in the seduction and rape of her own daughter. Because Till's loyalty to and responsibility for her mistress is so primary, it never occurs and need not occur to Sapphira that Till might be hurt or alarmed by the violence planned for her only child. That assumption is based on another — that slave women are not mothers; they are "natally dead," with no obligations to their offspring or their own parents.[9]

This relationship between mother and daughter jars the contemporary reader, who may not make the same assumptions or who is unaware of the forced distance between mother and child that slavery often required and that Cather assumes her readers take for granted. "Surrounding this dialogue is the silence of four hundred years. It leaps out of the novel's void and out of the void of historical discourse on slave parent-child relationships and pain." [10] Obviously, it is not just the text that is illuminated by reading the story from a slave's point of view, it is the story of America, its view of itself and the African American culture within it. To enable the story to be told from the slave's point of view would be to illuminate part of the story of us all. This point is often missed, even by those who recognize the distinctness of the African American experience.[11]

CONCLUSION

Morrison's conclusions can work for other groups as well, groups that are not necessarily owed the strong recognition that we are obliged to extend to African Americans and Native Americans. The world from the point of view of the homeless, the unemployed, the gay, the dwarf, the sick, and the dying are worlds that check the assumptions of the everyday experience of most of us. For schools to fail to explore these worlds is to provide students with a distorted understanding of the scope of their own experience. Perhaps not all of these stories can be told in any one school, but the telling of some of them is required to extend children's imagination beyond the limits of their community.

The problem for those who want to tell the story from the inside is not that others are telling it from the outside. Stories require comparative points of view, moments of tension, background and oppositional stories against which to work. And understanding requires more than simply hearing a story or sympathizing with the point of view it expresses. It also requires comparison, analysis, and criticism from both within and without. The problem arises when we are overwhelmed by the sheer volume of stories from the dominant centers of experience. The need is not to silence those who tell these stories but to create the conditions for quieted voices to be heard.

8. Citizenship Education and the Multicultural Ideal

Citizenship education is a way to stabilize a normative conception of a nation and its instrument of governing, the state. It does this by developing appropriate interpretations, competencies, and loyalties, that is, those that encourage individuals to think of themselves as *a* people and that justify, enable, protect, and defend their partiality toward one another. Citizenship education requires that an excess of loyalty be developed beyond that provided to the family or the cultural community in order to support largely invisible but pervasive state and national formations.

A goal of citizenship education in a liberal multicultural society is to stabilize a personal, social, and political habitat that is conducive to the maintenance and reproduction of a variety of group and cultural formations and that is supportive of many different conceptions of the good life.[1] This goal brings us back to two issues first raised in chapter 1 that I want to revisit in this chapter. The first is whether citizenship education in a liberal multicultural society can have any value content or whether it must simply relegate any instruction about values or the good life to particular cultural subgroups. The second is whether stability is likely in a liberal multicultural society unless citizenship education develops attachments that extend beyond individual cultural units to the nation itself. And then, if stability does require a national attachment, which I believe it does, what is the character of the national values that a democratic multicultural society needs to promote?

ON THE QUESTION OF THE CONTENT OF CITIZENSHIP EDUCATION IN A MULTICULTURAL SOCIETY

The question of whether citizenship education in a liberal multicultural society can have any national content arises because of a certain view of liberalism itself—that it should avoid promoting one set of values over others and should only teach children *about* the alternative ways of life available to them. The liberal multicultural nation is seen as an empty shell containing many different conceptions of the good but favoring none of them.

Given this vision, it would appear that there is nothing for the schools to promote beyond the idea of individual choice itself and the values of critical thinking. This view is consistent with certain trends in education today, including the prohibition on officially sponsored prayer and the secularization of holidays such as "winter break" that were formerly linked to religious events such as Christmas. These, however, are only some of the more obvious ways in which schools seem to be moving away from any content that appears to promote a national set of values and a national identity.

Consider, for example, the way particularism, a name that I associate with the idea that values are appropriately attached only to individuals or their local communities, appears in two otherwise apparently contradictory trends in modern educational policy. The first, often associated with conservative ideology, attempts to privatize education and assign responsibility for the teaching of values exclusively to the child's parents or the schools they select. The second, associated with the politics of identity and the political left, involves the belief that public schools have wrongly favored some people's identity over others, advancing, for example, the ideal of a heterogeneous two-parent family over alternative single-sex relationships. Although the political impulses behind these two movements differ drastically, each rejects the idea that the school should serve as an instrument for the development of a national identity promoting certain values over others. The first rejects public control of identity formation. The second rejects the promotion of any value content by public schools and requires that they be neutral and not privilege one particular way of life.

It is useful to note, however, that under almost any practical conception of the state there are always restrictions on the ways of life and conceptions of the good that people are allowed to practice. Polygamy, for example, is a practice that is prohibited in all liberal nation-states for reasons that have to do with accountability and the protection of women and children. This and many other prohibitions have to do with the obligation that states in general, liberal or otherwise, have to protect their citizens against harm. Education in a *liberal* state is obliged to devalue certain harmful practices.[2] Education in a liberal state, however, must go further than protection from harm; it must, I believe, advance certain conceptions of the good as essential components of the liberal state itself. In other words, as I argue in this chapter, education in a liberal multicultural state must not be neutral with regard to certain values, namely, those that are critical to the flourishing of a liberal, multicultural society. The problem is to understand how education in a liberal society may be partial and still be liberal.

THE PROBLEM OF STABILITY IN
A MULTICULTURAL SETTING

The issue of stability arises because of the concern that if multicultural education legitimizes multiple centers of allegiance but neglects a common national identity, the multicultural *nation* will not have the ability to support the multicultural *state*. That is, if the multicultural nation is not constituted through a single people but is only the name of a formation that holds within it many different cultural groups, then the emotional and intellectual commitment of the citizens will be insufficient to sustain order, stability, and cooperative endeavors across cultural and interest group boundaries. Some fear that a society that seeks to recognize groups rather than individuals will redirect loyalty away from a common national good to more particularistic cultural goods. The concern is similar to that raised in chapter 4: that multiculturalism encourages people to favor their own kind and encourages parochial group interests, but here it issues not just from a concern for a certain conception of fairness but from a concern for the unity of the nation.

The fear stems from a belief that the multicultural ideal requires too little of citizens because it views the nation only in terms of the groups that constitute it, and it fails thereby to see the nation as a unity that joins and transcends different cultural groups. To critics who hold this view, not only does multiculturalism divide people from one another, reducing their willing contributions to a transcultural good, but it also dissipates the moral energy needed day after day to renew a national identity. Moreover, these critics believe that it serves cultural chauvinism and national apathy. And, because it fails to see the nation as a unity, it is lax about educating for a national loyalty.

If these fears are to be addressed, then citizenship education in a multicultural society must have a specific moral content, and it must require complex conceptual skills and concrete moral commitments. These are skills and commitments that parents and

local cultural groups alone may not have sufficient reason to develop, and their importance provides a powerful case for a public
school system that attends to their development.

LOYALTY IN MULTICULTURAL NATIONS

Nationality is an ideal that transcends cultural difference and enables members of different ethnic groups to recognize each other as
sharing a common identity. Where such an identity is recognized
it allows networks of mutual aid and cooperation to flourish in an
apparently "spontaneous" way. The mechanisms that create and
maintain this "spontaneity" are complex, however, and national
identity can be fragile. Unlike the identity of those who belong to
the "traditional" family, national identity does not develop out of
face-to-face relations. And unlike the identity of those who belong
to the same community, it is not normally reinforced by immediate and present sanctions such as shame and ostracism. Rather,
national identity in a multicultural setting develops from the celebration of certain ideals that are conveyed by formal and informal
education.

The state reinforces one of the conditions of national
identity—the perception that without this identity, many benefits
would not otherwise be available. Specifically, it serves to minimize the harm that anticipation of a free rider causes, and it guards
against the downward spiral of noncooperation that such uncon-
trolled speculation brings with it.[3]

The problem of the free rider arises if I believe that you
are likely to accept the benefits of cooperation without contributing your full share, and as a result I am less willing to contribute
my full share. And similarly, if you start to believe the same of me,
then you will likely be unwilling to contribute your fair share, re-
inforcing my suspicion and my failing contribution. The problem
is especially acute where the actors are strangers to one another or
where they do not belong to the kind of local community where

less formal enforcement, such as shame or ostracism, can be effective. It is even more acute where they belong to different communities each of which demands special acknowledgment and each of which is able to exercise shame or ostracism on its own behalf.

Hence, just as there is a fear that without the multicultural *nation*, the multicultural *state* will not have sufficient support, there is also the concern that without a multicultural state, the multicultural nation will falter. Without the administrative and enforcement apparatus of the state, the legal and moral framework for cooperative activity across primary groups is threatened by the demands of the local cultural group, and the possibility increases that each group will stand to the nation as a free rider. Without the state, this threat inhibits the growth of excess loyalty, and without that loyalty the identification with the nation is unstable.

Since nations are imagined communities, their existence depends on this extra loyalty and the belief that as co-nationals, citizens have special ethical obligations to one another.[4] The development of this belief has been a large part of the domain of public education. It nurtures the (inter)subjective elements, the "will," required to enable the state to develop a framework for cooperative activity and mutual aid. When this subjectivity is fractured, the continuity of the nation is strained.

The object of citizenship education under a multicultural framework is to strengthen the links across and between different units within the nation and to thicken the concept of citizenship itself. As Yael Tamir writes:

> Democratic education in a multicultural state thus seems to demand three layers of education: a unified stratum of civic education (which in fact will be similar in all multicultural societies), a particularistic stratum of communal education, and a shared stratum of cross cultural education which will introduce children to the diversity in their own society.[5]

Tamir does not address the content of this education or whether, at the unified national level, it involves anything more than teaching children the *rules* of social, economic, and political action. The answer to this question depends on whether the liberal multicultural nation can be an ethical community. Such a community requires more than simply an understanding of abstract rules.

IS THE MULTICULTURAL NATION AN ETHICAL COMMUNITY?

A community consists of a group of people who are consciously engaged in a specific way of life and who are mutually concerned to maintain and reproduce the practices associated with it. Members of a community exercise partiality toward one another in those areas that are necessary to maintain and reproduce these practices. This partiality is justified to the members on the ground that it is necessary to maintain the community and its values. This, for example, is the role that ostracism serves in some religious communities. It protects the community's values and ensures their continued enjoyment by present and future members.[6] Partiality can also be justified to those outside the community on the ground that it expresses a general principle about the rights of others to be partial and to support their own communities' values and ways of life even though these will differ from community to community.[7]

The question of whether a liberal multicultural nation is a community has two answers, depending on the point of view from which it is addressed. To the extent that a liberal multicultural nation does not adhere to a single conception of the good but nurtures many different conceptions, it does not fit the conventional definition of a community formed around a certain conception of the good. From the point of view of a person standing within a local community and committed to a certain conception of the good, the multicultural state is not a community. Rather, it establishes the conditions for alternative communities to be formed and reproduced.

If, however, we grant that the multicultural nation is a special form of liberalism[8] and is, with liberalism, committed to the values of equal opportunity, freedom of association, and personal growth, then a different picture emerges. This picture requires us to stand outside of any particular local community and to see the multicultural nation as itself a community that legitimately exercises partiality in favor of its own way of life. It is not just that partiality is exercised when the application of basic principles is constrained by the principle of national membership, as was discussed in chapter 2. It is also exercised in the celebration and support of the conditions that enable these values to flourish, and it allows that in certain cases, preferences be given and incentives provided to subcommunities within it that seek to further such values.

Still, unlike traditional nation-states, the liberal multicultural nation must frequently, although not always, reject the temptation to use state power to enforce particular conceptions of the good, even its own. One important exception to this general rule occurs when there is a compelling national interest. Such an interest is present where a specific conception of the good is intentionally or predictably harmful to those inside or outside of the community[9] or where it would do violence to liberal, multicultural values. There will always be disagreement about whether one or another course of action is harmful or will do violence to the values of the nation. Nevertheless, the idea that we are citizens of the same liberal multicultural nation provides us with special obligations toward one another that are similar to those found in more conventional nation-states. As David Miller puts it:

> The . . . defense of nationality begins with the assumption that membership and attachments in general have ethical signifi-

cance. Because I identify with my family, my college, or my local community, I properly acknowledge obligations to members of these groups that are distinct from the obligations I owe to people generally. Seeing myself as a member, I feel a loyalty to the group and this expresses itself, among other things, in my giving special weight to the interests of fellow-members. So if my time is restricted and two students each ask if they can consult with me, I give priority to the one who belongs to my college. . . . These loyalties, and the obligations that go with them, are seen as mutual. I expect other members to give special weight to my interests in the same way as I give special weight to theirs.[10]

The obligations that people have as members of a national community are different from those that they have in terms of other relationships. Unlike the moral reproach that should be evoked, say, when we refuse to feed our own children or when we fail to lend support to a member of our religious congregation, we are not obliged to respond to the needs of all other citizens in the same direct way.

Although we owe certain obligations to other citizens that are not *owed* to noncitizens, many of these obligations may be met indirectly through state mediation. Whereas failing to do something we are obliged to do — such as giving our own children food — is a moral failing,[11] in many cases it is not a moral failing to neglect to give food to other hungry citizens — although offering such aid is often a morally worthy thing to do.

Our obligations as members of a national community differ from those we have as members of a family community, and it is perhaps because of this difference that people have difficulty understanding that the nation is an ethical community. As citizens our primary obligation is to maintain the institutions, practices, and values that provide the conditions for a useful and productive life for all other citizens, including the conditions that will assure that hunger is eliminated. This is an indirect responsibility, however, that requires us, say, to ensure that the care of the hungry will not be left to chance. Without this concern for the least fortunate among us, citizenship threatens to deteriorate into a set of reciprocal relationships that are sustainable only when their mutual benefits are obvious.

To neglect the nation as a bridge between different cultural groups divorces the state from its communal base and leaves the idea of the nation inchoate and impotent. Nationhood is held together in part by a shared set of beliefs and understandings that allow citizens from different cultural groups to acknowledge shared commitments, and the common school plays a critical role in this process.

THE SKILLS AND UNDERSTANDINGS OF THE MULTICULTURAL CITIZEN

Cultural Respect

There are at least two elements to citizenship education in a multicultural setting. The first involves developing cultural respect and the second, cultural engagement. Multicultural nations need citizenship education in which students learn to respect members of different groups without necessarily understanding their practices or agreeing with what they say or do. If respect does not extend further than understanding, there is constant interference with practices that are considered odd or unusual. Such respect is a basic element of political democracy.

This is an important point to make given the justified emphasis on dialogue among educational theorists.[12] Dialogue is an important element of educational democracy in a multicultural society. It serves to introduce students to the "diversity in their own society."[13] It is an educational good serving to make children aware of the practices of other groups. And, perhaps most important of all, it allows them to glimpse their own practices and norms as a cultural product that could well be otherwise.

The goal of dialogue has limits, however. For example, some groups may feel that their children's sense of identity with their local cultural unit is uncertain and that they are not yet ready to encounter alternative ways of life. Others may feel that their communal coherence requires separation and do not wish to encourage their children to engage in dialogue with people who are not members of their group. The value of respect does not preclude dialogue, and in many cases it serves to promote it. But dialogue must not serve as a precondition for respect. Whether people choose to engage in dialogue or not, they must respect the rights of those who are different from themselves, including the rights of those who reject for themselves the values of pluralism and multiculturalism — including the value of dialogue.

Students may learn respect in different ways and at different levels of understanding. At early levels, teachers may need to create models of respect by enabling students to treat all of their classmates, regardless of their cultural background, with consideration. The pedagogical issues are complex, and teachers need to strike a reasonable balance between requiring that children respect other children and respecting a child whose response to others does not meet a high standard of respect.[14]

This basic level of respect does not require students to understand *why* they must follow certain rules, but the public school needs to enable children at some stage of their education to understand the relationship between respect for cultural difference and the principles of a liberal, democratic society. They will also need to learn about the political and intellectual events out of which the idea of such a society developed.

Cultural Engagement

If all that one understands is the general principle that citizens must respect more than they can understand and more than they agree with, there are limited possibilities for cultural interaction. Respect is a necessary but not a sufficient condition for education in a multicultural setting. It may allow a person to grow within a culture, but it provides limited possibilities for cultural interaction. It requires no special provisions for interaction across cultural groups[15] and allows a radical separation between the cultural and the public. Although multiculturalism must allow for the possibility that some will choose cultural isolation, isolation is not a stance that it hopes to encourage. Moreover, the multicultural vision requires more than simply the general understandings that motivate the attitude of passive respect described above. It requires skills of active engagement that both draw insight from cultural variations and allow cultural differences to persist.

COGNITIVE SKILLS

Distinction Between Cultural Competence and Cultural Understanding

Consider, for example, the distinction between cultural competence and cultural understanding and the different roles that they play in educating students in a multicultural society.[16] The standard of competence is a native's ability to navigate the culture — to know what to expect in response to certain behavior and gestures, such as eye contact or smiling, and how to respond appropriately to them. The standard of understanding is a scholar's reconstruction of the meaning of cultural events, including a native's behavior.

Cultural Competence

Cultural competence involves the ability to recognize and participate in a way of life and to guide our own development by its conceptions of morality, performance, and excellence. The more competent we are the more smoothly we interact through gestures, expressions, and everyday linguistic utterances, and the smoother these interactions, the more open we are to learning through the cultural forms that they represent. Young children learn these forms through the routines that are practiced and reinforced by their elders, by engaging in cultural activities, and by participating in the critical life events and ceremonies of members of the cultural community. It is the standpoint of a fully acculturated adult — one who has learned the norms and practices from childhood — that constitutes the ideal of competence.

The ideal standard of competence, therefore, is the ability to learn through the developmental frameworks of the other culture as a child might learn — unmediated by previous cultural understandings. To accomplish this ideal more than once requires that we achieve a level of second-culture understanding at which translation back to the practices of the first culture is no longer required and at which learning moves forward through the concepts and apparatus available only through the second culture.

The ideal here is growth and development that are unmediated through the concepts of a first culture. It is not an ideal that many can achieve a second time, but it is important for students in a multicultural society to understand the way in which cultural familiarity empowers people and to experience some of their own cultural practices as if they were unfamiliar and strange. Although many students will not reach the level of competence that will enable them to navigate another culture with self-confident assurance, they can develop an appreciation for the effort and accomplishment that cultural practices require. This appreciation is the minimum that students should be expected to obtain from courses in foreign languages and literature and from engagement with cultures other than their own.

Cultural Understanding

Whereas the goal of cultural competence is to enter a different way of life, the goal of cultural understanding is to make the strange familiar — to bring that different way of life home. We *understand* another way of life from the point of view of something that is our own. When we want to understand a practice that is unfamiliar or strange, we try to relate it to something with which we are familiar and that we understand. Cultural understanding involves the same process, whether the culture is near or far in time or space. We seek connections that enable us to read signs and activity in terms that are familiar.

A person may have native competence without much understanding, as is the case with many intuitive people who know how to read and appropriately respond to the behavior of others but cannot say what the behavior means or why it means what it does. Similarly, a person may have a great deal of understanding without having any practiced competence. Historians who have studied the customs and practices of an ancient and extinct people in significant detail have acquired much understanding but no competence.

The Place of Cultural Understanding and Cultural Competence in Multicultural Education: Self-Knowledge

A person who is completely competent can navigate the culture intuitively, participate in its music, enjoy its stories, and carry on many conversations. A person who is fully competent can participate in the culture from the inside. Even this level of participation, however, is distinguishable from understanding the culture. When we understand another culture, we understand its core set of beliefs about self and other and we are able to translate these into particular patterns of behavior.

It takes an awareness of another culture to have a conception of one's own behavior as a cultural expression—this is the beginning of self-understanding. To develop this understanding requires that students develop an openness to the practices of the other culture without exclusively interpreting them through their own immediate aims, even though any fruitful dialogue will eventually involve bringing those aims back into focus. Nevertheless, their own aims are often the reason for the dialogue to take place, and their reassessment may well provide a reason for altering its nature. Here in the momentary decentering of their own culture is the core of cultural understanding. It is this act of decentering and coming to terms with otherness that is one of the major tasks for the education of a democratic public in a multicultural society.

Both cultural competence and cultural understanding are important elements of multicultural education for all groups. Students from the dominant group, however, because their behavior is taken as the norm, find that understanding is often more difficult and, therefore, needs systematic development. One often hopes that such understanding is accompanied by certain positive attitudes, but—and here the advocates of a minimalist view of democracy have a point—no education can fully prescribe how one should feel about what one has come to understand. Citizenship education can at least further attitudes of patience and openness toward the other by advancing the reflective insight that contrasting groups are joined in the simple fact that their different norms and behaviors are historically and culturally constructed.

Ultimately, knowledge of the other culture enables the student to see her own position as contingent and subject to reflexive development and change. To be educated for citizenship in a multicultural way means to understand the nature of this contingency and the possibilities for development and change that it provides. Hence, regardless of one's cultural foundation, there is something that all people who are educated in this way have in common — the recognition of a constructed contingent self whose understanding depends on an acknowledgment of otherness. Here we move beyond the decultured self and acknowledge a self that is always implicated in culture.

Groups that have claims to robust recognition also have a special claim to have their experiences serve as objects of cultural understanding for children of the dominant groups. Hence, for example, in the case of the ebonics dialect, mentioned earlier, it would be reasonable for white students to be expected to learn about its history, structure, and function within the African American community, just as they need to learn about African American contributions in other areas of American life.

MORAL UNDERSTANDING, DISCIPLINE, AND PREFERRED IDENTITY

Many political theorists and philosophers believe that justice in a liberal multicultural society provides only procedural moral requirements and that any substantive morality will come from the various cultural, religious, or ideological traditions that are represented in the society at large. If this belief is correct then citizenship education has but a minimal role to play in a multicultural society. Children will develop their ideas about values at home or within their cultural communities, while at school they will learn the basic social rules and the procedural constraints for expressing opinions and settling disputes.

That this is not completely adequate as a view of citizenship education can be seen by many of the cultural prohibitions, for example, polygamy, that are imposed by a liberal state as a result of the need to protect its citizens from injury or neglect. Even allowing for some obvious exceptions, this view wrongly associates the development of a specific conception of the good with cultural formations alone and fails to see how cultural doctrines are altered in substantial ways when introduced into the setting of a liberal multicultural society.

In order to understand the extent to which specific cultural doctrines are changed as a result of being placed in a liberal context, consider John Rawls's argument for liberal tolerance. Rawls argues for a version of liberal tolerance—one that disallows us from repressing views with which we disagree[17]—on the ground that tolerance is part of the overlapping consensus shared by those who hold different conceptions of the good. The consensus is one that endorses the conception of justice as fairness that Rawls elaborated in his earlier work, A Theory of Justice.[18] This overlapping consensus allows for a variety of different conceptions of the good to coexist without any one of them seeking to use state power to force its views on others.

The consensus does not arise, according to Rawls, because different comprehensive doctrines all contain a tolerance clause. Rather, it arises because reasonable people in a liberal society, committed to one or another comprehensive doctrine, will recognize the limitations of social institutions in selecting from "the full range of moral and political values that must be realized"[19] and because they will understand that no single institution or doctrine will be able to embrace them all. For this reason, according to Rawls, people in a liberal society are willing to support certain forms of tolerance and considerable levels of public neutrality when it comes to advancing particular conceptions of the good.

Yet the implication of Rawls's argument should not be that liberalism adds nothing to belief and serves only to enable people with different beliefs to coexist in the same society. Rather, it should be that when a comprehensive doctrine, one that contains a specific and detailed conception of the good, enters a liberal society, there is a profound educational change in the way believers relate to that doctrine and that the deliberate attempt to bring about this change is a major concern of citizenship education in a liberal society. Or, to put it differently, the reasonable people on whom the implementation of Rawls's notion of tolerance depends do not just spring up by accident. They are the product of specific educational work.

In a liberal society those who hold a comprehensive belief need to do so from two separate vantage points. They need to hold it from the vantage point of believers in the truth of that specific doctrine and to accept its teachings for themselves. Presumably this is the learning that they derive from their cultural group. They also must learn, however, to hold it from the general standpoint of *any* person who believes in *any* specific doctrine — not just this one — in a society where other people hold other doctrines. From this standpoint the social conditions and protections must be available to enable people to hold different and competing doctrines, and these conditions include the willingness of those who hold specific doctrines to support the conditions that enable others to hold opposite ones.

This, incidentally, is the truth in the quip that a liberal is a person who cannot take his own side in an argument. Liberals cannot take their own side only in the sense that there is also concern for the conditions that enable the opposing view to be expressed. Moreover, we are not all liberals in all things. There certainly may be times when I feel so committed to my own version of the truth that I find it difficult to hear other versions and am uncomfortable in allowing the other a voice. And, there are times when others are similarly unhappy with hearing my voice. In these cases liberalism provides a counter voice, one that endorses neither one side nor the other but rather delivers a message about maintaining multiple values and alternative viewpoints. And what allows me to remain a liberal is a concern for those general institutional structures that allow different voices to be heard on many issues.

From a strictly political standpoint this message looks like a procedural matter only, one having to do with the right of others to express their views. From an educational standpoint, however, to encourage multiple voices and beliefs involves a highly complex set of understandings that includes knowledge about people and the various ways in which they hold beliefs. It also includes knowledge about what those who hold certain doctrines can count on from the society at large and what society at large should be able to count on from them. It requires, among other things, an understanding that others adhere as strongly as I do to very different beliefs and that they believe strongly that I should hold these beliefs as well.

In developing this understanding it is helpful to have a sense of a possible future self—an "I" who no longer holds the beliefs I presently hold but rather holds their opposite with equally firm conviction and even better reasons. Because one cannot count on this conception of reasonableness to be a part of any one comprehensive doctrine, its achievement requires a special educational effort on the part of the larger society as a whole.

PREFERRED IDENTITY AND THE HYPHENATED AMERICAN

When people speak of the hyphenated American it is these understandings that should constitute the "American" side of the hyphen and that should constitute the preferred identity that citizenship education in a multicultural nation should undertake to achieve. Taking on the hyphen requires students to understand that the values that sustain multicultural societies are transcultural, liberal values and that they are rooted in historical developments that have occurred in many traditions and that are themselves cause for celebration. Because these values are subtle and easily misconstrued, careful attention is required for their development and continuation. Just how the American side of the equation is interpreted in a multicultural society is an extremely important matter, and one must guard against a reading that would limit public expression to the "American" side of the equation while relegating the rest to the private or the cultural.

SKILLS OF PUBLIC DISCOURSE

The problem, as Bruce Ackerman puts it, is one of "how people who disagree about the moral truth might nonetheless reasonably solve their ongoing problem of living together." [20] Ackerman suggests that the proper solution to the problem of moral disagreement that arises from cultural or other conflicts is to restrain public conversation, "simply say *nothing at all* about this disagreement and put the moral ideals that divide us off the conversational agenda of the liberal state." [21] We can, he believes, continue to talk to one another about these deep disagreements in the context of our private conversations, but we must agree that our public discourse will be more modest and use the public conversation "to identify normative premises all political participants find reasonable (or, at least not unreasonable)." [22]

I believe that Ackerman's view is too restrictive and that it makes an unreasonably sharp divide between allowable public discourse and more permissive private discourse. Moreover, it is hard to say whether his suggestion would provide any real solution to the heated debates of the day. For example, pro-choice and antiabortion groups are not deeply divided on the basic values involved in the abortion question. Each believes that murder is wrong. Rather, they are divided on questions of definition such as whether interfering with the development of the fetus is murder. If we limit the public debate to simply the principles on which there is agreement, then we have allowed nothing to be resolved and have actually curtailed the debate itself.

Curtailing public conversation in this way provides few spaces for people to talk across their moral and ideological differences and allows few opportunities for people to grow through their encounter with cultural difference. For a society that houses many cultural groups, it is an implicit commitment to an assimilationist view of public education. The reality, however, is that we no longer live in a society in which assimilation to an established model of discourse is meaningful in the context of highly conflicted issues such as abortion.

Given the impracticality of Ackerman's suggestion, the educational issue of how to teach students to talk together about their deepest cultural differences is even more critical. To know how to talk together does not, of course, guarantee that such discussions will be held, but it would increase the likelihood that some would want to hold them.

One friendly critic of Ackerman, Kenneth Strike, provides a more appealing account of public discourse and morality.[23] Strike also subscribes to the view that public language must be shaved of any thick moral point of view, but he agrees with those who criticize Ackerman for "preventing people from actually debating their disagreements."[24] He believes that debate can be accomplished by developing a shared civic language that, as he puts it, is "weakly rational," which means that it generally accepts "a diversity of moral languages"—religious and otherwise—and that "it asserts no claim of general superiority to these various moral language" and is able to be spoken by those who speak different moral languages.[25]

This civic language enables durable disagreements to persist without relegating some citizens "to second class status." Strike describes this language as a kind of "moral pidgin that can be spoken by people who deeply disagree about morally significant affairs, but who can find ways to speak with one another about civic matters narrowly construed."[26] The test of a public language is that it restrains justifications to arguments "that can be formulated in a shared civic language."[27] Generally, Strike believes that "people should sometimes forebear from asserting arguments in public that are more likely to divide than persuade."[28] He expresses concern, however, should this form of constraint go so far as to inhibit people from acting on their basic convictions, and he therefore seeks a form of civic morality that, although thin, would not discourage the development of more robust forms of local moralities.

Pluralism is essential to his total view of social life even though certain restraints are placed on its expression in the public realm. And this, he proposes, is especially the case for public officials, who have a responsibility to promote tolerance in civic life. Tolerance requires that "reasons must be constructable in diverse local moral languages in support of tolerance."[29] For Strike, civic morality arises only in those areas where local moralities overlap and form a consensus, and it requires that the principles can command wide agreement among people with radically different visions of the good life. Yet he also holds that civic language would form a dialectical relationship with various local moral languages where, as it seeks legitimacy, it would evolve in interaction with them. In this process, the civic language both takes the form of "a distinctive moral tradition in its own right" and invites a continuing opportunity to challenge and reconstruct the existing overlapping consensus.[30]

Strike's proposal meets some of the concerns addressed earlier to Ackerman. He does not place the strong restrictions on debate within the public sphere that Ackerman does, and the restriction he does place on the speech of some officials in the public sphere seems reasonable. Judges and public school teachers, for example, are provided a publicly supported platform that others do not enjoy and that is easy to abuse. They should be careful to avoid using that platform to advance strictly or discriminatory private agendas.

The lines between private and public speech are often difficult to draw, however, and there is often not a large separation between moral language and other forms of language, such as bureaucratic or technical language. Often the most effective, although not necessarily the most defensible, form of moral persuasion arrives bound together with seemingly technical discourse about means. And much of moral counterdiscourse involves showing how moral claims are imbedded in seemingly technical proposals where possible choices are hidden in the language of technical determinism.[31] This observation is especially important for teachers in a liberal society. For although they may be required to maintain discretion in advocating their own moral ideal, especially with young children, it is important to sensitize youngsters to the various ways in which moral claims may be packaged.

A form of instruction that is appropriate to a liberal, multicultural society teaches students to be aware of the different ways in which their own voice may be heard, the different understandings that different audiences may bring with them as they listen to their voice, and the different interpretations that may result from the experiences of different listeners. This kind of teaching allows culturally inspired insights to be extended while accommodating the cultural understandings of others. The way to teach students to engage in public discourse is not to require them to mute their own unique cultural voice but to teach them how to have that voice heard by others who may not agree with it.

AN UNDERSTANDING OF THE HISTORICAL BASES AND COMMUNAL UNDERPINNINGS OF THE LIBERAL MULTICULTURAL IDEAL

The political superstructure of liberalism is often confused with its moral foundation. It is this confusion that allows some critics and some defenders of liberalism alike to wrongly suppose that traditional communities have a thicker and ultimately more satisfying moral fabric. This mistake then leads to the view that liberalism can provide only a superficial moral education and that local communities and religious groups are the better arena for moral development to take place.[32] Of course, this view is viable only so long as one chooses to focus on the differences between liberalism and some particular community. As soon as one notices the vast array of differences in moral doctrine that exists between particular communities, and even when one looks at them from the point of view of one of those communities, liberalism looks no worse than most of the others and better than many. When one goes beyond the political superstructure of liberalism, the moral foundation provides ample material for moral education.

The political superstructure holds to the view that political institutions must respect differences and allow many different versions of the good to be expressed within the bounds of civility and public order. Yet the reason for advocating such respect arises not just out of the need for political compromise but out of an evolving understanding of the relationship between the communal and the individual good. Consider the history of the liberal concept of tolerance as an example of this relationship and of the way in which liberal values are historically rooted in a recognition of community and its importance.[33]

Tolerance was advanced by Locke first as a statement of the kinds of dispositions that a group of believers require if they are to form a true community. Belief should not be coerced because religious community requires a level of voluntary commitment. The fact that Locke's *A Letter Concerning Tolerance* was addressed to the believers themselves is an implicit indication of the importance he gave to the idea of community and the need to maintain it.

It is likely that neither Locke nor Mill, who advanced his ideas on tolerance as a prerequisite to both truth and individual growth, felt a great need to talk about the responsibility that the individual owes to the community largely because religious authority still played such a heavy role in assigning duties and responsibilities. The greater problem was to limit such authority in terms of its ability to command belief.

Dewey took the idea a step further, made the community primary, and rooted liberal democracy and education in its requirements for reproduction. Public morality is to be evaluated by the avenues it established between different communities of interest. It must therefore both protect local cultures and provide opportunities for contact between people of different cultural orientations and points of view. Public morality is more than just a broker between different private moralities. Its foundation is a commitment to individual growth within communities and to the open character of different local communities. It asks in return that any local community that makes a claim as a moral enterprise respect this foundation by providing its members with a conditional understanding of the character of its specific communal values. It must enable them to entertain the standpoint of any person who holds an unswerving commitment to any doctrine of belief. When this request is granted, then public morality both conditions respect for local communities and establishes the conditions for respect across local communities.

COMMITMENT TO A PUBLIC DISCOURSE

One of the problems with proposals that view the public morality as simply the point where various private or local moralities intersect is that they increase the likelihood that the deeper roots of the public morality will be neglected. And they also assure that the form of principled and disciplined behavior that public morality requires will be interpreted in terms of narrow pragmatic expediency.

It is true that liberal morality does not have positions on all matters of human concern. Whether there is a god, whether life exists after death, or whether there is, was, or will be a Messiah and who that Messiah is, was, or will be are all matters about which the public morality is silent. Silence on these matters does not mean indifference to the way discussions about them are carried out or to the climate in which those who do hold strong convictions are enabled to express them.

Sharing a national identity with people who are culturally different involves a mutual search for the terms under which we can live together and flourish both within and across our different communities. Citizenship education in a liberal, multicultural society involves developing a commitment to this mutual search and the skills needed to carry it out. The goal is to identify, preserve, and invent the communal conditions that are required for the growth and development of all citizens, including those whose backgrounds and cultural commitments will continue to differ from our own.

9. Conclusion: Common Schools and the Public Formation

Multicultural nations such as the United States need to recognize the possibility of cultural evolution and realignment and, if they are to reproduce themselves, they must build this recognition into the self-image and definition that is communicated to students in the common school. Since the teaching involved in this reproduction entails a conception not only of present realities but also of future possibilities, however, the standpoint from which content is to be selected is a contested issue.

We know that the future composition of the nation will be different from that of the past or the present, and we also know that many of the understandings and values that are today taken for granted will someday be different than they are now. We do not know, however, which ones will change and which ones will remain the same. Given this uncertainty, one of the most puzzling educational issues is how the character of the United States can be represented to its developing citizens.

The question cannot be addressed exclusively in terms of the object to be represented, as if there were something that was being represented but no agent doing the representing. Representation is done by people, and people represent from specific standpoints. The question of how to represent the nation — how to describe its history, aspirations, and ideals to future citizens — is also a question about whose standpoint will be acceptable and under what authorization.

The issue is further complicated because the uncertainty that marks the symbols of representation also marks the agents and their standpoint. There is no single agent, no class, race, ethnic group, or sex whose representation should be privileged in a society that sees itself as democratic and multicultural. There may, of course, be groups whose experiences have been underrepresented and who have a rightful claim to have their voices heard and their experiences told. This, however, is different from privileging their experience over others'. It is more like making space for it in a crowded room.

To speak in terms of certain groups being "underrepresented" and as having "a rightful claim" to have their voices heard provides a way to begin to address this issue. For to speak in these terms is to presuppose certain norms of discourse and also to assume the existence of a certain public that understands these norms. These norms and the discourse *about* them are a part of what is meant by the idea of a public, and the norms and the ways in which we discourse *through* them are significant components of the way democracy in multicultural nations is expressed. Norms such as inclusiveness, nondomination, open inquiry, cultural freedom, and autonomy constitute the standpoint from which issues of nationhood are addressed, and they are what is appealed to when national concerns are discussed.

THE PUBLIC AND COMMON KNOWLEDGE

Two components are involved in the education of a public. The first is an identification with the national experience, and the second is an active engagement with the issues involved in the material and moral climate of national life.

It is sometimes mistakenly assumed that a common store of knowledge about historical events, social issues, scientific facts, and technical skills is essential for the establishment of a national identity. This assumption frequently is the reason people are concerned when they learn that a significant number of schoolchildren do not know some fact that most adults take for granted. For example, a few years ago the *New York Times* and other newspapers reported with concern the percentage of high school students who could not correctly answer the question "When did Columbus set foot in the new world?" The reason for this concern is that people see such failure as a sign that national unity may be endangered. Given this concern, a number of people believe that the first step in creating a public is to provide students with the same factual knowledge and information.[1]

The belief that a storehouse of common knowledge is necessary to develop a public is wrong. We can look up the things that we do not know and we can forget those that we do know. The ability to maintain a particular piece of factual knowledge, no matter how significant for our national history, is of no great consequence for determining who we are as individuals. If I forget the date of the Battle of Gettysburg, I am still American.

Granted, it is meaningful to speak of gaps in our knowledge, and what counts as a gap for an American will be somewhat different than what counts as a gap for a French person. Yet we all have gaps, and we are no less American for this, and we are no more so when we fill some of them.[2] Given an idealized map of what every American "should" know drawn by some ideal super American citizen, we will all have gaps, and they will differ from one person to the next.

Jefferson's idea that a democratic public is a knowledgeable public does not require that people hold the same items and the same associations in their heads. A Japanese scholar of American studies may, in a sense, actually know more about some of the key events in American society than many citizens of this country. That the former is not a member of the American public, and the latter are, does not result from what they know but is a result of the different standpoints from which they hold their knowledge. In one case it is held in order to better understand and perhaps predict the behavior of the American nation. In the other it is held in order to contribute to making better national decisions. Insofar as schooling has a public-forming role its goals are to engage students, to teach them to attend to the wider effects of their individual and collective behavior, to teach them to care about those effects, to share this concern with others, to develop the skills and knowledge required to address this and similar concerns intelligently, and to do so in ways that are open to the concerns of others.

To *be* an American, that is, to submit to the nation's laws, is different than to *identify* oneself as an American and to participate in the public will formations that determine the direction of national action and inaction. This identification is active and requires an engagement with interpretations of events that comprise the American story. That there is an "American story" means not that there is one official understanding of the American experience but, rather, that those who are telling their versions of the story are doing so in order to contribute to better decision making on the part of the American nation and that they understand that they are part of those decisions. The concept is really "Americans' stories."

This requires us to recognize that the way in which "factual knowledge" is presented to students has much to do with how they come to conceive of their relationship to the nation. If teachers simply treat facts as items on a list without examining their meaning for different people — without any sense that some items could be different than they are — students will likely come to view themselves as passive agents of a national program, and they will wrongly come to believe that knowledge about the nation and its history is fully interpreted and understood. This belief is inconsistent with the self-conscious evolutionary quality of a multicultural nation and with the idea that with each new group new layers of interpretation and understanding are revealed.

THE FORMATION OF A DEMOCRATIC PUBLIC

An induction into a public in a consciously multicultural nation involves an active engagement with the materials and symbols of society. This requires that schools acknowledge the importance of local symbols as well as national ones. In some instances this involves using the classroom to inform children about the cultural and religious differences in their own community and exposing them to some of the aesthetic and artistic differences that exist. To learn about the nation means to learn about the different groups that comprise it and to experience these differences within their own local context. As they become members of a public, children learn to recognize these differences, to address them in ways that are sensitive to the styles and meanings of different groups, and to encourage others to participate in the process of national self-formation.

This means, among other things, that students must learn about the various meanings that people from different backgrounds might give to different events. They need to address these differences in ways that promote continuing discussion around these and other matters. And they need to do so in ways that enable both cultural and national identities to evolve intelligently in response to and in anticipation of a changing social and natural environment. The idea of such engagement is always to develop the ability of students to understand both their similarities and their differences with others and to provide opportunities to understand how these must sometimes be engaged in a discussion of common concerns.

A democratic public is constantly in a process of self-formation, and this means that it cannot count on knowledge of any single fact to be forever important for everyone to know. The ability to identify significant people or events is important because it is one sign that youngsters are actively and thoughtfully engaged in the cultural experience of the national community and are developing the skills required to participate in guiding its future conduct. If youngsters lose interest in the ongoing construction of their nation's history, both as events and as reconstructed texts, their own sense of efficacy is undermined and with it their capacity to participate in public-forming projects.

HAVING A COMMON IDENTITY

To draw on the same sources as others in developing a narrative is a part of what is meant by a common identity. You and I can communicate with one another easily when we share certain conceptual and normative frameworks that are taken for granted in our narratives about ourselves and in our everyday discourse. To hold a common identity self-consciously means that we are aware that we share these frameworks and that we employ them in our own day-to-day interactions.

At one stage, our awareness is similar to that which occurs when something occupies the periphery of our attention—like the steering wheel of a car when everything is going well and we are attending to the traffic in front of us. At other stages, the framework itself comes to our attention, for instance, when we encounter someone who does not reference the same normative or conceptual categories but who has other ways of making sense out of much of experience. Given this contrasting narrative mode we become more attentive to those features in our own framework that usually enable communication to occur but that appear to have broken down here.

At still another stage the common identity becomes an object for deliberation. We discuss what we believe should count as critical elements of our common identity—and whether any critical elements should be identified at all. In these cases we often call on our national identity as an assumed but unspecified unity that allows each of the participants to continue the quest. The appeal to nationhood and to our status as co-nationals reaches for an elusive yet effective structure that enables cooperative activities and communication to continue as we attend to the specific content of the framework. It is at this stage that schoolchildren need to become acquainted with the ways in which people from many different backgrounds and in the service of many different needs appeal to the nation as a framework for meaning and renewal.

From Lincoln honoring those who have sacrificed for national unity in his Gettysburg Address, to Malcolm X and Noam Chomsky reminding us of national failings, to Martin Luther King Jr. and Jesse Jackson holding out national promise and hope, children need to see the different meanings nationhood holds for different groups of people. They also need to understand how, despite differences, the idea of the nation provides a framework for a continuing discourse about meaning and value. Ultimately the signifiers of this identity are less important than are the principles of fairness and justice by which we evaluate the past and anticipate the future.

For example, the argument about whether Jefferson was a statesman or a hypocrite because of his ownership and treatment of slaves is not ultimately about Jefferson as a person but about whether, as a signifier of a national identity, he is an appropriate embodiment of defensible principles of fairness and justice. And the question whether he is representative of the national experience is a question about whether the national experience has been a sufficient embodiment of the principles of fairness and justice. As children come to enter a public they need to be able to separate the signifiers from their objects and to identify national successes and failures in terms of the principles that were advanced or violated.

Children also need to understand that identity is confined neither to national boundaries nor to the groups within them. What was said above about the way a nation holds out promise for unifying meaning could also be said of culture or of humankind, with the exception that nation-states also entail formal and enforceable instruments for collective action. Nevertheless, many features of our identity are shared across national boundaries and across distinct cultural groups.

Although webs of meaning become thinner as we move across distinct and nameable cultural boundaries, and although webs of mutual aid also thin out as we move across established and recognized national borders, they do not disappear. Every citizen of a multicultural state carries an identity that is larger than that of this single nation. When people become members of a public they need to attend to the extended identities of their fellow citizens.

NATIONAL IDENTITY AND THE PUBLIC SCHOOL
The identity of multicultural nations such as the United States is defined in part through their role in maintaining existing avenues of association and in developing those through which new individual and cultural alignments can emerge. Maintaining this identity requires citizens who are willing to deliberate about the way webs of meaning and mutual aid are constructed and who are able to evaluate present conditions against future possibilities.

This requires that schools provide opportunities for children to experience the values found in other cultural groups and in competing conceptions of the good life.[3] These two elements are related. In order to consider issues on their own merits students need to have available the range of alternatives that acquaintance with different ways of life entails, and in order to be able to choose from different conceptions of the good, students need to be able to consider evidence that may be uncomfortable for the prevailing authority in their own community.

HOW THE COMMON SCHOOL IS DIFFERENT
FROM OTHER SCHOOLS

The idea of the common school requires that students come to take responsibility for the conditions that affect us all and that instruction highlight shared as well as private concerns. For example, many virtues, such as good health habits, are important for everyone to acquire. They are conditions for leading a good and useful life, and we would expect children in private and religious schools to learn about the importance of health and how to maintain it.

We also expect children in the common school to learn about health, but we should expect them to do so for social as well as private reasons. Here students need to understand the social costs that are incurred when industry squanders health resources by polluting the atmosphere or by encouraging teenagers to buy tobacco products. Health education in a common school must teach about industrial and environmental policies that promote or retard good health, and it must enable children to understand that health is a social as well as an individual matter. Such teaching should occur in other schools as well, but only the common school has a socially grounded obligation to develop an informed and educated public.

One of the dangers of the recent trend to involve business in public education is that it may serve to compromise this teaching and exert a subtle influence on instruction. The solution is not to block business from participation in schools but to ensure that its participation is balanced by that of other interests (labor, environmental groups, and so on, including other business interests) and by ensuring that teachers, parents, administrators, and the community have control over the form and content of their participation.

Other goals take on a special character when they are developed within the common school. For example, careful and systematic inquiry involves virtues that are the same whether children are in a private or a public school. Respect for evidence, careful observation, and consideration of alternative explanations are some of these virtues. In the public school, however, inquiry should attach to additional virtues that are associated with active participation in the public sphere. If one person's voice is louder and more persistent than another's but no less qualified, or if, because of racial, ethnic, class, or gender differences, some people are listened to more attentively and taken more seriously than others, then teachers need to address these considerations and to teach students to become aware of the implications of these patterns of interaction for the quality of public life. William Galston notes that "the willingness to set forth one's own views intelligently and candidly as the basis for political persuasion rather than manipulation or coercion" is a critical factor in a democratic society.[4] This willingness is a learnt social product, however, and teachers involved in the creation of participants in public life need to develop an awareness of how everyone has a responsibility for creating a climate in which this willingness can arise.

The formation of a public sphere occurs in fragments, here and there, but it does not happen accidentally. The need to attend to the conditions for its creation is an important reason for public education. The learning involved in such attention is complex, involving not only the technical skills needed to build roads or interpret legal texts but also the skills needed to take on a certain standpoint that is neither natural nor easy to learn.

Jurgen Habermas writes: "A portion of the public sphere comes into being in every conversation in which private individuals assemble to form a public body."[5] But what makes a body a public one? If this conversation is to reflect public concerns it will require participants to take on a standpoint that extends beyond their immediate personal concerns. If you cannot depend on my actions to maintain a healthy environment, then the effects of your own environmental projects are reduced, and it becomes less appealing for you to expend your own time and money on behavior for which I receive a reciprocal but undeserved benefit.

This standpoint is not intuitively given. It requires instruction in order to understand that the way in which I orient my action affects the way in which you orient yours and that our public selves are created in this process of mutual orientation. If this standpoint is to have stability, it also requires that I understand that you are capable of deliberating from the same platform as well and that you understand that the way you orient your action affects the way in which I orient mine.

This learning is critical if modern multicultural societies are to avoid destructive cynicism and maintain a working commitment to democratic inclusion. Yet in a multicultural society where cultural differences provide conflicting signals and sometimes high levels of initial distrust, such learning involves knowing a great deal about the expressive traditions of other groups and their unique understanding of the national experience.

ON THE QUESTION OF INTRUSIVENESS

Some people fear that the values of inquiry will inevitably trespass on parents' rights to socialize children according to their own design. This fear is associated now with conservative Christians, but it is felt by others as well. They fear that the promotion of inquiry and inclusiveness threatens parental, religious, and communal authority because it encourages children to reflect on and be critical of the values they are taught at home and in their churches. As we saw in chapter 5, there are times when the state must advance certain values and enforce certain educational norms.

The question of what the state should have the authority to enforce is different, however, from the question what constitutes a good *public* education. Schools have a responsibility to offer the best education they can, but this does not mean that they always have the right to force that education on the children of reluctant parents. Force may be justified in meeting minimum educational standards, but whether it is justified beyond this will depend on the circumstances involved in each case.

The fear that teaching the values of critical inquiry will necessarily undermine parental authority is often unreasonable. As I mentioned in chapter 1, the intent of teaching children to be reflective and critical should be to teach them to be reflective and critical. It should not be to teach them to reject the culture of their parents or their community—although, as we saw in that chapter, it is likely that children who are exposed to a good public school education will relate to some of the values of their culture in ways that differ from their parents' ways.

It is questionable how influential schools are in leading children to forsake their cultural values or to discard their religious beliefs. Schools are probably much less influential in this regard than is popular culture, and insofar as schools introduce a critical component into issues of identity, it is more likely that it will lead students to be critical of mass culture. One simple reason for this is that mass culture is open and available for direct scrutiny and evaluation in formal and informal classroom discussion. A child's traditional culture is rarely the object of direct evaluation. It is possible, of course, that as children are exposed to alternative ways of life and different conceptions of the good they may come to new conclusions about the values that are taken for granted at home.

Nevertheless, the effects of the common school are not neutral across all cultural groups, and even without the rejection that is sometimes feared, the common school surely may change some children's relationship to their home culture. If the common school requires children to learn to judge important matters for themselves, it may well appear to be imposition to some members of authoritarian or patriarchal groups.

If children develop a more questioning attitude, the school has done its job regardless of the accommodations the student makes to her familiar environment. True, as I pointed out in the first chapter, this is more than just a procedural change. If the result of public education is greater tolerance toward practices that a group condemns without adequate support, this is a substantive change. This change need not be harmful to the tradition itself, however. A more open attitude toward one's own tradition is often what the tradition requires to maintain its vigor in a changing social and material environment. Although in some extreme cases the question of exposure to different ways of life raises certain legal issues concerning the right of parents to control the education of their children,[6] these need to be treated separately from the question of the educational benefits of such exposure.

EDUCATIONAL AUTHORITY AND TRADITIONAL CULTURE

Some members of traditional cultural groups will not always see liberal educational practice as simply a neutral reminder that there are other ways of life. To many traditionalists liberalism itself stands as a competing way of life, and hence to them the liberal educational agenda constitutes a monopoly on cultural practice. Many liberals try to deny this charge, arguing that liberalism is indeed only a procedural matter, one that is neutral regarding the merits of different cultures. This line of defense is inadequate and confusing.[7] It is inadequate not just because a good public education guided by liberal values does affect the character of the local community's values in the way I described in chapter 1, but because, somewhat like MacIntyre, this argument mistakenly assumes that there is an unbridgeable gulf between liberal and other traditional values.

Communitarians such as MacIntyre are right in their understanding of liberalism as a cultural form and not just a neutral political philosophy. It may require of itself a certain level of impartiality among competing local traditional cultures, but it also requires very deep-seated principles of social interaction and personal development, as well as practices that honor and valorize these principles. To ignore these is to provide an enfeebled view of liberalism and a confusing set of justifications. This is especially true when it comes to education. Hence, whereas there are many practices that the common school may *allow,* not all of which are liberal ones, there are certain attitudes, skills, and ways of understanding that it must *advance* as appropriate for all children.

When communitarians view the distance between traditional and liberal culture as always and inevitably insurmountable, they are mistaken. As a tradition of inquiry, liberalism is committed to the ideals of openness and equality. But these commitments are to be found within many segments of traditional cultures as well. There is a healthy dialogue in many groups between those who are wedded to hierarchical traditional forms and those who seek textual authority to advance new ways of understanding and organizing themselves. For example, feminist scholars in Islamic societies use sacred Islamic texts to counter the interpretation that supports male domination. Challenges such as these come from within traditional culture and yet call on concerns that are mirrored in liberal thought as well. These challenges require a strong commitment to the norms of the group as well as an ability to distance oneself from their immediate expressions and beliefs.[8] They count as liberal challenges because they are open to ideas that do not fit neatly into the received wisdom of the group and allow themselves to be surprised by the anomalies that they experience.

These challenges from the inside of traditional culture are also important in the revitalization of liberalism. If liberalism depends on people choosing different conceptions of the good, then there must be different conceptions from which to choose. When people have the possibility of renewing their local cultural traditions from inside they can avoid the alienation entailed when they are forced to abandon many important features of their cultural life in order to live in the modern world. Although a multicultural society celebrates its different cultural traditions, sharp boundaries between cultures are not desirable at all levels of interaction, and dialogue within and across cultural boundaries is the more desirable state of affairs. When dialogue within cultural traditions draws on insights across cultural traditions, the interaction allows new conceptions of the good to emerge within a continuing appreciation of the old.

CONCLUSION: INSTRUCTION IN DEMOCRACY

Instruction in democracy involves confidence in Habermas's ideal of the unmanipulated, uncoerced consent of the governed.[9] It also involves the recognition that both manipulation and coercion may take different forms. The ideal of unmanipulated and uncoerced consent provides a moral picture of the way things are supposed to work, and the picture is an essential component of life in a democratic society. Even when honored in the breach, it serves as a standard announcing that something has gone wrong and as a benchmark by which to judge the practices of educational, cultural, and political leaders against their own professed principles. And it provides the material for initiating a critique of local cultures as well as of national institutions.

It is naive to think that we actually live in a democracy all the time and to ignore the many institutional practices that are essentially nondemocratic — from the military, to the corporation, to many aspects of the institution of schooling. Yet although we may not live in a democracy all of the time, we can try to dwell democratically in the place where we do live. Part of what it means to dwell in a democracy is to understand when it is appropriate to appeal to democratic principles and when it is not.

Part of learning how to dwell in a democracy is learning subtle distinctions between nondemocratic practices and antidemocratic ones. The former seek spaces within democracy for traditional and authoritative norms to operate, whereas the latter seek to shut down any space in which democracy develops, and it seeks to do so undemocratically. For example, even though democratic attitudes may be rejected in certain homes, it is often inappropriate and intrusive for a school authority to directly criticize a particular family or group for its paternalistic and undemocratic customs. It is important, however, for teachers in their classrooms to advance the kind of critical and reflective thinking that is associated with democratic ways of life, even if it has implications that are in tension with family practices.

Another aspect of dwelling democratically involves a concern for fairness across differences in class, gender, race, or culture. Sometimes fairness is contrasted with partiality and the first is assigned to liberal democratic societies, the second to premodern, traditional ones. This contrast is used to applaud the liberal ideal as one of the conditions of material progress, and it is what is often appealed to when people voice criticism of affirmative action programs, for example. They see these programs as reverting to outdated ideas that distribute rights and goods on the basis of one's membership in a religious or cultural group rather than on the basis of competence.[10]

Both the advocates and the critics of liberalism are wrong

on this point. Fairness is not antithetical to the notion of partiality but actually requires it under certain conditions. Fairness implies more than the notion that the pros and cons of a decision be placed on a balance and left for an independent party to judge. Fairness must also be concerned that different parties have reasonable opportunities to make their own case, to exercise partiality in their own cause, and to contribute to a discourse that defines what we should count as a pro or as a con.

Hence, one of the functions of the common school is to teach students how to advance their own ideas and to speak and write in an authentic and convincing manner. In other words, the common school has a role in teaching students how to advance their own concerns — including cultural ones — and to express themselves in ways that ring true. It does this by teaching them to express their own opinions, drawing on their own personal and cultural experience while also keeping in mind the character of the audience that will hear their concerns and act on them. Partiality is an important component of fairness, and the common school must be involved in teaching students both to speak from the knowledge that their cultural identity provides and, as audience, to hear the voices of others. It is also an important component of national identity. Learning to express the concerns and values that arise from one's own standpoint in a way that is available to people from other standpoints is clearly one of the avenues for the evolution of new forms of affiliation and association that the liberal multicultural nation stands to protect and that constitutes an important component of its moral identity. It is within and across this medley of difference that the common school continues the dialogue begun during the American Revolution about the nature of national unity and the character of national identity.

Notes

CHAPTER 1 EDUCATION: CULTURAL DIFFERENCE AND NATIONAL IDENTITY

[1] See James A. Banks and Cherry A. McGee Banks, eds., *Handbook of Research on Multicultural Education* (New York: Macmillan, 1995).

[2] These include Eamonn Callan, T. McLaughlin, Kevin McDonough, Kenneth Strike, Yael Tamir, and John White.

[3] Nicholas Appleton, "Cultural Pluralism: Must We Know What We Mean?" *Philosophy of Education, 1976: Proceedings of the Thirty-second Annual Meeting of the Philosophy of Education Society* (Urbana: University of Illinois Press, 1976), p. 161. See also James A. Banks, *Teaching Strategies for Ethnic Studies* (Boston: Allyn and Bacon, 1975), pp. 10–13.

[4] For an informative analysis of different conceptions of pluralism see Nicholas Appleton, *Cultural Pluralism in Education* (New York: Longman, 1883), pp. 23–29, 72–76. The view that he identifies as corporate pluralism is close to what I refer to here as multiculturalism. Multiculturalism, however, does not restrict individual intercourse across group boundaries in the way in which corporate pluralism as defined by Appleton seems to. Appleton's description of liberal pluralism is what I mean by *pluralism*.

[5] As quoted in David Tyack, "Constructing Difference: Historical Reflections on Schooling and Social Diversity," *Teachers College Record* 95, no. 1 (fall 1993): 8–33.

[6] See, e.g., Barbara A. Sizemore, "Shattering the Melting Pot Myth," in *Teaching Ethnic Studies*, ed. James Banks (Washington, D.C.: National Council for the Social Studies, 1973), pp. 73–100.

[7] Stokely Carmichael and C. V. Hamilton, *Black Power* (New York: Random House, 1967), p. 44.

[8] Horace Kallen, *Culture and Democracy in the United States* (New York: Boni and Liveright, 1924), p. 51; Michael Walzer, "What Does It Mean to Be an 'American'?" *Social Research* 57, no. 3 (1990): 593–614.

[9] Arthur Schlesinger Jr., *The Disuniting of America: Reflections on a Multicultural Society* (New York: Norton, 1992).

[10] This concern is voiced most prominently by Schlesinger; see ibid. Yet Schlesinger's early book on Andrew Jackson (*The Age of Jackson* [Boston: Little, Brown, 1945]) virtually ignores Jackson's role in the assault on Native American culture.

[11] Will Kymlicka, *Multicultural Citizenship* (Oxford: Clarendon, 1995), p. 50. Kymlicka is actually describing what he sees as a dominant form of contemporary liberalism.

[12] Ibid., 51. Kymlicka traces this concern to, among others, Wilhelm von Humboldt

and Giuseppe Mazzini. See also Charles Taylor, *Multiculturalism and the Politics of Recognition* (Princeton: Princeton University Press, 1992). Taylor traces this connection back to Herder.

[13] Schlesinger, *Disuniting of America.*

[14] Even to philosophical liberals such as Will Kymlicka and to libertarians such as Iris Young cultural recognition is the precondition of a rich and fulfilling and diverse America.

[15] David Miller, *On Nationality* (Oxford: Oxford University Press, 1995), p. 139.

[16] Arjun Appadurai, "Patriotism and Its Future," *Public Culture* 5 (1993): 411–29.

CHAPTER 2 NATURE OF NATIONAL IDENTITY AND CITIZENSHIP EDUCATION

[1] Dumas Malone, *Jefferson and His Times*, vol. 6, *The Sage of Monticello* (Boston: Little, Brown, 1981), p. 248.

[2] Ralph Waldo Emerson, *Uncollected Lectures* (New York: William Edwin Rudge, 1932), p. 6.

[3] Ibid., p. 7.

[4] Roy J. Honeywell, ed., *Educational Works of Thomas Jefferson* (New York: Russell and Russell, 1931), p. 13.

[5] "Everyone" did not, of course, include slaves or Native Americans.

[6] Honeywell, *Educational Works*, p. 13.

[7] Ibid.

[8] See Michael W. Apple, *Ideology and Curriculum* (London: Routledge and Kegan Paul, 1979); Pierre Bourdieu and Jean-Claude Passeron, *Reproduction in Education, Society, and Culture* (London: Sage, 1977); Samuel Bowles and Herbert Gintis, *Schooling in Capitalist America: Educational Reform and the Contradictions of Economic Life* (New York: Basic, 1976); Walter Feinberg, *Reason and Rhetoric* (New York: John Wiley, 1974); Michael Katz, *The Irony of Early School Reform* (Cambridge: Harvard University Press, 1968).

[9] The strong relation between national identity and the common school does not contradict other claims about the use or misuse of public education. For example, some historians and sociologists have argued for a tight connection between the development of the public school and the need for a new kind of workforce that arose with industry and capitalism. The evidence for this claim is abundant, and the development of the skills and attitudes needed to change from an agrarian to an industrial and capitalist nation was certainly a major reason for the expansion of public schools. It is important, however, to highlight the fact that it was *the nation* that was the focal point of this development. The object was not just economic growth as such, but national economic growth, and the need was to develop a new workforce that would identify with these national goals.

[10] Ernest Gellner, *Thought and Change* (Chicago: University of Chicago Press, 1965), p. 169.

[11] Benedict Anderson, *Imagined Communities* (London: Verso, 1992), p. 7.

[12] Ibid., emphasis in original.

[13] Ibid.

[14] Ibid., p. 45.

[15] I am following Anderson here.

[16] Anderson, *Imagined Communities*, pp. 35–36.

[17] John Dewey, *Democracy and Education* (New York: Macmillan, 1963).

[18] Kwame Anthony Appiah, "Cosmopolitan Patriots," in Martha C. Nussbaum and respondents, *For Love of Country: Debating the Limits of Patriotism,* ed. J. Cohen (Boston: Beacon, 1996), pp. 27–28.

[19] Ibid., p. 28.

[20] Fernand Braudel, *The Wheels of Commerce: Civilization and Capitalism, 15th–18th Century,* vol. 2 (New York: Harper and Row, 1979), pp. 514–68.

[21] As quoted in ibid., p. 560.

[22] Ibid., pp. 362–63.

[23] A number of scholars have argued that the role of the school was really more sinister than this and that it was largely established to create the attitudes required of workers in an industrial society. See Katz, *Irony of Early School Reform.* This argument does not counter the point that I am making. The workers who were to be created were also to be created as citizens with a certain conception of and loyalty to the county. What the argument suggests is that some of the principled reasons for public schools were often violated.

[24] I am indebted to Jefferson McMahan for the idea of co-national partiality.

[25] There is the considerable question of when nations arose and their connection to nationalism. Anderson sometimes seems to argue that they are coterminous with the doctrine of nationalism. Others, such as Scruton, argue that nations existed well before nationalism developed as a doctrine. (See Roger Scruton, *The Philosopher at Dover Beach* [New York: St. Martin's, 1990], p. 304). The answer may depend on how we think about the doctrine of nationalism and whether it must be expressed only in systematic form or whether it can also be expressed in the informal convictions and acts of individual people, which later become systematized.

[26] This is to distinguish *multiplying* from a parrotlike repetition of responses one has heard.

[27] Today this judgment might be disputed by certain postmodernist theorists who would object to the evaluative implication of the term *higher.*

[28] Luria puts the issue in other terms, such as prelogical v. logical thinking or primitive v. higher-order thought. My point, however, is to show how the need to widen coordinated action alters the kind of thought that is required.

[29] A. R. Luria, *Cognitive Development: Its Cultural and Social Foundations*, ed. Michael Cole (Cambridge: Harvard University Press, 1976), pp. 107–109.

[30] A. R. Luria, *The Making of Mind: A Personal Account of Soviet Psychology*, ed. Michael Cole and Sheila Cole (Cambridge: Harvard University Press, 1979), p. 71.

[31] Emile Durkheim, *Moral Education: A Study in the Theory and Application of the Sociology of Education* (New York: Free Press, 1973), p. 4. Appreciation also to my colleagues Bob Jones at the University of Illinois and Eric Bredo at the University of Virginia for helpful discussions about Durkheim. Jones's unpublished essay "Moral Education: The 'Whole Man' of the Future" was most helpful.

[32] For a discussion of Green's views see Peter Gordon and John White, *Philosophers as Educational Reformers: The Influence of Idealism on British Educational Thought and Practice* (London: Routledge and Kegan Paul, 1979), p. 77.

[33] Durkheim, *Moral Education*, pp. 10–11.

[34] Ibid., p. 76.

[35] Ibid., p. 79.

[36] Ibid., pp. 82–83.

[37] Ibid., pp. 68–69.

[38] John Dewey, "Evolution and Ethics," *The Monist* 8, no. 3 (April 1898): 321–41, at 326.

[39] Ibid., p. 327.

[40] See Robert B. Westbrook, *John Dewey and American Democracy* (Ithaca: Cornell University Press, 1991).

[41] Katz, *Irony of Early School Reform*.

[42] Bourdieu and Passeron, *Reproduction in Education, Society, and Culture*.

CHAPTER 3 CULTURAL DIFFERENCE

[1] Durkheim was not unaware of the importance of community, as is evidenced in his famous comments on suicide. See Emile Durkheim, *Selected Writings*, Giddons, ed. (Cambridge: Cambridge University Press, 1988), p. 113.

[2] See, e.g., the collection edited by Michael F. D. Young, *Knowledge and Control: New Directions for the Sociology of Education* (London: Collier-Macmillan, 1971); Paul Willis, *Learning to Labor: How Working Class Kids Get Working Class Jobs* (London: Saxon House, 1978); Elizabeth Ellsworth, "Why Doesn't This Feel Like Empowerment?" *Harvard Educational Review* 59, no. 3 (August 1989): 297–324; Pierre Bourdieu and Jean-Claude Passeron, *Reproduction in Education, Society, and Culture* (London: Sage, 1977).

[3] Jonathan Glover, *I: The Philosophy and Psychology of Personal Identity* (Harmondsworth: Penguin, 1988), p. 175.

[4] Will Kymlicka, *Multicultural Citizenship* (Oxford: Oxford University Press, 1995), p. 52.

[5] See Lucy Suchman, "Response to Vera and Simon's Situated Action: A Symbolic Interpretation," *Cognitive Science* 17, no. 1 (January–March, 1993): 71–75, at 72.

[6] Shirley Brice Heath, *Ways with Words: Language, Life, and Work in Communities and Classrooms* (Cambridge: Cambridge University Press, 1985), p. 84. Heath fits the strong culturalist view in many respects, especially in presenting all cultural forms as if they were a consistent whole and in terms of her silence when obviously normative issues arise. It would be wrong to think of her strictly in these terms, however, for there is little to suggest that schools are inevitably an instrument of imposition and symbolic violence. The best way to read her is to see her silence on certain critical issues as a methodological device to better understand cultural formations and then to find ways to use this understanding to guide school practice in ways that minimize the violence and impositional possibilities of schooling.

[7] Ibid., p. 84.

[8] Ibid., p. 85.

[9] Ibid., p. 185.

[10] Ibid., p. 187.

[11] Ibid., p. 189.

[12] Appreciation goes to Mark Briod for this example.

[13] Laura Bohannan, "Shakespeare in the Bush," in A. Ternes, ed., *Ants, Indians, and Little Dinosaurs* (New York: C. Scribner's Sons, 1975), pp. 203–16.

[14] Richard Shweder, *Thinking Through Cultures: Expeditions in Cultural Psychology* (Cambridge: Harvard University Press, 1991), p. 6.

[15] Takeo Doi, *The Anatomy of Dependence,* trans. John Bestor (Tokyo: Kodansha International, 1971), p. 7.

[16] Shweder, *Thinking Through Cultures,* p. 7.

[17] Charles Taylor, *Multiculturalism and the Politics of Recognition* (Princeton: Princeton University Press, 1992).

[18] The relation between honor and dignity is treated in a number of different and important works. See, e.g., Benedict Anderson, *Imagined Communities* (London: Verso, 1992). See also Taylor, *Multiculturalism and the Politics of Recognition,* and Charles Taylor, *The Ethics of Authenticity* (Cambridge: Cambridge University Press, 1992). For a literary treatment of the issue see Kazuo Ishiguro, *The Remains of the Day* (New York: Random House, 1990).

[19] Shweder, *Thinking Through Cultures,* pp. 61–62.

[20] This is the point of the slogan "no pain, no gain."

[21] I discuss this in detail in chapter 5.

[22] This is what makes Shirley Brice Heath's work interesting for teachers, since she actually used the cultural meanings developed at home to develop curricular material for children at school.

[23] This point is well made by Will Kymlicka, *Liberalism, Community, and Culture* (Oxford: Clarendon, 1991), p. 4.

[24] J. Waldron, *Liberal Rights: Collected Papers, 1981–1991* (Cambridge: Cambridge University Press, 1993), p. 355.

[25] See Eva Hoffmann, *Lost in Translation: A Life in a New Language* (New York: E. P. Dutton, 1989).

CHAPTER 4 THE POSSIBILITY OF MORAL EDUCATION IN A LIBERAL SOCIETY

Some segments of this chapter were published previously as "The Communitarian Challenge to Liberal Social and Educational Theory," *The Peabody Journal of Education* 70, no. 4 (summer 1995): 34–55.

[1] Some liberals are now trying to incorporate the communitarian concerns and to argue that neutrality is not central to liberalism. Some of these theorists, such as William Galston, argue that the liberal state is committed to a distinctive conception of the good. See, e.g., Galston, *Liberal Purposes: Goods, Virtues, and Diversity in the Liberal State* (Cambridge: Cambridge University Press, 1991).

[2] M. A. Glendon, *Rights Talk: The Impoverishment of Political Discourse* (New York: Free Press, 1991), p. xi.

[3] Lawrence Kohlberg, *Essays on Moral Development,* vol. 1, *The Philosophy of Moral Development* (San Francisco: Harper and Row, 1981).

[4] Carol Gilligan, *In a Different Voice: Psychological Theory and Women's Development* (Cambridge: Harvard University Press, 1982); Nel Noddings, *Caring: A Feminine Approach to Ethics and Moral Education* (Berkeley: University of California Press, 1984).

[5] Alasdair MacIntyre, *After Virtue* (Notre Dame: University of Notre Dame Press, 1981).

[6] John Rawls, *A Theory of Justice* (Cambridge: Harvard University Press, 1971).

[7] Robert Nozick, *Anarchy, State and Utopia* (New York: Basic, 1974).

[8] It is true that in general MacIntyre wants to avoid this totally incommensurate view, but when it comes to his analysis of liberalism, he often seems to be assuming it.

[9] Alasdair MacIntyre, *Whose Justice? Which Rationality?* (Notre Dame: University of Notre Dame Press, 1988).

[10] Ibid., p. 321.

[11] Ibid., p. 335.

[12] Ibid., p. 339.

[13] One must wonder about the accuracy of this point. Does MacIntyre mean to suggest, for example, that the concept of hypocrisy simply does not exist in preliberal society or, if it does, that it is not seen as a vice? Or does he mean to suggest that in earlier societies people were always compelled by the logic of their argument to do the right thing and hence hypocrisy was never a practical concern?

[14] Note, for example, the excommunication of Rev. Tissa Balasuriya for holding to a doctrine of religious relativism. *New York Times,* 7 January 1997, p. 1.

[15] MacIntyre, *Whose Justice?*, p. 348.

[16] Ibid., p. 345.

[17] Ibid., p. 344.

[18] For an excellent treatment of these issues, see James D. Wallace, *Ethical Norms, Particular Cases* (Ithaca: Cornell University Press, 1996).

[19] My appreciation to Maria Seferian for suggesting this possibility.

[20] Kohlberg, *Essays on Moral Development*.

[21] Ibid.

[22] Alasdair MacIntyre, "Is Patriotism a Virtue?" Lindley Lecture, Department of Philosophy, University of Kansas, 1984.

[23] Jon. 3:6 AV (KJV).

[24] MacIntyre, *Whose Justice?*

[25] In fairness to MacIntyre, this is not an error to be associated with his position since he does speak of the benefits of being raised in two competing positions. His concern is the judgment of traditions, not the benefits that occur through their interaction. See "Relativism, Power and Philosophy," in *The Proceedings and Addresses of the American Philosophical Association* (Newark, Del.: American Philosophical Association, Sept. 1985).

[26] William Butler Yeats, "An Irishman Foresees His Death," in Alexander W. Allison, et al., eds., *The Norton Anthology of Poetry.* 3d ed. (New York: W. W. Norton, 1983), p. 517.

[27] See chapter 2.

[28] A series of discussions with Jefferson MacMahan has been helpful in sensitizing me to this issue.

[29] See Thomas Nagel, *The View from Nowhere* (New York: Oxford University Press, 1986).

[30] Roger Scruton, *The Philosopher at Dover Beach* (New York: St. Martin's, 1990), p. 302.

[31] Without penalty is not the same as without cost.

CHAPTER 5 AIMS OF MULTICULTURAL EDUCATION

[1] *New York Times*, 20 January 1997, p. 1.

[2] Granted, the *Times* may be biased in its reporting, or it may slant its reports on Africa more negatively than it does those on other places, but the point remains. There are times when more and better information leads to less rather than more respect.

[3] John Ogbu, "Immigrant and Involuntary Minorities in Comparative Perspective," in *Minority Status and Schooling: A Comparative Study of Immigrant and Involuntary Minorities*, ed. Margaret Gibson and John Ogbu (New York: Garland, 1991).

[4] Walter Feinberg, *Japan and the Pursuit of a New American Identity: Work and Education in a Multicultural Age* (New York: Routledge, 1993).

[5] Arthur Schlesinger Jr., *The Disuniting of America: Reflections on a Multicultural Society* (New York: Norton, 1992).

[6] This objection is put graphically by Diane Ravitch: "I recall reading an interview . . . with a talented black runner. She said that her model is Mikhail Baryshnikov. She admires him because he is a magnificent athlete. He is not black; he is not female; he is not American-born; he is not even a runner. But he inspired her because of the way he trained and used his body." "Multiculturalism: E Pluribus Plures," *American Scholar* 59, no. 3 (summer 1990): p. 354.

[7] Schlesinger, *Disuniting of America.*

[8] Ravitch, "Multiculturalism," p. 342.

[9] Ibid.

[10] Ibid., p. 344. Ravitch overstates this point. It is standard educational practice to speak not just in terms of nations but of wider social and historical units called "civilizations." Courses in Western civilization or Asian civilization are standard in high schools and colleges and, although the context and the priority given to these units may be altered by a multicultural framework, the units themselves are familiar. What is more problematic is the assumption that these units are self-contained and that there is not considerable influence across the different areas. The failure to acknowledge this leads to the mistake of believing that such units are containers for essentially different types of people.

[11] Eva Hoffman, *Lost in Translation: A Life in a New Language* (New York: Penguin, 1989), pp. 107–8.

[12] Paul Heelas, "Introduction: Detraditionalization and Its Rivals," in Paul Heelas, Scott Lash, and Paul Morris, *Detraditionalization* (Oxford: Blackwell, 1996), p. 3.

[13] Ibid.

[14] Ibid., p. 4.

[15] I use this awkward phrasing because I suspect that there are different ways in which to be "traditional" and that they vary considerably in how they conform to the "ideal of the traditional society" as described by modernist writers.

[16] Jonathan Glover, *I: The Philosophy and Psychology of Personal Identity* (London: Penguin, 1991), pp. 197–98.

[17] Ibid., pp. 60–61, for Glover's understanding of personhood.

[18] Ibid., p. 161.

[19] Nelson Goodman, *Ways of Worldmaking* (Indianapolis: Hackett, 1978).

[20] This view was put forth, for example, by Arthur Jensen in a famous article on intelligence (Jensen, "How Much Can We Boost IQ and Scholastic Achievement?" *Harvard Educational Review* 39, no. 1 [winter 1969]: 1–123). Jensen argues that

people with low intelligence can learn many of the same things as people with high intelligence, although they must learn them differently. The former must learn them associatively, through rote memory, whereas the latter may learn them using higher-order conceptual skills such as problem solving. One of the many difficulties with this argument is that it is wrong in its belief that people are learning the same things. Rather, since thinking involves going beyond the given and rote learning requires one to stay with the given, one group is learning to think and the other is not. See Walter Feinberg, *Understanding Education* (Cambridge: Cambridge University Press, 1981) for an analysis of this issue.

[21] Researchers such as Cole and Scribner make a convincing case that what appears to be an example of illogical thinking is often something considerably more complex and complicated and that it is hard to imagine how people could survive without some reasonably sophisticated, even if possibly preverbal, forms of expression. The issue of whether someone is actually engaged in familiar (to us) modes of thinking or whether cultures inhibit certain ways of thinking is an open question. Michael Cole and Sylvia Scribner, *Culture and Thought: A Psychological Introduction* (New York: John Wiley and Sons, 1974), pp. 161–63.

[22] Ibid., p. 161.

[23] Carol Gilligan, *In a Different Voice: Psychological Theory and Women's Development* (Cambridge: Harvard University Press, 1982).

[24] Cole and Scribner, *Culture and Thought*, p. 143, describing the ideas of A. F. C. Wallace. Also see p. 163 for a fine reconstruction of an apparently nonlogical response into a perfectly coherent logical form.

[25] Note Ludwig Wittgenstein's criticism of James G. Frazer's *Golden Bough*, in *Philosophical Occasions*, ed. James Carl Klagge and Alfred Nordmann (Indianapolis: Hackett, 1993), pp. 115–55.

[26] These examples are taken from a talk by Ali Mazrui titled "Afrocentrism and Multiculturalism" given at the University of Wisconsin, Madison, June 1992.

[27] For a useful discussion of this see Will Kymlicka, *Multicultural Citizenship* (Oxford: Oxford University Press, 1995), p. 77.

[28] This is also true of cultures in which two or three cultural forms may share center stage, as, perhaps, in Switzerland. A person who participates largely in some other cultural form will still be disadvantaged.

[29] William E. Connolly, *Identity/Difference: Democratic Negotiations of Political Paradox* (Ithaca: Cornell University Press, 1991), p. 94.

CHAPTER 6 UNCOMMON IDENTITIES: HARD CASES

[1] *Wisconsin v. Yoder*, 406 U.S. 205 (1972).

[2] *Mozert v. Hawkins County Board of Education*, 827 F.2d 1058 (1987).

[3] *Mozert* parents wanted schools to provide alternative material for their children, but the main issue was whether the children should be required to read material to which their parents objected.

[4] I am drawing on David Miller's definition of multiculturalism; see David Miller, *On Nationality* (Oxford: Oxford University Press, 1995), p. 131.

[5] Think, for example, of the shock registered in the film *The Crying Game* when the male lead discovers that his beautiful lover has a penis. Since nothing else has changed, some extraterrestrial observer might wonder why this has precipitated such a large emotional change. The only thing that makes it understandable is our knowledge that men are supposed to love women and that women are not supposed to have penises.

[6] I believe that this is the birth order that is supposed to signal a faith healer.

[7] I use quotation marks to indicate that both need and culture are in contention in this dispute.

[8] Harlan Lane, *The Mask of Benevolence* (New York: Knopf, 1992), p. 267.

[9] Ibid., p. 12.

[10] Ibid., p. 142.

[11] Ibid., p. 93.

[12] See Will Kymlicka, *Multicultural Citizenship* (Oxford: Clarendon, 1995), p. 7.

[13] For an insightful treatment of the problem of standing, see Judith N. Shklar, *American Citizenship: The Quest for Inclusion* (Cambridge: Harvard University Press, 1991); Walter Feinberg, "Affirmative Action and Beyond: A Defense of Race- and Gender-Based Affirmative Action," *Teachers College Record* (spring 1996): 362–99.

[14] Molefi Kete Asante, *The Afrocentric Idea* (Philadelphia: Temple University Press, 1987).

[15] I am not denying here that some other cultures may have been violated as severely. The culture of traditional immigrant groups, however, does not fit this mold.

CHAPTER 7 ON ROBUST RECOGNITION AND STORYTELLING

[1] Michael Morton, *Herder and the Poetics of Thought: Unity and Diversity in* On Diligence in Several Learned Languages (University Park: Pennsylvania State University Press, 1989), p. 43.

[2] See Elizabeth Ellsworth, "Why Doesn't This Feel Like Empowerment?" *Harvard Educational Review* 59, no. 3 (August 1989): 297–324.

[3] Thomas S. Kuhn, *The Structure of Scientific Revolutions* (Chicago: University of Chicago Press, 1962).

[4] Michel Foucault, *The Archaeology of Knowledge and the Discourse on Language* (New York: Harper and Row, 1972), p. 22.

[5] Paulo Freire, *The Pedagogy of the Oppressed* (New York: Herder and Herder, 1968).

[6] Ibid. What is inaccurate about this label is that even Freire understands that the silence exists only in certain kinds of settings—those that are public or rehearsed. These are settings in which the script calls forth the dominant voice and marks others as less important or trivial.

[7] This is even true of stories that tell of influential past civilizations. This is because they are past, and what is interesting is not just the story that is told about them but the fact that they are no longer present to tell it about themselves. One of the implications obviously is that to hold the exclusive story of a still-living group is to treat them as a dead object.

[8] I am following Toni Morrison's description of the novel here in *Playing in the Dark* (Cambridge: Harvard University Press, 1992), pp. 18–21.

[9] Ibid., p. 21.

[10] Ibid., p. 22.

[11] For example, Nathan Glazer, in a chapter that is admirable for its self-critical standpoint, still holds that "multiculturalism is the *price* America is paying for its inability or unwillingness to incorporate into its society African Americans." Nathan Glazer, *We Are All Multiculturalists Now* (Cambridge: Harvard University Press, 1997), p. 147, emphasis mine.

CHAPTER 8 CITIZENSHIP EDUCATION AND THE MULTICULTURAL IDEAL

[1] I am thankful to Fred Lighthall for the term *habitat*. It is similar, of course, to Pierre Bourdieu's *habitus*. The term is so loaded with conspiratorial and fatalistic overtones in Bourdieu, however, that it is not helpful in addressing normative questions.

[2] For an interesting paper addressing this issue see David Blacker, "Fanaticism and Schooling in the Democratic State," *American Journal of Education,* forthcoming. I also examine this issue in Walter Feinberg, "Dewey and Democracy at the Dawn of the Twenty-first Century," *Educational Theory* 43, no. 2 (spring 1993): 195–216 (an essay review of Robert W. Westbrook, *John Dewey and American Democracy*).

[3] The standard term for such a person is *free rider*. One problem that the state addresses is that of the mutual perception that someone else is a free rider. This perception then adds incentive to becoming a free rider oneself, thereby encouraging the originally perceived free rider to become an actual one. The state is in place in part to inhibit this downward spiral.

[4] See chapter 2.

[5] Yael Tamir, "Two Concepts of Multiculturalism," in *Democratic Education in a Multicultural State,* ed. Yael Tamir (Oxford: Blackwell, 1995), p. 8.

[6] Jeremy Waldron, *Liberal Rights: Collected Papers, 1981–1991* (Cambridge: Cambridge University Press, 1993).

[7] See Thomas Nagel, *The View from Nowhere* (New York: Oxford University Press,

1986), for an extended treatment of the justification of partiality along these lines.

8 See especially chapter 5.

9 This formulation raises two obvious questions. The first is what to count as harmful. For example, hate speech may be said to have a harmful effect because, among other things, it raises anxiety levels. Yet there are good reasons for limiting the state's intervention in matters of speech, reasons that have to do with practical matters such as the difficulty of defining "hate" speech. For example, what should be done about speech that may be accurate in minor respects yet is so distorted as to produce the feelings associated with hate speech? Or, should the same standards apply to the speech of dominant majorities against endangered minorities as those that apply to endangered minorities against majorities? The other question involves who should be considered a member of the community. Children constitute an uncertain category here. Certainly they are critical for the group's continued existence. The fact that they have not chosen the group in any unconditional sense, however, suggests that their membership is not the same as that of adult members, who have at least a formal right of exit.

10 David Miller, *On Nationality* (Oxford: Oxford University Press, 1995), p. 65.

11 This comment is meant only to apply to individuals within the nation. I believe that quite a different morality applies to the nation as a collectivity in relation to other national collectivities. Here moral failing is quite likely when it comes to failure to provide mutual aid.

12 Nick C. Burbules, *Dialogue in Teaching: Theory and Practice* (New York: Teachers College Press, 1993).

13 Tamir, "Two Concepts of Multiculturalism," p. 8.

14 This problem is spelled out in a most compelling way by Vivian Gussin Paley, *You Can't Say You Can't Play* (Cambridge: Harvard University Press, 1992).

15 The term "exclusively" is used here to distinguish this form of pluralism from that described in chapter 6, which strives to make room for cultural expression within a public context.

16 I am drawing on material that I developed in my *Japan and the Pursuit of a New American Identity* (London: Routledge, Chapmann and Hall, 1993).

17 John Rawls, *Political Liberalism* (New York: Columbia University Press, 1993), p. 60. Rawls includes a rather lengthy discussion of what will count as reasonable and comprehensive beliefs, pp. 47–66.

18 John Rawls, *A Theory of Justice* (Cambridge: Harvard University Press, 1971). *Justice as fairness* is the term Rawls gives for the two principles of justice that he advocates.

19 Rawls, *Political Liberalism*, p. 57.

20 Bruce Ackerman, "Why Dialogue?" *The Journal of Philosophy* 86, no. 1 (January 1989): 8.

21 Ibid., p. 16.

22 Ibid., p. 17.

23 Kenneth Strike, "On the Construction of Public Speech: Pluralism and Public Response," *Educational Theory* 44, no. 1 (winter 1994): 1–26.

24 Ibid., p. 14.

25 Ibid., p. 13.

26 Ibid., p. 14.

27 Ibid., p. 15.

28 Ibid.

29 Ibid.

30 Ibid., p. 17.

31 For an example of how moral language is imbedded in technical language in education, see the first part of my *Understanding Education* (Cambridge: Cambridge University press, 1982). Here I show how claims about IQ scores and how to treat difference are as much moral as technical issues, even if the technical claims were to be more or less correct.

32 See the treatment in chapter 4 of Alisdair MacIntyre, *Whose Justice? Which Rationality?* (Notre Dame: University of Notre Dame Press, 1988).

33 For this discussion I am drawing on Susan Mendus, *Toleration and the Limits of Liberalism* (Atlantic Highlands, N.J.: Humanities Press, 1989), pp. 22–43, and John Locke, *A Letter Concerning Tolerance,* ed. J. Tully (Indianapolis: Hackett, 1983).

CHAPTER 9 CONCLUSION: COMMON SCHOOLS AND THE PUBLIC FORMATION

1 This view has gained a considerable amount of currency recently because it can be presented in seemingly neutral, utilitarian terms — i.e., what is needed to get ahead in America. See E. D. Hirsch Jr., *Cultural Literacy: What Every American Needs to Know* (Boston: Houghton Mifflin, 1987); E. D. Hirsch Jr., *The Schools We Need and Why We Don't Have Them* (New York: Doubleday, 1996).

2 Hirsch claims in his first book that such factoids are necessary for economic advancement. His second book seems to step back slightly from this unsupported assertion.

3 See Amy Gutmann, *Democratic Education* (Princeton: Princeton University Press, 1987).

4 William Galston, *Liberal Purposes: Good, Virtues, and Duties in the Liberal State* (Cambridge: Cambridge University Press, 1991), p. 227.

5 Jurgen Habermas, "The Public Sphere: An Encyclopedia Article" (1964), *New German Critique* l (n.d.): 49.

6 See chapter 6.

7 See chapter 1 for a different argument for the same point.

8 It does not mean discarding those beliefs callously when they fail one or two experi-

ential tests. See, e.g., Imre Lakatos, "Falsification and the Methodology of Scientific Research Programmes," in Imre Lakatos and Allan Musgrave, *Criticism and the Growth of Knowledge* (Cambridge: Cambridge University Press, 1970), pp. 91–197.

9 See Jurgen Habermas, *Communication and the Evolution of Society*, trans. Thomas McCarthy (Boston: Beacon, 1979), pp. 178–206.

10 For an analysis of some of the problems with this kind of criticism, see Walter Feinberg, *On Higher Ground: Education and the Case for Affirmative Action* (New York: Teachers College Press, 1997).

Index